Logical Family

Praise for *Logical Family*

"I fell in love with Maupin's effervescent *Tales of the City* decades ago, and his genius turn at memoir is no less compelling. *Logical Family* is a must-read."   —Mary Karr

"Engaging and revelatory, Maupin's memoir is a delight, punctuating a distinguished career in letters."   —*San Francisco Chronicle*

"A book for any of us, gay or straight, who have had to find our family. Maupin is one of America's finest storytellers, and the story of his life is a story as fascinating, as delightful, and as compulsive as any of the tales he has made up for us."   —Neil Gaiman

"Wise, witty, and beautifully told."   —*People*, Book of the Week

"A sweetly frank and funny memoir by a storyteller in the first rank."
                                                  —*O, The Oprah Magazine*

"Entertaining. . . . Wry and sharply drawn. . . . There is a good deal of what one expects from Maupin, wit and heartache rolled up into a tidy package, so that any anecdote can bring an ache of longing and a belly laugh all in the same paragraph. There is also vivid, sharp writing."   —*New York Times Book Review*

"*Logical Family* gives selflessly of such heartrending experience as it journeys through Maupin's life."   —*Slate*

"Vivid and charming."   —*Minneapolis Star Tribune*

"Maupin is a gifted storyteller. His memoir packs much into 289 pages. . . . Humorous and poignant by turns."
                                          —*Charlotte News & Observer*

"Engrossing and emotional. . . . The story is told with such clarity that even those unfamiliar with Maupin's work can appreciate his life experiences. . . . The true prize here is the cleverness with which Maupin bares his soul. Maupin ties the bonds of joy and heartache he shares with both his families (biological and 'logical'), and in so doing he has crafted a nuanced reflection on what it means to love and be loved in a flawed but beautiful world."

—*Publishers Weekly* (starred review)

"There could be no more appropriate title for Maupin's own tale, which relates his coming of age from a rigidly conservative Southern childhood to one of the most notable writers of the twentieth century. Maupin writes vibrantly . . . with just the right amounts of humor, thoughtfulness, and poignancy."

—*Library Journal* (starred review)

"Maupin is a sympathetic and soulful storyteller. His account of a past struggle for equality is especially important in our fraught present."

—*BookPage*

"Master storyteller Armistead Maupin—the man who defined the difference between 'a biological family' and 'a logical family,' who is both gifted with fearless art and the ability to speak for millions—finally tells his own story. *Logical Family* is a sweet, filthy peach of a memoir from a cultural explosion of a man."

—Caitlin Moran

"The unflinchingly honest, often humorous, and ultimately powerful memoir of one of the most influential American writers of our time."

—*The Advocate*

"It is easy to understand Maupin's reputation for geniality, given his openheartedness as a person and his honesty as a writer; and that will make this delightful chronicle attractive to a wide range of readers, whether they're familiar with his fiction or not."

—*Booklist*

"*Logical Family* is a beautiful memoir—so tender and funny and dignified and kind that it left me a little weepy."

—Alan Cumming

Logical Family

A MEMOIR

Armistead Maupin

HARPER PERENNIAL

NEW YORK • LONDON • TORONTO • SYDNEY • NEW DELHI • AUCKLAND

HARPER ⬤ PERENNIAL

A hardcover edition of this book was published in 2017 by
HarperCollins Publishers.

LOGICAL FAMILY. Copyright © 2017 by Literary Bent, LLC. All rights reserved.
Printed in the United States of America. No part of this book may be used
or reproduced in any manner whatsoever without written permission except
in the case of brief quotations embodied in critical articles and reviews.
For information, address HarperCollins Publishers, 195 Broadway,
New York, NY 10007.

HarperCollins books may be purchased for educational, business, or
sales promotional use. For information, please e-mail the Special Markets
Department at SPsales@harpercollins.com.

FIRST HARPER PERENNIAL EDITION PUBLISHED 2018.

Designed by Bonni Leon-Berman

Library of Congress Cataloging-in-Publication Data has been applied for.
ISBN 978-0-06-239125-4 (pbk.)

18 19 20 21 22   LSC   10 9 8 7 6 5 4 3 2 1

For Christopher Turner,

my beloved husband

AUTHOR'S NOTE

This is largely an account of my youth, that is to say the thirty-some years it took me to claim my truth. (In a few places in the narrative I've skipped forward briefly for the sake of completing a tale.) You may already have read some of these remembrances—in interviews and newspaper essays, or thinly disguised in one of my novels—so please know I reserve the right to plagiarize myself. I have reconstructed long-ago scenes and conversations to the best of my ability. I've tried not to imagine anyone's thoughts but my own.

Logical Family

PROLOGUE

WHEN I WAS A BOY IN Raleigh I was afraid of being locked in Oakwood Cemetery overnight. Every Sunday after church, when our blue-tailed white Pontiac cruised through the entrance, I fretted about the sign posted above us: GATES LOCKED AT 6 PM. I never voiced this fear to my parents, but it hovered over me like a threatening storm cloud all afternoon. *What if we lose track of the time?* That could easily happen as we plucked dandelions from my grandfather's grave or posed sullenly for Daddy's never-ending slides, rigid as garden gnomes. Our family plot was on a rise with the other Nice Families, a respectable distance from the gate, so the caretaker, a runny-eyed old man who kept a spittoon in his granite cubbyhole, might overlook us when he left for home. That enormous gate would clang shut, and we would be trapped there all night, eating acorns for survival, drinking dew off the lilies—my brother, my sister, my parents, and me—Cemetery Family Robinson.

This was not your usual ghoulish graveyard terror, since I found the cemetery anything but spooky. I loved its winding lanes and tilting stones, the way its pale-green dells were flecked with pink in the spring. I reveled in its rich hieroglyphics, all those corroding angels and renegade jonquils, the palpable antiquity of the place. This was our family seat, after all, the ground to which I would return someday, permanently planted among my ancestors. So what was so scary about that? Folks in Raleigh might assume it had to do with the way my grandfather had died. But I wouldn't learn about that until later, when I was well into my teens and the matter of *why* we came to the cemetery every Sunday would finally be explained. Even then, though, my focus would remain on the writing on the stones, not on what actually lay in the boxes beneath them.

Oakwood Cemetery was not just the landscape of our past but also the very blueprint of our family for years to come. My father would eventually lay out the rules for his children in a self-published family history called "Prologue," so named for a famous line in *The Tempest*: "What's past is prologue." Antonio uses the phrase to explain his intention to commit murder. My father used it to justify bragging about his ancestors, and he murdered the truth more than once in the process.

"One thing is certain," the old man wrote after rattling off a roll call of all the lawyers, governors, planters, and generals in our family, "is that wherever one of these men met success, there was a self-effacing and goodly lady by his side."

Back then I was still too young to realize that there would never be a lady by my side, goodly or otherwise. Nor would I have noticed how the old man had summarily reduced his wife and daughter to dutiful handmaidens. I felt only this shapeless longing, an oddly grown-up *ennui* born of alienation and silence. Some children experience this feeling very early on, long before we learn its name and finally let our headstrong hearts lead the way to True North. We grow up as another species entirely, lone gazelles lost amid the buffalo herd of our closest kin. Sooner or later, though, no matter where in the world we live, we must join the diaspora, venturing beyond our biological family to find our logical one, the one that actually makes sense for us. We *have* to, if we are to live without squandering our lives.

So maybe I was beginning to understand something on those Sunday afternoons in the cemetery. Maybe I sensed I didn't belong there, now or forever, that my true genealogy lay somewhere beyond these gates, with another tribe.

ONE

MY MOTHER HELPED ME WITH MY very first effort at writing. We were living in a duplex in Raleigh, on Forest Road, near the new shopping center. Out in California a three-year-old girl had fallen down an abandoned well, and I was determined to console her. I was only a few years older than this child, so my mother must have taken dictation. I couldn't begin to tell what I said. What *could* I have said?

I'm sorry you fell down a well.

Please don't be sad.

I hope they get you out soon.

What I *do* remember is how I'd pictured this letter being delivered: someone dropping it directly into the well, like a wishful coin consigned to a fountain, before it drifted down through the clammy darkness into the little girl's outstretched hands. I figured she would be expecting the letter, awaiting my words of comfort. And my words, if I just chose them carefully enough, would save her in the end.

I suppose my mother must have heard a mailing address on the radio, one provided by the family. Either that or she never mailed the letter at all, intending it only as an exercise in empathy, a homemade remedy for her heartsick, overimaginative child.

The point is: I remember nothing, happy or sad, about the fate of Little Kathy Fiscus. A quick Googling reveals her name and the fact that her attempted rescue in 1949 was one of the first calamities ever to be broadcast live on television. I know now that the well was only eighteen inches wide and that the rescuers recovered Kathy's body a hundred feet beneath the field where she'd been playing three days earlier. The doctor who broke the news to thousands of rapt onlookers said she had died of suffocation only hours after "the last time her voice was heard." A haunting detail, but one I don't remember. I would surely have remembered that voice.

My mother must have changed the subject as soon as the truth was known, distracting me with a Little Golden Book or an antiques store. (I enjoyed antiquing at a revealingly early age.) My mother spent most of her life withholding things, shielding her children and her husband from uncomfortable truths. I'm sure she must have learned this at the feet of her own mother, an English suffragette who had a few doozies of her own to hide. Still, my mother believed in the curative power of letters. She must have written thousands over the years. When she wasn't at The Bargain Box, selling used clothes for the Junior League, or hosting a radio panel show for teenagers, you could hear her writing in her den, clattering away on a millipede of a typewriter that popped out of a desk like a Victorian magic act.

I remember the letters she sent me at summer camp and how I reread them daily like a soldier at the front. There were four or five pages sometimes, covering the front and the back, the type inevitably crawling up the margins to a sideways ballpoint finale. *Love, Mummie.* That signature was my undoing at camp. Another boy spotted it, and since no kid in his right mind called his mother Mummie, there were immediate taunts about moldy pharaohs in their tombs, complete with bedsheet impersonations. My mother, who called her own mother Mummie, never knew of my humiliation. By the time I was a teenager I had decided to call her Mither, a name that struck me as elegant and ironic, so the joke could not possibly be on me. I did the same thing with my father who became Pap after years of being called Daddy, a name only children would use. I was learning to build my manly armor with words, being careful, so careful, like my mother.

Her letters were my only balm at Camp Seagull. Those were days of random self-disgrace in the prickly Carolina heat, days of capsized sailboats and fumbled baseballs and arrows landing short of their mark. There was one other kid who felt like a friend, another miserable ectomorph, but he bunked in another cabin, so our time together was limited. Sometimes we would meet up at twilight to walk along the shore of the Neuse River, away from our torturers, swapping notes on the universe as we poked in the sand for sharks' teeth. (*What was his name, goddammit?* He looked me up in San Francisco in the early eighties, when a few published novels and a listed phone number made me easy to find. He told me he was gay like me but not very good at it. He liked my books, he said. He seemed so profoundly sad. I'm wondering if he ever made it past the plague, or if he lives with the virus, or if he died in one of the other ways, or if he's on Facebook right now, like so many people I never expected to hear from again, posting videos of cute interspecies friendships.)

When he wasn't around, this nameless boy, I would linger in the mess hall after supper and vanish into the comforting whir and flicker of a movie. They were usually war movies, my least favorite kind, but there was always a moment when the gunfire stopped and a lady appeared, a wife or a girlfriend, speaking softly amid soft music. How I craved a woman's gentleness in that all-boy bedlam. I even considered sharing my anguish with Miss Lil, the wife of Cap'n Wyatt, the camp director. She was the only lady around, and not nearly as glamorous as my mother, but she bore a passing resemblance to Dale Evans and might be a sympathetic ear.

I never worked up the nerve. Nor did I share my homesickness with my mother, though she seemed to sense it from afar. Her letters soothed me with detailed visions of my imminent deliverance: "We'll put a mattress in the back of the Country Squire so you can stretch out and read to your heart's content. I'll have all your favorites, darling—lots of Little Lulus and Uncle Scrooges. Don't say I don't mollycoddle you!" I never said that, never even used the word. It was Daddy who believed that sensitive boys could be permanently warped by sympathy. What was the point in making a man out of me if my mother unraveled it with her love?

On the way back to Raleigh, battling in the back of the station wagon with my brother and sister, I felt the sweet relief of our family made whole again. When we played Cow Poker or read aloud the Burma Shave signs, or, in the case of Mummie and me, lobbied my father passionately for a stop at a flea market, it was easy enough to believe that life could always be like this. It was easy to forget that camp had made me glimpse the hardest truth of all: that my mother's absence would one day be permanent. I had done the arithmetic more than once, lying in bed after taps. She was in her late thirties; in another fifty years she would be dead.

As it turned out my figures were off considerably.

My mother must have known who I was even then. She called me her little Ferdinand, the Disney bull who sat in the pasture and smelled the flowers rather than go out and fight in the ring. It took me another quarter of a century to level with her. It makes sense that I chose to do so in a letter, getting the words exactly right, the way she had taught me. My letter was a work of fiction addressed to a fictional character in "Tales of the City," but I had poured my heart into it with such naked intimacy that I knew she would realize that the message was meant for her.

I waited for a response, but none came. Not a letter or a phone call that might speak to the long unspoken. Though what right had I, really, to expect an answer? The letter had appeared in a San Francisco newspaper, where millions of people could see it, including my parents in Raleigh, who subscribed to the paper because of my work, but it could hardly be described as an act of bravery. I had avoided the chance of rejection by addressing my message to everyone and no one.

I had thrown it down a well, and there was no voice from the bottom.

TWO

WHEN I WAS SIX, WE MOVED across town to a nicer neighborhood called Budleigh, where our new L-shaped ranch house aspired to colonial charm with dark-green shutters and a superfluous cupola like one you might find on a Howard Johnson's. With the leftover lumber my father built a playhouse in the backyard that was big enough to hold all three of us kids. For me, it was also a playhouse in the theatrical sense, since there was a porch along one edge that worked wonderfully as a stage. Above the porch, above *everything*, Daddy had emblazoned a message with my mother's red nail polish: SAVE YOUR CONFEDERATE MONEY! THE SOUTH WILL RISE AGAIN. I already knew this was not especially suited to a production of *Jack and the Beanstalk*, but I was determined to make the best of what I'd been given.

My brother and sister were too young for the theater, so my costar was Freddy Fletcher from down the street. I played Jack, and Freddy played the bean seller and the Giant. Freddy couldn't act worth a damn, but he offered other advantages. His father was in show business—an announcer down at WRAL Radio—so, amazingly, the Fletchers had their own mimeograph machine at home. Freddy and I cranked out flyers by the dozens and got giggly drunk on the sweet purple fumes as we passed them out door-to-door on Gloucester Road.

One afternoon, Mr. Fletcher came by our rehearsals after his morning at the station. He was bald and smoked cigars and reminded me of Dennis the Menace's next-door neighbor in the Sunday funnies. We played our beanstalk scene for him, the one where I climb a bamboo pole to the roof of the playhouse, and he seemed impressed. The next day, though, Freddy showed up with a strange proposal.

"I'll give you five bucks for something."

I told him he didn't have five bucks. I knew this because Freddy and I got the same allowance, and I didn't have five bucks either. I had probably already spent my last quarter on a matinee of *Rear Window* and a box of Red Hots at the Village Theater. We were both paupers. We didn't run around with that kind of money.

Freddy corrected himself. "My *daddy* will give you five bucks." He pointed to my father's message above the playhouse. "If you'll get rid of that."

When I asked him what was wrong with that, he just shrugged and went home. I wondered if his father thought the inscription was disrespectful of the South, but that was stupid, since nobody respected the South more than Daddy did. It was just for fun, anyway, like Daddy's cartoon in the bathroom: the grumpy old Rebel soldier with a Confederate flag and the caption that said: "Forget, Hell!"

That night I told Daddy about Mr. Fletcher's offer. He was sitting on a stool at the counter between our kitchen and family room, where, almost every night, he sipped bourbon on the rocks and scarfed Triscuits and cheese from a wooden salad bowl. When he heard my story, his face balled up like a big pink fist.

"Fred Fletcher said that? That he would *pay* you?"

I shrugged. "That's what Freddy said."

"Did he say why the hell why?"

I shook my head warily. Daddy's scattershot anger could be unnerving. Even when he wasn't mad at *you*, he sounded like he might be.

"How did he even know about the goddamn thing?"

I told him. Mr. Fletcher came by to watch our rehearsal.

"Presumptuous sonofabitch!"

I hesitated a moment before asking: "Are they Yankees or something?"

"Hell, no." Daddy thrust a Triscuit into his mouth and chewed ferociously. "They're from Fuquay Springs. They're just *common*."

Common was worse than Yankee in Daddy's book. Some Yankees were fine, he said—the genteel ones from New England—but common was just plain common.

Mr. Fletcher's offer—his "five-buck bribe," as Daddy described it to Mummie—was never discussed again. The nail-polish manifesto stayed intact, and Mr. Fletcher didn't come to *Jack and the Beanstalk* when it opened the next day. His wife, Marjie (whose name *did* sound a little common once I'd thought about it), arrived on her own with a tray of Rice Krispies treats. I wondered if she'd be upset, but she smiled at me pleasantly as I waited by the playhouse for my entrance.

I was costumed in Rit-dyed green tights and one of Daddy's old white shirts, cinched at the waist with my webbed Boy Scout belt. I was trying to go over my lines, but I was distracted by Daddy as he yelled at my mother about Mr. Fletcher. (Mummie referred to this as "addressing the jury," though never to Daddy's face.)

". . . sonofabitch thinks he can pay my son to renounce his heritage!"

"All right, darling, lower your voice." Mummie knew that Marjie Fletcher was seated nearby, and Daddy, of course, knew it, too. He wanted her to hear this.

"You ever listen to that goddamn thing? *'Tempus Fugit!'* He can tempus my fugit."

I recognized the name of Mr. Fletcher's radio program.

"It's goddamn ridiculous. Fairy tales for grown-ups. Does all the voices, too. Calls himself the Fairy Tale Man. Nobody takes him seriously."

"Sounds sweet," my mother offered.

"It ain't sweet. It's propaganda. You know what that means? Tempus fugit? Time flies, that's what. Nothing remains the same. That's Communist right there!"

My mother caught my eye, hoping for a way out. "Look," she said brightly. "There's Teddy! Doesn't he look stalwart?"

Daddy would not be silenced. "I don't listen to the damn fool thing, but Hank Haywood heard it down at the Sphinx Club. All these forest creatures rompin' around in harmony . . . but it ain't about that at all. It's about lettin' niggers in the schools."

"Be quiet, Armistead!" My mother's forefinger shot to her lips like a scarlet-tipped musket raised in warning. She didn't approve of that word. Not in public, not with Marjie Fletcher sitting within earshot. Once, down at a cottage at Wrightsville Beach, I used the word in a row with our maid's daughter, a skinny girl three years my senior. My mother overheard it and yanked me away by the wrist.

"You do not use that word, Teddy. Ever."

"She took my steam shovel."

"I don't care. You don't use that word. You hurt her feelings."

"Daddy says it all the time."

"It doesn't matter," she said. "He's your father."

That was her explanation for so many things.

I banned the N-word from my vocabulary, but there were further intricacies to be learned about race, and my mother set me straight on those as well. When I referred to someone as a "colored lady," she corrected me gently: "No, darling, she's a colored woman. There are no colored ladies. Only white ladies are ladies."

It was all so complicated.

WHEN GROWN-UPS TALKED about Daddy they often liked to use the word *unreconstructed*. For a long time I didn't understand what that meant, historically speaking, but it sounded like someone who had been taken apart and never put back together. *Unreconstructed.* Most folks used the word with humor and affection, but sometimes they would inject a disdainful note as if Daddy had somehow gone too far. I figured them to be Yankee sympathizers—or, like my Maupin cousins up in Cincinnati, actual Yankees—so I paid no mind to them. Yankees didn't get it.

I had sort of hoped that Freddy would turn out to be a Yankee. I myself had been accused of that, so I would have enjoyed turning the tables. Since I had been born in Washington, D.C., while Daddy was skippering a minesweeper in the Pacific, some of the kids at Ravenscroft School said that made me a Yankee. (Washington, after all, had been *the capital of the North*.) I had no choice but to take my accusers to our living room and show them the portrait over our Roman brick fireplace.

"That's Grandpa Branch. He was a Confederate general who died at Antietam. A Yankee sniper shot him off his horse when he was talking to General Lee. They put his body on display downtown in the Capitol. Mimi still sleeps in his bed."

Then I would take them to my grandmother's room and show them the bed itself, a sleigh bed with a chipped mahogany veneer that exposed the pale, dry bones beneath. "It's very old," I would tell them. "It was made by slaves in our family."

That's how my father always put it: *slaves in our family.*

I had copied his language because I thought it made us sound genteel but compassionate, the sort of kindly slaveholders who embraced their human property as family. Exactly *where* we held the slaves—or even where that bed had been made—was not entirely clear to me, but no one ever challenged the claim. Grandpa Branch's house, a gratifyingly white-columned mansion with its own North

Carolina historical marker, still stood down on Hillsborough Street, but it was nowhere near a cotton field. When I tried to picture house slaves doing whatever they were supposed to do, the image failed to materialize, since I'd never even been inside the house. It was a funeral home now, and a shabby one at that. It catered to Baptists and Holy Rollers, Daddy said, so none of us was ever likely to be found there, dead or alive.

This was disappointing, since my grandmother had told me so much about this house. General Sherman, she said, had been quartered there on his bloody March to the Sea. The Yankee general had been a friend of Grandpa Branch back when they were both in the U.S. Army, so he had accepted the kind hospitality of Grandma Branch and placed guards around the house to protect it from his own plundering troops. (I've often wondered about the sleeping arrangement—it was not the sort of thing I would have asked Mimi—but who could have faulted the hapless widow for being "hospitable" when her life and home were at stake.)

This was Mimi's own grandmother, so the story felt thrillingly current every time she told it, as if she herself had heard Sherman and Grandma Branch swapping pleasantries over hotcakes at the breakfast table before he went about his daily pillaging. Mimi always ended the story by saying that the weathercock on the steeple of Christ Church was the last poultry left in town after Sherman's army left.

I loved telling friends about the time Mimi rode on Jefferson Davis's catafalque. I wasn't completely clear on what a catafalque *was*, but I imagined it to be a sort of coffin-on-wheels with a platform for passengers. The Confederate president had been dead and buried in a New Orleans cemetery for almost four years when his widow decided he should be moved back to the Capital of the Confederacy. So, nearly thirty years after the South had fallen, the remains of its president were transplanted slightly to the north in a grand public spectacle that was part funeral procession, part whistle-stop tour. Mimi, by virtue of her slain Rebel grandfather, was invited to ride on this sacred box of bones when it passed through Raleigh. She was five years old. What she remembered, from the middle of the next century, was a starchy dress and the way her mother had scolded her when she smiled and waved merrily to the mourners along Hillsborough Street.

There was still evidence of this history in Mimi's room, most of it contained in a chest of drawers that looked like the big-shouldered sister of Grandpa Branch's sleigh bed. Even as a boy, I was allowed to explore this treasure trove in the name of family research. I found sepia photographs mounted on cardboard and letters from Civil War days, one of which—I forget whose—I took downtown to the Hall of History for lamination before returning it to the dresser. The bottom drawer held shoe boxes of typewritten letters bound with crumbling rubber bands. I found them less interesting than the others, since they were all from the 1930s, barely a decade older than I was. They were mostly testimonials from local organizations on the occasion of Mimi's husband's death: what a fine man he had been, what a fine husband and father, what a sterling citizen. They were so laden with bland civic hyperbole that I lost interest in them, never considering what might have motivated such overstatement. Besides, I had no face for my grandfather. We didn't talk about him; there was no portrait of him over the fireplace.

Mimi was a sweet, bent-over little thing, uncomplaining as the day was long, with a hearing aid in her slip as clunky as a bar of Ivory soap. She got increasingly shaky and doty as I moved toward my teen years. That's how my mother put it: shaky and doty, delicate shorthand for Parkinson's and Alzheimer's. When Mimi's mind played tricks on her, it usually did so before bedtime, so my father, alerted by my mother, would storm off to Mimi's room to fix things. Behind the closed door you could hear only Daddy's half of the conversation, but that's all you needed.

"Goddammit, Mama, they are not investigating you! . . . I don't care what you heard, that's ridiculous. . . . When? Who said that? . . . The goddamn Christ Church prayer group is not investigating you, Mama. . . . All right, the Women's Auxiliary, they aren't investigating you either! This is crazy talk, Mama. Nobody's doin' any such thing."

I knew my father was right, but I never stopped to think about why Mimi's nocturnal terrors made him so angry, why he seemed to take them personally. One night, after a trip to the kitchen for Bosco and milk and a sandwich, I heard an odd sound coming from Mimi's room. I stopped at the end of the hallway and listened. The sound came and went, an intermittent squeak, like that little noise dogs make when they're dreaming. It took me a while to figure out what Mimi was doing, right there in Grandpa Branch's big sleigh bed, and it was deeply unsettling.

Old ladies were not supposed to cry in their sleep like little children.

I GOT OFF easily, I guess, as Southern boyhoods went, since my father never insisted on guns or sports. He rarely ever talked about either, in fact, explaining that the pistol in his bedroom was intended only for protection from intruders. This suited me fine, since I was humiliated by the compulsory ball games at recess, and I could fall into guilty despair if I killed so much as a fly in a windowsill. I didn't even like fishing. The sight of a fish flapping and gasping on a dock, dying alone, away from its family, was cause for great anguish. My delicacy in this regard cannot have gone unnoticed by my father, but I don't remember him ever remarking on it; maybe he thought it would eventually recede with the arrival of testosterone.

He had to summon new reserves of strength when, in my teens, I decided I needed a stained-glass window for my bedroom. I had seen the windows at Ye Blue Tartane, a "European-style" motor court in Petersburg, Virginia, and wanted the same Olde Worlde charm for my bedroom. My father, with only a trace of a sigh, agreed to take me to Raleigh's sole purveyor of stained glass, a workshop in the country where an old man in suspenders made windows for Baptist churches. I chose various textures of green, red, and purple glass, then told the glazier exactly how I wanted the squares and rectangles arranged. Daddy watched this process in silence, frowning a little now and then. What must he have been thinking?

I was in the middle of a crafty period back then. I concocted natural vegetable dyes on the stove in the kitchen, turning skeins of yarn gold and purple with onion skins and bark and berries. I loved the whole process: waiting for the colors to turn out, then fixing them with alum and admiring the results when the yarn was dry and soft and bunched up again. I couldn't knit, so I never actually made anything with the yarn. But I pinned the skeins to a piece of stiff cardboard with labels, like a rock collection, and submitted it to the Broughton Science Fair. They told me it didn't quite fit any of their categories and I should think about submitting it to the Arts Fair. The Arts Fair told me roughly the same thing, only they suggested I try a Sewing Fair, at which point I decided it was probably safer to enjoy my pretty yarn in private.

It's not like Daddy didn't like beautiful things himself. He built a bamboo bridge over our muddy creek and a lych-gate at the bottom of the garden. His azaleas were the envy of the neighborhood. On the way back from the beach he would stop and buy specimen plants at the nursery at Orton Plantation, a bona fide piece of the Old South that could easily be transplanted to Raleigh. Following his example, I harvested a tangle of Spanish moss from an oak tree behind an Esso station and brought it home with visions of an antebellum transformation in our backyard. Daddy was dubious, but I was determined to show him. I draped the stuff among our dogwoods like Christmas tinsel and waited for it to flourish, fluffing it a little from time to time, sprinkling it with the hose. It took weeks for the gray-green strands to shrivel into black filaments, so I never knew the exact moment of its death, just the unfixable fact of it. My youth would be like that, the slow decay of cherished myths—about politics and race, about love itself—until nothing was left but compost from which something authentic could finally begin to grow.

WHICH IS NOT to say that I didn't love being Southern as a child. I loved it as much as anything, as much as the Hardy Boys and fountain Cokes and Rosemary Clooney in *White Christmas*. I read and reread a book called *Tar Heel Ghosts*, true North Carolina stories of eerie lights along railroad tracks, and faces reappearing in windows, and a perfectly circular path in the pinewoods where nothing grew and objects left on the path before midnight would be gone by dawn. I loved the idea that the landscape itself was part of the story, a surviving portal into the past that you could see and touch. I was especially enchanted by an old lead mine on the edge of town, a muddy tunnel barely wide enough for a boy to wriggle in on his belly, where graphite had once been dug for use in Rebel gunpowder. My patriotism alone demanded I explore it. The tunnel turned out to be only a dozen feet long, but it was a wonder those dripping pencil-gray walls never swallowed me up like Little Kathy in the well, a candidate for some other kid's letter of consolation. (Daddy would surely have told the press that at least I had died the way I would have wanted, entombed in Confederate gunpowder.)

I was just as enthralled by Christ Church, the neo-Gothic stone pile on Capitol Square that our family had attended since before the Civil War. It was my own version of the House of Usher, smelling exotically of musty velvet and lilies and linseed oil. It was there that I earned my God and Country Award as a Boy Scout, religiously squeezing Elmer's Glue into the cracked spines of prayer books. Sometimes my friend Clark and I snuck into the bell tower or crawled under the floorboards looking for Bishop Ravenscroft, who was said to be buried beneath the altar.

You could still see my father's tooth marks in Pew 17, where, as a small boy, he had gnawed on the wood in boredom during long communion services on his knees. I learned about those tooth marks when Daddy cited them as proof of our dominion over Pew 17. We had always been in Pew 17, he said, and everyone knew that except those common-as-pigs'-tracks newcomers who had brazenly sat in our pew one Sunday when we stayed home. The old man had heard about this from Miss Nell and Miss Elizabeth Hinsdale, the spinster sisters who occupied the pew in front of us, each adorned with an entire dead creature—furry head, tail, paws, and everything. Once we knew of the pew invaders, our church attendance improved dramatically, and the mood at home grew more urgent on Sunday mornings.

"Goddammit, Diana, get 'em in the car. That goddamn house painter is gonna beat us to the pew."

My parents were not especially religious. They would not like to read that here, but they weren't. It was just something we were supposed to do. My father had given me a prayer book for my confirmation, one his own father had given him, but it was more of a familial ritual than anything to do with a private God. My mother was famously kind and loving, an innately good-hearted person, but the guidance she whispered in my ear during church largely focused on my appearance. *Look reverent,* was what I heard most often, which irked me, since I knew I was great at looking reverent. I was an acolyte, personally trained by Reverend Sapp. I knew how to look plenty reverent when snuffing out a candle. Brides-to-be, in fact, sometimes requested me by name for their weddings.

Reverend Daniel Sapp was a gentle, willowy man who was beloved for spending hours at the bedsides of the sick and dying. Most folks, out of affection and familiarity, mashed his first and last names into a single word: Dansapp. The fact that he had a wife and children was usually enough to absolve him from the widespread suspicion that he might be "that way," though there was reason for such speculation, given his fondness for camp. When greeting his flock after the service, Dansapp referred to his cassock as his "dress," especially if it was something in raspberry. He got a kick out of inviting new parishioners to his office to see his "collection of cocks." There, to their great relief, they would behold his array of rooster figurines, an affectionate nod to the historic weathercock on the steeple.

My mother's concerns about my demeanor in church escalated in my early teens when I decided to ditch ordinary Episcopalianism for the High Church version. I began crossing myself with such casual aplomb that I might have been doing it for years. This brought puzzled sideways frowns from Mummie, but she let my unilateral act of rebellion pass without comment. I'm sure she knew it would not last long, and it didn't. I got totally hung up on transubstantiation, the part about the wafer literally turning to flesh in my mouth. I would address this concern twenty years later in *More Tales of the City*, when I invented a group of High Church Episcopalians who took their faith so seriously that they ate actual body parts—stolen medical waste—on a catwalk high above the altar in San Francisco's Grace Cathedral. In another sixteen years, when the *More Tales* miniseries was filmed, I would be asked to play the priest in that scene. My deficiencies as an actor made this moment awkward enough, but the severed rubber foot that was dropped on me bounced absurdly when it hit the altar. Our French-Canadian director had no sympathy when I confessed to feeling queasy about the scene. "You wrote it," he said with a Gallic shrug.

Until the day she died my mother never stopped worrying about how I appeared to the world. When I was in my early teens she sat me down and told me gently that I shouldn't see so much of my friend Eddie. At first I thought this was because Eddie was a Yankee (by way of Minneapolis and Miami) who vehemently disapproved of the Confederate monument on Capitol Square and whose parents had Danish modern furniture in their house. But then she spelled it out for me: Eddie was "a little bit sissy," and if we were close friends, *"people might get the wrong idea."* I had never had that idea myself; I just thought he liked movies.

I know my mother thought she was worrying in my own best interest, as she did with all of us. When acne arrived, as promised, she saw my despair (and my early abuse of Clearasil as a concealer) and taught me to clear my face of oil with a splash of Mennen's Skin Bracer on a quilted cotton pad. Then she went on lengthy reconnaissance missions, hunting blackheads like a mother monkey hunting fleas, popping them with her nails and holding up the waxy proof of her labors. "Look, darling. We got him good. Wait a sec, don't move. There's one more teeny one here on your neck." The process was humiliating, and often unnerving. Sometimes, when we were talking, I realized she wasn't looking at me at all, just patrolling my pores for the enemy. She could pounce unexpectedly, too, forcing me to swat her away with gangly mortification.

She also fretted over the way I walked, sort of slew-footed with my feet turned out like a duck—very much the way I still walk, as a matter of fact. There was nothing physically wrong with me, she said; it was just a bad habit I could break by consciously turning my feet straight until it became second nature. She had lots of time to test this theory when the family spent a week at Shrine Mont, an Episcopal retreat in the mountains of Virginia. On the way to the dining room or the slimy-green swimming pool, my mother would linger a few paces behind. "Turn 'em straight, darling," she would call like a cheery drill sergeant; or sometimes, "Much better!" just to keep my spirits up. I was unconvinced. Nothing about this awkward exercise would ever become second nature to me. If you want to feel even more like a duck, try walking like a pigeon.

It was maybe a year later that our doctor noticed something amiss in the cleft of my butt, up at the very top, near the bottom of my back, a dimple of sorts that apparently was the vestigial remnant of the glands birds use for preening their feathers. Lots of perfectly normal young men had these, my mother assured me, but they could sometimes become infected. And, since tens of thousands of servicemen had been hospitalized during the Second World War with "Jeeps Disease" (so named because it was thought to be caused by bouncing in a Jeep), my "pigeon preener" (as my mother cheerfully called it) would automatically exempt me from service. This distressed my father, who had big plans for me, military-wise, when the time came.

Not to worry, said the doctor. He could perform a simple operation in his office, just a few stitches with the shades drawn, and no one would be the wiser. I knew already that there was another way to be disqualified for military service, but that would not betray me unless

I waited too long to get married. My father got married when he was twenty-six, so I figured that was how long I would have before anyone became suspicious. In the meantime, I took my cues from Dear Abby, who had recently told her readers that parents should be concerned if their sixteen-year-old child had never kissed a member of the opposite sex. That was all the expert advice I needed. I took a girl I barely knew to Roy's Drive-In and gave her desultory kisses while the windows fogged up. It felt like earning a merit badge.

I knew I was mentally ill. I had read it somewhere in a magazine. I'd heard that there were ways to treat it, too, if a psychiatrist was alerted early enough. But I couldn't bring myself to tell my parents, even if it could save me from permanent insanity. There were mornings when I woke up thinking, *Tonight I'll tell them. After supper, maybe, or after* Gunsmoke, *when Tony and Jane and Mimi are in bed.* But I never found the nerve. (Had I done so, I would no doubt have other stories to tell you now, ones about homoerotic slide shows with electroshock devices that attached, ever so correctively, to my genitals.)

I decided that one way to thwart my inevitable shame would be to become paralyzed from the waist down. If I couldn't use that part of me, no one, including my wife-to-be, could have unrealistic expectations. I would have lots of sympathy, too, as well as an air of nobility. Exactly *how* I was to achieve paralysis was never clear to me. A car wreck, perhaps, if it wasn't a really bad one. Polio might work, too, though people rarely got that anymore; we had had the shots.

I can pinpoint the day when I knew there would be no fixing me. It was a muggy summer afternoon, and I had just dropped Mimi off at the beauty parlor in the old Carolina Hotel on Nash Square. Killing time, I wandered into the newsstand—the "blind stand," as they were called back then, since they were traditionally staffed by blind people. There, prominently displayed on a rack, was a magazine called *Demigods* with a blond, bare-chested man staring at me from the cover. I had seen photos of shirtless men before—in the Sears catalog, for instance—but this guy was not there in the name of haberdashery. He was lolling in bed amid a tangle of satin sheets, and, quite clearly, he wanted me.

Since the blind cashier was the only other person in the room, I could easily have flipped through that magazine. Hell, I could have *bought* the damned thing. I could have told him it was *Time* or *Field & Stream*, left a few coins in his dish, and sailed out of the room with my prize. But I knew that the blind had other senses that were highly developed. What if the mere sound of my footfall had betrayed my exact location and object of my lust? What if he could *smell* me loitering there?

I fled the magazine and the newsstand with a feeble *Thank you, sir* just to make it clear to him that I hadn't been shoplifting, and sought refuge from my panic in my new car, a cherry-red VW bug that enveloped me like a blast furnace when I unlocked the door. I turned on the radio to collect myself, only to hear a song called "Walk on the Wild Side," which seemed the perfect soundtrack for the moment, since it proclaimed with sultry trombones that I had already begun my slide into hell. (This was not the famous Lou Reed song but an earlier one of the same name, written for a movie starring Jane Fonda as a New Orleans hooker.)

How could I argue with that? I had seen the abyss now, and it was blond and bare-chested. Apparently, there were whole magazines out there devoted to my secret mental illness—or, as the state of North Carolina had officially phrased it, "the unspeakable crime against nature." I knew that term already because of my trigonometry teacher, a man I still think of as the meanest teacher I ever had. On the very first day of class he appeared to delight in our confusion over our daunting new subject and threatened to flunk us all if we didn't get a grip on it, and quick.

I remember how overwhelmed I felt, how completely at his mercy. And I can still feel the flood of relief that came a week later when another teacher showed up, unannounced, to replace him. Most of us assumed his dismissal had to do with his sadistic teaching methods, until an item appeared in the morning paper. He had been arrested for crimes against nature in William B. Umstead State Park, on the edge of town. When the word spread around class, I remember making a flippant joke about defacing trees, but it was no joke to me. This was my own dark forest, bristling with hideous demons; this was the very man I did not want to be.

When I returned to the Carolina Hotel that muggy afternoon, I steered clear of the blind stand. I went straight to the beauty parlor, where Mimi was already waiting for me, her thin, mouse-colored hair artfully arranged above her sweet, plain face. I told her how pretty she looked and asked if she wanted to go for a drive. So we went to Oakwood Cemetery, where, at the nursery greenhouse just outside the gate, I bought myself a potted cactus as I often did on our weekly Sunday visits. (I had many such cacti in my bedroom window, a phalanx of telltale phalluses facing the world in stoic silence.) In the cemetery Mimi stood by her husband's grave for several minutes, looking her best for him, until the weighing-down heat of the afternoon finally got too much for us.

We stopped for milkshakes at the Krispy Kreme on our way home. Even as a teenager I loved doing things like this with Mimi. We went to see *Lili* at the Village Theatre, bonding over it so completely that we might have been on a date. To this day I can conjure Mimi up by singing the song that Leslie Caron sang in the movie, the one about love and how sad it is. Mimi, I realize, must have found that all too true.

Forty years after that disturbing moment at the blind stand, I told that story to my friend Nick Hongola. Nick had served as caregiver for an elderly gay man, who, having no further need for his circa-1960s porn, had bequeathed his collection to Nick. "That name rings a bell," Nick said with an impish smile, and the next day he showed up at my house with an old issue of *Demigods* magazine. It wasn't just any issue, either—it was *the very one*—and my secret cover boy was just as splendid as I'd remembered (the arms, the chest, the rakish curl across his forehead), though his name, Larry Kunz, left a little something to be desired. As for those satin sheets, they proved not to be sheets at all but a plastic shower curtain wrapped around his waist. He was not even in bed, in fact—that was the edge of a bathtub he was sitting on.

I was well into my fifties by then, but I tore through that magazine like a kid under a Christmas tree. Sadly, there were no other photos of the unfortunately named Mr. Kunz, but there were lots of other strapping young bucks decked out in sailor caps and pendulous posing straps. Their names were sexier, too, though possibly suspect— names like Troy Saxon and Mike Nificent. I got a kick out of the page of exotic mail-order gifts, items seemingly indispensable to the manly household of 1962: an Indian pith helmet; an antiques dealers' handbook; a twenty-one-inch imported Italian pepper mill; a musical cigarette box that played "Smoke Gets in Your Eyes." It was like one of those pages in my old comic books where sea monkeys and joy buzzers and X-ray glasses lured gullible children with the promise of power and popularity.

But what struck me most about that fading artifact was how profoundly innocent it seemed to me in late middle age. I was hard-pressed to remember how the very sight of *Demigods* had once scorched me with shame and dread, invoking that awful war chant of a word— *ho-mo-sex-u-al*—that I'd been trying so hard not to hear. How could I have guessed then that the thing I feared most in myself would one day be the source of my greatest joy, the inspiration for my life's work.

THREE

I HAD AN AWFUL RECURRING NIGHTMARE as a child. Nothing with a narrative of any kind, just a crushing, bone-gray weight that roared in my ears like a jet engine and sent me running down the hallway in the dark to the refuge of my parents' big Sears & Roebuck French provincial bed. There was nothing I could articulate that they could dispel on the spot, so sometimes I would sleep between them all night. Or I would wake up in my own bed in the morning without quite knowing how I got there. This nightmare didn't happen often, but the feeling of it was recognizable when it returned, an amorphous terror without a plot or a cast of characters.

As I grew older I learned about self-hypnosis and began putting myself to sleep with stories. They were serials, actually, each one taking up where I had left off the night before. There was one I called "The Secret Crossroads," a mystery in the woods inspired by the Hardy Boys, and another took place under the sea, like the movies I loved at the time where strong Greek sponge fishermen bubbled around in diving helmets and got the bends if they came up too fast. I still play with stories just before sleep, believing, I suppose, that the unconscious mind will offer assistance.

So storytelling came first; writing more or less crept up on me. When I was nine I kept a diary with a green vinyl cover and a little lock with a key. I'm pretty sure I got the idea from *Little Lulu*, but I didn't stick with it longer than a few months, no longer than I've ever stuck with a diary. I didn't exactly pour my heart out. I wrote about movies I had seen, and stuff I ate for lunch, and a murder case that Bobby Ballance and I were solving on the bus on the way home from school. There were several cases, so we rotated them as we saw fit, reciting the clues into a reel-to-reel tape recorder at Bobby's house, the first device of its kind I had ever seen. The diary refers to the Skippy Goldston Case, and since I have no idea what or who it involved, I'll have to ask Bobby about it the next time we connect on Facebook.

At roughly the same time—or was it earlier?—I was allowed to take shirt cardboards from Daddy's dresser to serve as storyboards for my "Little Tallulah" comics. I had updated my favorite comic heroine by merging her with my favorite radio star, a funny lady with a voice like a man, who soothed me every week on *The Big Show* with her closing rendition of "May the Good Lord Bless and Keep You." Her benediction meant everything to me, since she seemed so warm and forgiving.

I had begun to mouth off to my parents as soon as I started going to school, and Daddy got so mad sometimes he would haul off and slap me hard. I knew how to handle this. I would whimper very softly in my room, keeping it pitiful until my mother sent my father in to make amends. He never apologized, just sat on the edge of the bed and called me "Sport" and talked about buying me the bullwhip I wanted so badly, or about the little shelf he would build for my radio once we got the bunk beds. Once, after another slapping, I punished him in a different way by smashing an ashtray I had made for him in school. It was a plaster handprint of my hand, painted shiny pink, and Daddy's cigarette ashes were supposed to go in the indentations. The destruction of this keepsake really hurt him, I believed, and I felt bad for days, since it was not an action I could take back, even if I made him another ashtray.

In fifth grade at Ravenscroft School, where children of Old Raleigh families attended class in a war-surplus Quonset hut, Mrs. Robertson encouraged us to write by giving us picture postcards with paintings from art museums. She called this exercise Word Pictures. I chose a postcard from the Old West, a night scene with a dark-blue sky above a main street saloon that glowed like a lantern. I wrote about the tinkling of the piano and the boots clomping on the wooden sidewalk and the shadow of a stranger coming into town. Mrs. Robertson went nuts over it, reading it aloud, very slowly, to the class. I had never before felt so good about anything.

There were two short pieces in the seventh grade, both of which were mimeographed and distributed. One was an autumnal mood piece, just a paragraph, but heavy on the scenery, using words like *myriad* and *azure* that no one uses after the seventh grade. The piece came to a halt, rather rhythmically, I thought, with two short sentences: "All is calm. Tranquility reigns." The other piece was a poem, even shorter than the paragraph, about a boy who worships a girl as a goddess until he sees a vaccination mark on her arm and realizes she is not immortal. Three guesses what was going on there. I needed credible excuses, and fast, for why I didn't have a girlfriend yet, and perfectionism seemed as good as any. I loved girls too much to actually go steady with one. Privately, I assured myself that I would fall in love when I met a girl who looked like Kim Novak in *Vertigo*. Good one, since no one looked like Kim Novak in *Vertigo*; though, as of this writing, Miss Novak still makes a valiant effort.

Mrs. Peacock—Mrs. Phyllis Peacock—was that teacher writers write about, the one who singled them out in class and heaped praise upon them and predicted a great career to the everlasting eye-rolling annoyance of everyone else in class. Two of her previous graduates of Senior English, Reynolds Price and Anne Tyler, had already received this anointment; all three of us eulogized Mrs. Peacock to the press when she died at ninety-four, in 1998, after half a century of teaching. She was a tiny dynamo, more hummingbird than peacock, really, and she flitted about the room with goofy histrionic flair, sometimes jumping onto chairs to make her point. A lot of kids giggled at her behind her back, but they weren't the ones getting "Orchids to You" written on their essays, complete with a drawing of an orchid.

I wonder now if Mrs. Peacock sensed what a wallflower I was, despite my efforts at sophisticated banter in class. She once asked me to research the origins of the maypole and report back to the class the next day. I knew nothing at all—only that debutantes danced around a maypole at the Terpsichorean Ball, as did the girls at St. Mary's Junior College, where my sister, Jane, was expected to go. When I asked my parents about maypoles at dinner, my father snorted, and my mother blushed and giggled. That night, when I went to my room, I found that Mummie had left a volume of the *Encyclopædia Britannica* on my bed, opened to an entry titled "Phallic Symbols." We never spoke about it after that. And the next morning, when I made my report to Mrs. Peacock, she listened, wide-eyed and seemingly enthralled by my account of pagans and penises, as if she had never imagined such a thing.

Her big finale for the year was to assign us literary-themed performance pieces at the school auditorium. I was already comfortable onstage, thanks to the Raleigh Little Theatre, where, at thirteen, I had been cast in their production of *The Desperate Hours*. I had played a suburban boy who was kidnapped by thugs and, all too briefly for my taste, manhandled by them. For Mrs. Peacock's assignment, I paired off with my friend Sarah Pierce, a smart girl known for her large breasts, and we created a stage piece about Sleep in Literature. We dressed all in white, and made Doric columns by covering Pine State Ice Cream cartons with marble Con-Tact paper and stacking them on volleyball poles from the gym. We recited everything about sleep that I could find in *Bartlett's Familiar Quotations* and ended with a passage from Tennyson's "The Lotos-Eaters," which I had committed to memory. The poem was about narcotic blossoms that made stranded sailors forgetful of home; according to Mrs. Peacock, Tennyson had chosen his words for their lulling, soporific quality.

"There is sweet music here that softer falls / Than petals from blown roses on the grass, / Or night-dews on still waters between walls / Of shadowy granite, in a gleaming pass; . . ."

When I was done, I looked into the audience to see Mrs. Peacock feigning sleep in the front row, her head tilted to one side. After a moment or two, she "woke" theatrically, like a storybook princess shaking off a spell, and began to applaud.

I used that poem when I wrote *Tales of the City*, almost fifteen years later. Mrs. Madrigal, the landlady at 28 Barbary Lane, recites it to her baffled new tenant, Mary Ann Singleton. Several years after that book was published, I did my first Raleigh book signing at a downtown bookstore. To my amazement there was something of a line, thanks to the publicity in *The Front Page*, North Carolina's first gay newspaper. Even more amazingly, Mrs. Peacock was there. She twiddled her fingers at me but insisted on waiting her turn when the two men ahead of her, both dressed head-to-toe in black leather, graciously offered her their place in line.

I WAS BLESSED with women like that in my youth, fairy godmothers who taught me how to nourish my incipient fairy heart. My mother's mother, the English suffragist, was an elegant, fey spirit from a time when past lives were all the rage. I was the oldest of Grannie's nineteen grandchildren, the first of us to fall under her seductive spell. She took me to see the first run of *Singin' in the Rain*, and had even let me go back twice on my own so I could master the lyrics of all my favorite songs. Since that time she had often theorized that I was the reincarnation of her beloved cousin Curtis back in England. Her *bachelor* cousin Curtis. Her extremely *artistic* bachelor cousin Curtis.

At six I had watched Grannie rise like a genie from a trapdoor in the stage of the Raleigh Little Theatre. (She had driven all the way from Virginia in her beige Ford to visit her daughter's family and take the lead in *The Madwoman of Chaillot*. I remember her huge aluminum suitcase with its sharp corners and uncomfortable wire handle that always made Daddy cuss when he hauled it into the house.) She was this stately little partridge of a woman, but there she was on opening night levitating from a cellar in Paris and playing to the kid in the third row. I was no stranger to theater—I had played a nonspeaking role on that very stage the year before as one of the murdered children in *Medea*—but Grannie's booming melodramatic delivery, coupled with my first whiff of stage smoke, came as a revelation to a boy already starved for enchantment. I was beside myself.

I don't know if she was anything more than a dedicated amateur. She must have been good at playing "the Madwoman," because she had played it once before at the Alexandria Little Theatre. When she came to visit us in Raleigh, she and my mother, also a little theater actress, referred to "the Madwoman" so off-handedly that it might have been someone they knew. When my mother played Eliza Doolittle, Grannie helped her with her Cockney accent. They could be actresses together, those two—that was their bond—and I'm sure it had offered them both, at different times, blessed relief from bombastic husbands. An actress had rehearsals, after all. An actress could be away from home for reasons other than the Junior League and the Piggly Wiggly. I can remember my father's growly discontent as he served up the chicken divan casserole our mother had left behind on one of her rehearsal nights. "Your mama's down at the theater with the goddamn fairies."

The summer I turned ten my parents put me on a train to Virginia so I could stay with Grannie for several weeks. Looking back, that strikes me as out of the ordinary. Had Grannie actually requested this visit, or had there been a crisis at home, some unmentionable "female operation" that necessitated a long-term child-sitter? I had already figured out that ladies kept family secrets even theater-loving boys were not allowed to hear. Whatever the reason, I was thrilled about it, since I would have the Madwoman all to myself. It would be just the two of us when we went to the Smithsonian or down to the Hot Shoppe in Shirlington for roast young tom turkey with all the trimmin's, and hot dogs in exotic rectangular buns.

Virginia was just as steaming hot as North Carolina, but Grannie built a nest out of old mattresses in her cool basement laundry room where I could curl up with my "Uncle Scrooge" comics and feast on buttered bread and iced tea, addictions that have followed me down the years. It was there that Grannie first began reading my palm, gently interrogating me about all my lives, past and present. As much as anything, palmistry was her excuse for offering tactful wisdom. When I grew older and Grannie visited Raleigh more frequently, I watched with pride as she read the palms of many others: my school friends, our maid Camilla, and once, during one of my parents' parties, the governor of North Carolina. Sometimes she dispensed with personal contact altogether and cruised for palms in public places, sneaking a peek on the fly. I was with her once on a crosstown bus when she nearly fell out of her seat in her effort to eavesdrop on an interesting hand on the other side of the aisle.

My own readings became a regular affair, the equivalent of a semi-annual checkup. I'm sure that was because Grannie wasn't getting the answers she really wanted. When she studied my lifeline and asked me about career choices, my reply would be the same for many years:

"I want to be a lawyer like Daddy." Whereupon, she would manage a feeble smile and close my fingers like a book she was done with for the evening. She rarely interceded in family matters, especially ones that might challenge my father's game plan, but she knew about me. She *knew*.

By the time I was thirteen I knew about me, too. I had begun to have dreams about kissing grown-up gas-station attendants, a development that disturbed me since it wasn't just messing around the way boys did on camping trips; it was flat-out romance. I learned the hard way to put a towel behind the toilet tank to keep it from banging against the wall when I jerked off in the morning. My father had called me on this over breakfast: "What was that thumping I heard this morning, son? You spent an awful long time in the crapper." He must have been thinking, with some degree of relief, that this was the advent of Girls for me. At the time, it was unimaginable to me that he could have known what was going on, much less tease me about it, but I was mortified just the same. Five years later I saw him inflict similar torment on my thirteen-year-old sister when he found a box of Kotex in her suitcase on a family trip. Such matters were never discussed in our family, but as soon as one of us arrived at a scary new rite of passage, the old man was there to greet us with a knowing leer. He seemed to enjoy making us uncomfortable. He was a pissed-off, shut-down guy, but I never stopped to think about why. All I knew—all I thought about, really—was that sooner or later I was bound to disappoint him.

Thus Grannie became a comfort in the minefield of my adolescence. Alone among my family and friends, she made no assumptions (and held no expectations) about my blossoming masculinity. When my father referred to Reverend Sapp as a "fairy nice fellow," Grannie registered disproval with a scolding glance and a soft "Oh, Armistead, must you?" Once, when she and I attended a garden party at Mount Vernon (not George Washington's house but a slightly smaller replica in a fancy Raleigh neighborhood), we spotted a woman in spike heels tottering ahead of us on a perfect green lawn. She was a pale-pink hallucination, a tipsy flamingo on the run, perfumed and powdered to the nth degree. As soon as she was out of earshot, Grannie turned to me with a sly smile and murmured, "Any woman who is all woman or any man who is all man is a complete monster unfit for human company."

This was the South in 1958, and I had never heard such a thing.

FOUR

IT WAS MY FRIEND CLARK WHO told me how my Southern grandfather had died. Clark, if you remember, was the one who had taken me spelunking beneath Christ Church. He was a bit of a self-styled rogue, a stoop-shouldered, hatchet-faced boy with a perpetual wild hair up his ass. He had a way of goading me into action, or at least into acquiescence, by muttering the same challenge every time: "Have you no spirit of adventure?" He said that before he drove our pickup into the surf at Carolina Beach and when he proposed a BB-gun fight between tents on an Explorer camping trip. Never mind that the pickup got stuck in the sand or that a BB got lodged in the cartilage of another boy's ear and had to be dug out, with considerable effort, using the pointy end of a church key—Clark had a way of forgetting his fiascoes.

Clark idolized my father. His own father was a soft-spoken architect who worked in a converted brick water tower downtown, so my father's constant bombast and engagement with everything and everybody must have been attractive to Clark. Both of us, I suppose, longed for what was conspicuously missing at home.

One day, as I often did after school, I walked through the woods to Clark's house. When I asked him about a fresh scratch on the side of his face, he dismissed it manfully as nothing, then led me down to Nicotine Alley, his secret smoking place in the woods. There, lighting a Lucky and speaking in the mumbling tones of a B-movie hood, he told me he'd been in a fight with another kid, a kid whose name I didn't recognize. Clark said he had been defending my father's honor.

"About what?"

"He called him 'the suicide's son.'"

"What do you mean?"

"You know. Because your granddaddy killed himself."

I was dumbfounded. "How do you know that?"

Clark just shrugged. "Everybody knows that."

Everybody did know that, including Mummie, who was on her Stauffer machine when I got home that afternoon. A Stauffer machine was a vinyl-covered bench that looked like a modern massage table, only lower, with a center part that moved from side to side at various speeds in the name of exercise. It was wildly comic to us kids, since Mummie looked like a horizontal hula girl when she used it.

I stopped at the door of her walk-in closet, not far from the head of the Stauffer machine, which seemed to be set at its highest speed. My mother was always svelte and beautiful, so I couldn't imagine why she thought she needed it. In those days people often said she looked like Elizabeth Taylor.

I got to the point right away.

"Did Daddy's daddy kill himself?"

"Oh, Teddy . . . you frightened me!"

"Sorry."

She turned off the machine and sat up on the bench in her terry-cloth jumpsuit. "Who told you that?"

"Clark."

"Well, that was very naughty of him."

"He wasn't being mean. He was defending Daddy. Is it true?"

She told me she didn't know much about it herself. My father had spoken of it only once, just before they got married, and she had never raised the subject again, realizing it would be too painful for Daddy. It had happened at home, she said, at night, while Mimi and her other two children were in the house. He had used a shotgun. Daddy was nineteen and away at college, so an old family retainer had driven to Chapel Hill to break the news in person. "Your daddy done kilt hisself."

Zebedee, I thought. *That must have been Zebedee.*

I had met Zebedee only once, when Daddy had suddenly taken a different route to a nursery to stop in front of a rundown house in the country. A skinny old black man had come out of the house, recognized Daddy, and thrown his hat to the ground in a gesture of amazement and joy. They clearly had not seen each other for years. Daddy got out of the car to talk to him, but I couldn't hear their conversation. Afterward all he said to me was: "Zebedee used to work for us. Fine fella."

I asked my mother if they knew why my grandfather had killed himself.

"Not really, but . . . it was during the Depression. And he had too many old ladies to deal with. That might have been part of it."

"Old ladies?"

"Who lived at the house. Aunts and such. Mimi's folks. It may have gotten too much for him. I don't know, darling."

I couldn't imagine why he would kill himself because of old ladies. That was another family house I couldn't begin to picture, since I had seen it only from the road. Daddy's father had built it in the twenties, out at the far end of Clark Avenue, near Meredith College. It was a big brick place with square white columns set back among oak trees. I could see Daddy with Zebedee in a Model T, heading home to that house, wondering what remnants of his father were still on the walls, realizing he had just become the man of the house, whether he wanted it or not.

Mummie could see where my vivid little mind was going.

"And you mustn't ask Daddy about it, darling. Do you understand? We don't need the details."

Maybe *she* didn't, but I did. I was thinking about those overwrought condolence letters in Mimi's dresser and the time I'd heard Mimi weeping in her sleep and her persistent delusion that the ladies of Christ Church were investigating her. Daddy wasn't the only person who'd been left with a mess to clean up. And what about his brother and sister, who had still been young children at the time? Had they all heard the shot? Who got there first? Yes, a few details would have been useful, but Mummie was a lifelong list keeper of Things That Might Hurt Your Father, and she was very clear about this one. He shouldn't have to think about this ever again.

At least Daddy's rage finally had a reason. Twenty years after his father's suicide he was still lashing out at the world, at goddamn integrationists and goddamn Communists and mild old Fred Fletcher with his subversive philosophy of tempus fugit. Tempus would never fugit for my father; it was stuck in 1933.

Unreconstructed.

And something else occurred to me once I'd learned about my grandfather: Daddy had a way of threatening to die whenever he argued with my mother or endured the pouting disapproval of his children. "Well, you don't have to worry about me, anyway. I won't be around much longer." I had never taken this seriously, considering it little more than histrionics over his high cholesterol, whatever *that* was. Now I wondered if suicide might run in the family, if the gun he kept in the bedroom closet, right there on the shelf above the Stauffer machine, might do the job one day. Whenever Daddy blew up at dinner and stomped off to the bedroom in a blind fury, I would consciously count the seconds after he left, as if marking the distance between a flash of lightning and the terrible thunder that was certain to follow.

The truth about my grandfather made me look at my father through different eyes. He seemed more breakable to me now, more broken; but rather than question the values that had sprung from his trauma, I chose to embrace them completely. He needed me on his side, after all, and I needed him to love me, so I resolved to follow in his conservative footsteps. There was already a national movement afoot to take back the country from the Communist sympathizers, and I would be part of it.

I started reading my father's copies of *Human Events* (where, at this very moment, Ann Coulter is writing love letters to Donald Trump) and studied the flyers that Daddy got in the mail from the John Birch Society. When, at sixteen, I was named student City Manager of Raleigh for a day, I told a reporter that young right-wingers like me would soon be of voting age, and that should serve as fair warning to liberal politicians who wanted big government and socialism. I had just read *1984* and *Brave New World*, so I thought that's what we were fighting against, a totalitarian regime that wouldn't stop at putting rats on your face. My father's face was flushed with pride when he read my adolescent war cry in the morning paper.

"Attaboy, son! You tell those sonsabitches!"

Not long thereafter the old man gave me a book called *Race and Reason: A Yankee View*. It was written by someone named Carleton Putnam, a businessman who eventually ran Delta Air Lines, and who was, in fact, a Yankee—a smart one, to boot, according to my father, since he went to Princeton and Columbia, and was an aristocrat, and wasn't afraid to speak the goddamn truth. This made him a perfect last-ditch voice for the cause of segregation. Putnam had studied the skulls of whites and Negroes and come to the conclusion that Negroes needed another five hundred billion years of evolution before they could breed with the whites without damaging bloodlines. This timetable served everyone, he argued, black and white alike, since it let the races evolve at their own rate and achieve their highest biological destinies.

Or something.

My father loved *Race and Reason*. It was his go-to political tract on the subject of race, his *Uncle Tom's Cabin*. It didn't mince words, he said, but it was written in such a calm scholarly voice that it sounded, well, reasonable—just as the title implied. It wasn't racist to make a case for segregation, just reasonable.

Daddy's own thoughts on racial mixing tended to run to the practical side:

"Don't worry, son. If you ever knock up a little nigger gal, we can send her to Puerto Rico for the operation."

It seems to me now that this was his feeble effort at wishful thinking. I'm pretty sure Daddy already knew that I would not be knocking up *anyone* in the next five hundred billion years, but he didn't want discrimination to stand in the way of my manly fulfillment. Poontang was different, he said. Poontang was fine.

THERE WERE STILL plenty of white people in Raleigh who thought (and talked) the way my father did, but their ranks had been diminishing since the mid-fifties, when the Supreme Court had ruled for the desegregation of public schools. It was easier for me to accept my father's bigotry as gospel because I had never known a black person beyond our maid Camilla, a thin, soft-spoken spinster with whom I watched *American Bandstand* every afternoon after school. She insisted on coming in the back door, calling herself "an old-fashioned colored lady." Sometimes, when we dropped off our old clothes at Camilla's house, I saw her brother Lovelace, who worked as a porter for the Seaboard Railroad. Beyond them, not one black person. Not in the Boy Scouts or my private grade school or either of my public high schools, junior or senior. Black folks were almost as invisible to me as queers were to everyone else in the South, including other queers. In 2008, when I was invited back to Broughton High as a guest of the Gay-Straight Alliance, an African-American girl was astonished to learn that there had been no kids of her color in the school when I was there forty-five years earlier. No more astonished than I, certainly, that LGBT kids were now walking the hallways of Broughton in HERE AND QUEER T-shirts.

The South makes social progress, like everywhere else, though it does its level best not to notice it while it's going on. Only later, when it stands a serious risk of looking like a total asshole, does it claim to have always been on the side of decency and justice. (The same style of black-on-silver historical marker that identifies the home of my slavery-defending Grandpa Branch now celebrates the site of a 1960 sit-in at a Woolworth's in Greensboro.) It's hard for the South to get things right from the start, because, ever since the Civil War, it has taught itself to equate righteousness with losing. *We must be on the right track, y'all, because everyone else is against us.* In my seventy-two years I have heard Southerners offer this excuse for everything from segregation to miscegenation laws to the "religious liberty" currently invoked in the name of subjugating gay people. And in every instance, when the Supreme Court reminds them that decent Americans don't act in this way anymore, they haul out the states' rights flag and brandish it in a Rebel-gray fog of amnesia.

When my father died in 2005, one of his obituaries said he'd always been sorry he'd been born too late to fight for the Confederacy. He meant that. And in a sense he achieved it. If slavery could not be preserved as an institution, at least he could still fight to see that those folks stayed in their proper place. That's what he thought he was doing, I suppose, on the unforgettable Sunday when he marched the whole family out of Christ Church in the middle of one of Dansapp's sermons.

Christ Church had never completely excluded black people from its services. There was a steep, dark balcony that had once been a slave gallery, and black folks were still seated there on occasion, if they were, say, the beloved family maid of someone getting married or buried. They were never offered communion at the rail. Dansapp thought it was time for that to change, and stated as much in his sermon, creeping up on the subject with talk of Christian love for our Negro brothers and sisters. When my father realized what was up, he muttered an order to my mother.

"Let's go. Right now!"

Mummie was as confused as the rest of us and didn't immediately respond.

"Diana, goddammit! We ain't listenin' to this!"

Gathering her wits and her children, my mother organized our exit from Pew 17. I was a teenager and fully capable of backtalk, but I headed down the aisle like a dutiful duckling, still wondering if Daddy could be right about this. What if the races weren't meant to be together in church or anywhere else? What if Dansapp was a troublemaker trying to upset the natural order of society and my father was just the only one brave enough to take a stand? I figured at least a few other families would join us in our righteous exodus, but the Maupins were the only ones leaving the church. There were a few quick backward glances from the congregation to see what we were doing before their heads jerked back to the pulpit. Only Reverend Sapp never took his eyes off us, smiling serenely and swaying ever so slightly, as he often did for emphasis during pauses in his sermons. I don't remember how he had dressed for this pivotal moment, but it was probably something in raspberry.

Things got quiet in the Country Squire on the way home. We had suffered public humiliation and everyone knew it. I wasn't surprised when we didn't stop to pay our respects at Oakwood Cemetery, and I was glad, really, since all I wanted was to be home in the privacy of my room with the consolation of Ian and Enid, my Java Temple birds. There was still lunch to be surmounted, however, so back at the house my mother split the funny papers between her children and set about making egg-salad sandwiches in the kitchen. The rest of us staked out places in the Chimney Room (so named because Daddy thought Family Room sounded common).

No one said a word. I stared out the window at the big poplar down by the creek. Daddy sat in the red leather armchair under his Confederate flag, gripping the arms as if he were about to take off in an airplane. I knew he was tallying his losses, counting the traitors who had not followed us out of the church. Some of them were Daddy's oldest friends, well-bred folks from the Terpsichorean Club he had known since childhood. Some of them must have seen him there on the day of his father's funeral, twenty-some years earlier, when a coffin full of God-knows-what had been solemnly hauled past Daddy in Pew 17. Some of them might have been pallbearers.

Eventually, Daddy got out of his chair and came to the window, where I was sitting. He gazed down at the creek for a moment.

"Looks like the rain has played hell with the dam again."

This was how he ran from subjects too painful to face. He just veered away abruptly and waited for us to follow, as if nothing had happened.

"Yes sir," I said, looking at the creek. "It's already down by a couple of feet."

Daddy had built a cement dam across the creek, creating a small murky pond that had become a home for crawfish and copperheads.

The copperheads would sun themselves on the dam until Daddy came down from the house and chopped their heads off with a pickax. The dam was always eroding around the muddy edges, so Daddy was constantly prying planks out of the basement—cannibalizing the house, in effect—to plug up the persistent leaks.

He clamped a hand on my shoulder. "I could use some hep with this, sport."

(My father was an educated man but he had learned to say "hep" instead of "help" and "ain't" instead of "am not" when addressing a jury. It made him sound folksy, I suppose, like a man of the people, not the aristocrat he fancied himself.)

So I wolfed down my egg-salad sandwich and followed him to the basement, where he picked up a crowbar and began to pry two-by-fours from his workbench. Then we set off for the creek, where I handed him the planks and watched him plug the unpluggable. It was a moment of father-and-son intimacy, or as close as we could get to one. The two of us against the unrelenting forces of nature.

The endurance of that dam was the least of my father's many illusions. For years he nursed the idea that he would one day run for governor of North Carolina. I fantasized about this with my "sissy" friend Eddie, imagining us down at the red-brick Victorian governor's mansion on Blount Street watching *The Twilight Zone* on television. But I knew, deep down, that the old man's chances of being governor were slim to nonexistent, given his work as a lobbyist at the state legislature.

Among his less-than-appealing clients was the North Carolina Outdoor Advertising Association, so his primary job was to get legislators to refuse federal subsidies in exchange for the banning of billboards on the new interstate highways. It was all about free enterprise, he said; farmers should be able to build whatever the hell they wanted on their own damn land. The federal government was running amok. And those rest stops the feds proposed for limited advertising would be crawling with robbers in the parking lot and sexual predators in the toilets.

It was a winning argument, given that Southerners, despite their tolerance of what I recall as some of the nastiest public toilets in the land, have always been fretful about who's in the next stall. (It was black folks when I was a kid; nowadays it's trans people.) But even my father's eloquent fearmongering was no match for the growing unpopularity of billboards, which were blocking the very scenery they advertised in places like Cherokee and Blowing Rock. Daddy didn't get this, the way he didn't get so many things. That's why our garden was the place I could love him the most. We could talk about day lilies and busted dams, and leave his lost causes alone for a while. It was so much easier to believe him there.

I'm sure no one was surprised when Daddy brought his family back to Christ Church on the Sunday after he ordered us out of the service. For one thing, he was too proud to surrender the pew to the Goddamn Housepainter. His insistence on the way things had always been done may have sent him storming out of the church, but that's just what would bring him back. He needed Christ Church; it was one of his constancies.

FIVE

IN THE SUMMER BEFORE WE LEFT for college, Clark and I went to work for the North Carolina Civil War Centennial Commission. The job was a perfect way to keep on romancing the Confederacy, since we helped preserve artifacts from a blockade runner that had been sunk in the ocean off the coast of Fort Fisher. These were war provisions that never made it to the Confederacy from England: muskets and fancy-handled knives and brass tourniquet screws that had been salvaged from the deep exactly a hundred years after they went under. Our task was to lower them into ditches filled with formaldehyde in the mosquito-ruled woods of Fort Fisher. This was half a century ago, I have to remind myself, a time so removed from the present that a team of zealous young volunteers recently returned to the site for a new act of earnest archaeology: excavating the very ditch Clark and I had eventually abandoned.

We lived with the Navy diving team in a shabby apartment house in the coastal town of Kure Beach. Our room was so sparsely furnished that we made shelves from wooden fish crates we found discarded at a dock. We gave them a good scrubbing and were proud of their rustic, maritime appearance until their scent reasserted itself. Clark, typically, refused to be discouraged and sprayed the crates with an aerosol deodorizer he found on top of the toilet. The end result was pine-scented fish guts, so we were forced to discard our only effort at decorating.

That was the summer that Clark drove the pickup into the surf. The rest of the time we used it to travel between our apartment and the preservation site, or sometimes to pick up provisions for the diving team in some rusty inferno of a shipyard on the Cape Fear River.

I think of Clark in that truck, singing exuberantly, even though (or maybe because) we didn't have a radio. Sometimes we would sing together. Clark never showed the slightest embarrassment about sentimentality. He could sing "Twilight Time" as we drove home through the moonlit salt marshes and not have to joke about it. He held no attraction for me, nor I for him. I just loved his company. He made me think how nice it would be to live with a boy forever.

I can see us there in that ditch of formaldehyde, holding the ends of a heavy block of rust that had once been a case of rifles. The metal was brittle, so we had to lower it slowly to keep from breaking it. The mosquitoes, meanwhile, were bellying up to the bar. Clark had chosen this moment to challenge, once again, my virginity.

"I just don't get it."

"I told you. I'm saving it."

"For what?"

"Marriage."

A mosquito buzzed around my ear, looking for a meaty spot.

"You're crazy, man. We're in our sexual prime."

"Some things are better, you know, when you restrain yourself."

Oh, what a prissy Aunt Pittypat I was. Clark's mud-spattered shoulders were bending under the weight of the rifle case, making him more sunken-chested than usual. He was no better at this than I was, but he managed to throw me a look.

"No way I'm gonna restrain myself from pussy."

A mosquito drilled into my arm. I held the rifle case in one hand, so I could use the other to swat the invader. Skeeter blood exploded lavishly across my arm. Clark barely took notice as I finally regained control of the case with both hands.

All he says is: "I hope you're at least eatin' some."

"Eatin' what?"

"Pussy!"

We lowered the rifle case together until it disappeared into the orange muck. I hoped this would finally bring an end to Clark's campaign, but no such luck.

"You know what I always say: Show me a man who doesn't eat out his wife, and I'll show you a wife I can steal from that man."

I couldn't picture skinny geeky Clark stealing anyone's wife. I couldn't picture pussy, for that matter, but I was fairly certain I didn't want to eat any.

My focus that summer was on the youngest Navy diver on the team, a smooth-chested blond who gave off the same heat as that guy on the cover of *Demigods*. When he hosed off his goggles and wetsuit outside the apartment house, I would find ways to talk to him—small talk about our tinny-tasting tap water, or the sword he'd just recovered from the ocean—and I would say "Oh, man!" more than I ever had, because I thought it might make me sound like a real guy, and I could buy more time with him. I hoped, too, that it would keep him from noticing how often I glanced at the glinting golden hairs on his arms and the peninsular bulge in his cotton shorts—shorts that were once red but had faded to pink from the sun.

I might have jerked off to the thought of those shorts at bedtime had I been home in Raleigh. There the only danger would be that my mother would enter my room in the morning and tell me, as she once had done, that it smelled like a tomcat in there. But Clark and I shared a room at Kure Beach, so I kept my hands off myself that summer. I was worried that he would hear the springs creaking and tease me about it and, even worse, bring up pussy again. Most nights we just drifted off in our fish crate–stinking quarters to one of two albums I had brought from Raleigh: the soundtrack of *Houseboat*, starring Sophia Loren and Cary Grant, and a selection of performances at the

Monterey Folk Festival, including Leadbelly and Joan Baez. Strange, I know, that I would be grooving to lefty movement songs, but art was already seeping into my consciousness in a way that rational thought could not.

There would be no demigods on the menu that summer. A big evening on the town was a movie in a dinky theater smelling of Coppertone and carpet mold. Clark and I saw *Summer and Smoke* there, buzzed on Busch Bavarians from the diner next door, and right there in the cool, mildewed dark, Tennessee Williams crept into my tight-assed teenaged heart. This was an unexpected thing. A few months earlier I had written an essay for English class that railed against Williams and Faulkner and other Southern writers who, in my learned teenaged estimation, had maligned and misrepresented our beloved homeland. Mrs. Peacock said I made "an interesting case" and sent it to an English teachers' magazine, where it won an award and appeared in actual print. I had officially disapproved of Tennessee Williams, yet here I sat, giving it up to him completely—stunned by the realization that I was not Laurence Harvey in this film; I was Geraldine Page. I was the lonely spinster, Miss Alma, whose yearning for love would always destroy the chance of it; and I was headed off to college in the fall.

I felt so old that summer. Older, maybe, than I would ever feel again. I know high school seems like the end of everything for some kids, certainly the ones who've left their glory days on the gridiron or under a crepe-paper bower at the Queen of Hearts Ball. That's not how it was for me. I felt old because I had strangled my youth, and I could not for the life of me imagine what lay ahead.

I certainly could not have imagined that I would one day meet Tennessee Williams in the flesh. It happened in San Francisco in 1977, when he was working on a soon-to-be-panned play called *This*

Is (An Entertainment) at the American Conservatory Theater. I was beginning to become known locally and so had been invited to an opening at a small South of Market art gallery. I don't remember the artwork, but it had a wannabe transgressive flavor, leaning toward leather, and there, under brutal white lights, I spotted the playwright in a crowd of shiny-faced people, all scrambling to be photographed with him. He had plastered a smile on his face, but he looked bereft and empty. Trapped. It was the most chilling image of fame I had ever seen thus far. I left the gallery and leaned against a car in the parking lot to smoke a joint. Williams made his escape a few minutes later. When he saw what I was doing he approached and inquired in the softest of tones:

"Would you mind terribly?"

I told him not at all, so we shared the joint for several minutes, talking about nothing more than the moon in the sky. I did not try to introduce myself or be one of those fans he had fled. I knew he would prefer the kindness of a stranger.

DURING MY COLLEGE days at Chapel Hill I dated two girls who both bore the middle name of Armistead. We weren't directly related, though the two of them were related to each other; they were sisters. (Armistead was a distinguished old family name in Virginia, so their parents couldn't resist the urge to use it twice.) I didn't date these sisters at the same time; I waited a respectful interval between them. They were both blond and Candice Bergen–y. I took one of them—I forget which—on a walk through the snowy woods of Battle Park and kissed her on a bridge above a creek, where our breaths mingled like ghosts in the air. I wanted this to be a love scene out of *All That Heaven Allows*, which it sort of was, come to think of it, since Rock Hudson and the first Mrs. Ronald Reagan had about as much sexual chemistry in that movie as me and the lovely Miss Somebody Armistead Somebody.

I wonder sometimes if these sisters ever swapped notes and discovered that these romantic fizzles had been my fault entirely. I hope so. They deserved more than a guy who got off on the incestuousness of our names and wondered if passion could be summoned on the spot by the manipulation of pretty winter scenery.

I was just as chaste with the one other girl I remember dating in college, and my motives were just as dubious. Kim was the daughter of a famous forties bandleader who lived with his wife, the beautiful girl singer in his band, in a big antebellum house on East Franklin Street. I was too young to remember their heyday, but I still found it glamorous to go to their house. Sometimes, when picking up their daughter, I lingered longer than most boys would, making conversation. They were Christian Scientists and a little dowdy by then, but I found glamor in the fact that they both had been in the movies, however briefly. I was dating *them*, in effect; their daughter was entirely secondary.

So college was a sexless curriculum for me. The lust that crept in around the edges of my consciousness was purely accidental. One afternoon, looking for a place to pee on campus, I discovered a toilet in the basement of Bingham Hall, the English building. I was the only person there, but the stalls were lacquered with yellowing semen and graffiti samizdats so vividly detailed that they could qualify as novellas. As it happened, I was majoring in English, so I returned to this funky-smelling glade more than once, though I never met another person there, just the latest installment of the serials on the walls. I would move from stall to stall, catching up on things, wondering about the men who so brazenly created this literature.

Luckily, my friend Clark was a fellow freshman at Chapel Hill, so

I wasn't a total loner. It soon became patently clear that neither of us was cool enough to pledge a fraternity, so we joined forces with our friend Jim, who was equally ineligible, to form a merry band of three. We called ourselves The Cabal, since we had just learned that exotic-sounding word, and we thought it would fit us perfectly as bold conservative freedom fighters. I was the most vocal of the three, so it was decided, mostly by Clark, that I would run as the candidate from Grimes Dormitory for the Student Legislature. We printed black-and-white posters that advertised me as "A Representative Who'll Represent." I still have no idea what that meant. Mostly it afforded an opportunity for my detractors to add the word *Fascists* to the end of the slogan. That's how ruthless they were, those liberal, Commie-loving bastards.

My Modern Civilization professor, Bill Geer, was a firebrand leftist whose classroom theatrics were widely known across the campus. It was easy to think of him as a Marxist, since he *looked* like Karl Marx, with his bald pate and frizzy white beard and deceptively twinkly eyes. I sparred with him in class on a regular basis and eventually came to look forward to that, since it gave me a sense of identity. One day, to my complete amazement, he invited me to lunch at the faculty dining hall, where we continued to spar, but on a more personal level.

"Did your father warn you about me?"

This threw me, of course. "You, specifically?"

He smiled. *Just in the abstract.* "All us pinkos in Chapel Hill."

I shrugged. It was embarrassing to be asked this directly, since it was true.

"I'm a lot more like you than you know. I'm from Jonesville, South Carolina." Mr. Geer drawled out the name of his pissant country town to emphasize his point. "My daddy sent me to The Citadel."

I told him my father had briefly considered that hard-assed military college in Charleston for me. My brother, Tony, an athletic mesomorph who was much more of a team player, would enroll at The Citadel a few years later.

"You're better off here. They don't let you sass your teachers there. They make you drop and do push-ups."

Mr. Geer was smiling at me with wry affection. I realized that he actually liked me, and, even more amazingly, that I liked him. This man thrived on open combat, the vigorous clash of ideas. That's what he believed a university was all about. He loved the fact that we could challenge each other and still be friends.

There was something more to it than that, but I would not figure that out until fifteen years later, when Mr. Geer looked me up in San Francisco. His wife of thirty years had died two years earlier, and he had since made a practice of flying to California for occasional fortnights at Esalen, the loosey-goosey New Age spa retreat above the cliffs at Big Sur. "I can finally be myself there," he told me. "It's a great relief."

We were drinking wine on the deck of my rooftop studio on Russian Hill. Below us, in the amber light of evening, there were cargo ships gliding out to sea through the Golden Gate. I was proud of my little home—a place so miniscule that I called it a "pentshack"—and I was thrilled when I realized why Mr. Geer had sought me out again. He was in his early sixties, I in my early thirties. I had been an openly gay writer long enough for the gossip to circulate widely in North Carolina.

"I'm proud of you," he said, lifting his glass.

I thanked him with a smile. "Took me long enough, didn't it?"

"You and me both," he said.

And, just like that, he came out to me. It occurred to me then that we had both found it easier to camouflage our queerness on the fringes of academia—he on the left, I on the right. Our constant political grandstanding had been a distraction from a deeper, more difficult truth, the one that had to be hidden at any cost.

SOMEWHERE IN THE middle of my freshman year, I launched a column in *The Daily Tar Heel* called "A View from the Hill." It was meant to be funny, but, like most comedic efforts created by conservatives, it wasn't. I didn't know that at the time. I thought I had created a side-splitting hybrid of Art Buchwald and William F. Buckley. Of course I didn't jump into serious right-wingery right away. I needed to feel out my audience first, test the waters. The early columns were mostly satiric parables about campus life. In the very first one I lampooned the dean of men, calling him Batdean in homage to the new TV show that was all the rage in the dorms.

Later, I expanded my impertinence to the dean of women, Kitty Carmichael (whom I dubbed Kitty Galore in a naughty nod to James Bond), because of her rigid enforcement of the university's Carolina Code. The Carolina Code required students to be "Carolina ladies and gentlemen at all times." For the boys, that meant blue jeans were never worn on campus. The girls, poor things, could never be seen in shorts, even when leaving gym class; so they had to wear their London Fogs (they *all* had London Fogs) when crossing the quads. With their pale calves winking below their pale raincoats (yes, they all had pale calves), they looked like a flock of flashers. In that heyday of panty raids, hordes of slobbering men could descend on the women's dorms, demanding that panties be thrown out the window, and the administration would look the other way. That was just boys being boys. But gym shorts? No way.

I found this absurd, and said so in "A View from the Hill," where I invented a coed who had been charged, posthumously, with unCarolinaladylike behavior when she fell to her death from her third-floor dorm window . . . in a pair of gym shorts! She had been attending to a plant in her window box—"mulching her nandina"—when she lost her balance. You would think that such a fearless defender of women's rights would be progressive in other regards, but you would be so wrong.

My conservatism found its most strident voice in Student Legislature, where I railed against Socialists and peaceniks in the Students for a Democratic Society and the National Student Association. When the Student Legislature called for a boycott of local segregated restaurants and motels, I sponsored a counterresolution defending such establishments on the grounds that the concept of free enterprise entitled them to run their businesses as they saw fit. It was very much the same argument you hear today from bakers who refuse to bake cakes for same-sex weddings. I didn't stoop so low as to quote the Bible, but plenty of people did in those days, citing religious reasons for the races to remain apart. My "brave stance" against these "radical social agitators" even won the praise of a television commentator in Raleigh, an outspoken archconservative who was fond of saying, on his nightly broadcast, that nowadays UNC stood for the University of Negroes and Communists.

So who was this Armistead Maupin, Jr.? It's easy enough to say that he was still angling for the love of his father, because, obviously, he was. But he was twenty years old and out in the world, and he should have known better. I have a hard time liking him now, though I do remember as senior-class vice president, he worked to have a bronze statue erected on campus to his hero Thomas Wolfe, another restless underclassman who had grown up to write novels, and who, incidentally, had lived in Asheville when my mother lived there as a girl. And I still relate to a sentimental young Armistead who greeted the arrival of spring on campus with a sappy song called "Today" by The New Christy Minstrels, or that song from *The Fantasticks* about being "a tender and callow fellow." He was callow all right, but his heart was still closed to the possibility of real tenderness. The lid was locked down for fear of what might escape.

Or so it seemed, until someone named Roger Davis came along in my senior year.

Roger was a fellow student legislator who lived in one of the big new high-rise dormitories on the edge of campus. He had discovered that such places were dehumanizing, so he had renamed his dorm "Maverick House" and ordered Carolina-blue cowboy hats for the residents to wear at ball games and pep rallies, turning them into a fraternity of sorts, and becoming, in the process, a charismatic leader. His smooth Frankie Avalon hair and soulful, deep-set eyes enchanted everyone, male or female, who ever spent time in his presence. He seemed to like me, too. Sometimes, after legislative sessions, we would deliberately walk together across campus, talking about everything and nothing, until I headed off to my apartment and he returned to his brothers at Maverick House. I was in love with him, I suppose, in my own crippled way, but I never dared tell him how I felt.

News traveled slowly in those days, so I didn't hear about the accident until the morning after it happened. *The Daily Tar Heel* posted photos of the charred carcass of the "death car" on the front page. The car had leapt the median strip near the Glen-Lennox Shopping Center, rolled over several times, torn through a four-by-four sign-post, and, finally, struck a massive concrete abutment. Roger was still alive when they got him out, but not for long. This had been a "one-car accident," the paper said tellingly, and the speedometer had been stuck at ninety miles per hour. That made no sense at all, since, despite his affection for cowboy hats, Roger wasn't some car-crazy country boy. He was from Fort Lauderdale, the cosmopolitan beach town from *Where the Boys Are.*

The whole campus was rocked by the news. I attended a memorial service during which a toothy coed with a histrionic streak recited the famous lines from *Romeo and Juliet*: "and, when he shall die, / Take him and cut him out in little stars, / And he will make the face of heaven so fine / That all the world will be in love with night . . ." It was a beautiful sentiment, and a lot of people cried, but I resented the way she milked it so shamelessly. She sounded like a Miss America contestant performing in the Talent Competition, and I was sure she had come nowhere close to being Roger's Juliet.

Afterward, I wandered aimlessly through the crunching brown leaves of late October as I tried to sort it out. The whole episode might have remained cloaked in official discretion had I not run across Chief Arthur J. Beaumont, the campus security officer, in my grief-addled ramble. Chief Beaumont was a stubby fire hydrant of a man who spewed blunt talk as freely as a hydrant spews water. He had been one of the first responders at the scene of the accident, he said, and it wasn't an accident at all—it was suicide. "The kid was queer," he added, as if that naturally explained it.

The awful part is: I wanted it to be true. I wanted Roger to have been like me. There were too many questions I could have asked but didn't. Had Roger been caught in the act with someone? Had he left a note? Had he been tormented by an unspoken love for another man? I wasn't deluded enough to think that I might be that man, but I wondered if someone out there was mourning him as intensely as I was, or at least in the same secret way. And what if I had told Roger how I felt about him? Could I have saved his life with my love? Could that moment have been the start of something unimaginably wonderful?

Our own place in Fort Lauderdale after college, a life of manly tenderness in the ocean air?

In a daze, I left Chief Beaumont and went back to my apartment on Gimghoul Road, where I escaped into the welcome amnesia of an afternoon nap. The place was in the basement of an old townie couple's bungalow, so there was plumbing that crisscrossed the ceiling, gurgling away whenever it pleased. I had embraced this design challenge by making a rustic wooden sign that said PIPE DREAM that I hung on the ivied wall outside the door. I never really called it that, though. The place had a typical apartment address—the house number paired with the letter "A"—so I dubbed it the A-Hole early on, and it stuck with all my friends.

It must have been a toilet flushing that stirred me. I lay there in bed, staring at the ceiling, until I heard footsteps on the path outside my little high-up window. Then the footsteps stopped for a moment as my visitor perused the PIPE DREAM sign. He issued a boyish chuckle before he rapped on the door.

I recognized that chuckle, so I hurried to the living room to open the door.

"Nice place," said Roger, grinning at me as he gazed into the room. "Gee. See what you mean about those pipes."

It took me a while to state the obvious. "I thought you were dead."

"Stupid *Tar Heel*," he said with a shrug. "They mixed me up with another Roger Davis. Guy over in Old East. I figured you'd want to know right away."

He opened his arms to give me the hug I needed so badly. We stayed there for a long time, breathing in unison, chest to chest. I even dared to stroke the back of his head as I told him how glad I was to see him again, how I thought for sure I'd lost him forever, how I wanted to tell him, right now, what his friendship meant to me, because life could be short and cruel and love should never be left unspoken.

I held on to him until the sheer perfection of the moment compelled me, as it almost always does, to wake up.

I RECOUNTED THE story of this dream later that year, in an empty classroom where a panel of three professors sat solemnly behind a long desk. I came unprepared with notes of any kind. I just stood at a podium and spilled it all out as candidly as possible. I named Roger, of course, since everyone knew about his death, but I left out the part about Chief Beaumont and Roger's possible suicide, and the part about me loving Roger and hoping against hope that he loved me back. I made it a story about unexpressed friendship and cruel fate and the redemptive power of dreams when all else fails. Without telling them the whole truth, I tapped into my wounded heart and let them see it for a full ten minutes, exactly.

That's how I won the Mangum Medal for Oratory, the university's oldest student award and the one of which I remain most proud to this day. It was my first real lesson in storytelling, in connecting intimately with an audience.

Let them see enough of the truth to make them believe you.

SIX

MY FATHER NEVER LIKED ME TO say I had flunked out of law school. He preferred to say dropped out, and, technically, both things were true. My grades had been mediocre at best during my first law term at Chapel Hill, where I had been president of my class, but the lone question on my Equity final exam struck me as too boring to examine for the next two hours, not to mention for the rest of my life. I had really been enjoying Fellini matinees at the Carolina Theatre for the past nine months and realized, in a flash of insight, that I wanted to keep on doing that. I wrote a now very quaint-sounding sentence in my bluebook—"My mind just blew"—then walked out of the classroom and thumbed home to Raleigh on the old two-lane blacktop. When I told Daddy I wouldn't be coming to work in the law firm, he took it better than I had expected. "Oh, hell, son, you're right. I don't blame you. It *is* boring. I just thought you might liven up the office." It was the nicest lie he ever told me, since I knew how much he loved his practice and how much his heart was breaking.

If one of Daddy's dreams for me had just been dashed, at least I knew what the other one was. It was time to put on a uniform. The Vietnam War was at full tilt, so I could have been drafted at any time, but no one, myself included, liked the idea of me as an enlisted man at war, so I applied for Naval Officer Candidate School in Newport, Rhode Island. Actually, it was Mummie who applied, filling out the forms the way she had done for Camp Hemlock and Boy's State. She worked quickly to save me from imminent death in a foreign jungle, assembling my undergraduate honors and most respectable references. When she gave me the finished forms to sign, I noticed they had asked me to check the diseases in my medical history. My mother had checked only one: Tonsillitis. All the other boxes were empty, including Cancer, Epilepsy, Vertigo, and Homosexual Tendencies. If that phrase had given her the slightest pause, she didn't show it. Or maybe she figured that a question left unasked of me wasn't really a lie in the grand scheme of things. Either that or she believed it wasn't pertinent to the present. No different, really, from the tiny scar at the top my butt crack where there had once been a gland for preening my feathers.

I WAS ACCEPTED to officers' school in Newport, beginning in the fall. That meant I had a summer to kill and the chance to make pocket money. It made perfect sense to apply for a writing job at WRAL, the television station whose commentator (and executive vice president) had praised my conservative activism at Chapel Hill.

The station was red brick and low slung, surrounded by landscaped grounds. Out back, behind the parking lot, there was an enormous public azalea garden amid a stand of tall pine trees. The garden was the pride and joy of old Mr. Fletcher, the station owner, whose grandson, Freddy, had once starred with me in my backyard productions. On the day I reported for work, the parking lot was oppressively hot, but I lingered for a moment in the VW to let Jim Morrison finish singing "Light My Fire." Looking back, it's comical to think that the Doors were my soundtrack for that moment, considering the politics of my new boss. Hell, considering my own politics, not to mention my tenacious virginity. My fire had yet to be lit by anyone. I may have traveled through the sixties loving Dylan and Baez, the Beatles and the Mamas & the Papas, but I had somehow detached myself completely from the humanistic message at the core of their art. I was not making my own kind of music, as Mama Cass had so strongly advised; I was making someone else's.

Inside the building I headed down an air-conditioned hallway past oversized color posters of the station's newscasters, all of them, male and female, wearing wide smiles and carefully lacquered hair. At one point, through an open doorway, I caught a glimpse of the studio itself, an exotic jungle of cables and booms that led to a backdrop that said VIEWPOINT. I recognized it immediately, since my new boss performed against it every night. I was in showbiz now—or a form of it, at least—and this would be the first time anyone would pay me for being a writer.

I didn't go directly to the newsroom. I wanted to thank the commentator for giving me the job, so I went to his office and stood in the door until he looked up from his typewriter. He wrote his own editorials, well-crafted little essays, really, that were designed to delight his fans and enrage his enemies. He had been a sportswriter when he was young and, later, city desk editor at the *News and Observer*, so he knew the ropes when it came to journalism. He was giving me a break, and I knew it. When he saw me, he stopped typing and smiled. It wasn't the world's best smile. His teeth were crooked, and his mouth hitched to one side when he talked, causing a pearly residue to form in the one corner that I did my best to ignore. He was only in his forties then, but he had a certain old-timey courtliness that people found charming. He wore enormous black glasses that overwhelmed his face.

"Come in, Armistead. Have a seat. Good to have you aboard."

He had been in the Navy himself, so, like my father, he was tickled by the notion that I would soon be heading off to service at sea.

I already had several family connections with him. His daughter Jane had been a friend of mine in high school. His wife, Dot, had recently approached my mother about organizing Wake County's first SPCA with five thousand dollars left in an old lady's will. There wasn't a real shelter yet, just a farm out on Six Forks Road where stray animals were boarded until they could be placed, but my mother was determined to fix that. My father, in fact, had drawn up the incorporation papers.

All of this must have helped get me the job, but it was my college writing in *The Daily Tar Heel* that seemed to have done the trick. My new employer told me that afternoon that he saw me as the hope of the future, the natural heir to James Jackson Kilpatrick, the syndicated columnist in Richmond who would rise to fame a decade later as the right-wing side of "Point/Counterpoint" on *60 Minutes*. I considered this a great compliment at the time, though I knew there was an element of charity in his praise. He was laying it on thick, because he didn't want me to be ashamed of having failed abysmally at my legal career. I was going to be writer, he said, and a damn good one, and he was proud to be sending me down that road.

I was hired as a reporter in the newsroom, though I rarely appeared on camera—just the back of my head sometimes as I held a mic and asked probing questions at, say, a flower show or a Kiwanis Club meeting. Mimi was tickled to find me on television, since she had recently been moved from Grandpa Branch's mahogany sleigh bed to a green cinder-block room at the Mayview Convalescent Home, where a small black-and-white set had become her portal to the world. Sometimes I visited her during the news hour, just so I could sit in front of the set with her and point to the back of my head and make her smile and say, "I declare, would you look at that?" one more time, as if the back of my head were the most amazing thing in the world.

She got used to finding me there. Pretty soon, thanks to her dementia, she began to see the whole family on television. She saw my mother and sister in a fashion show, my brother drag racing with his high school buddies. One afternoon I arrived at Mayview to find her in a state of extreme distress, shaking even more than usual, because she had just seen my father being killed by "a mob of angry nigras." (My guess was that she had just seen her first civil rights demonstration.) There was nothing I could do to shake the notion that her son was dead, so I asked Daddy to come down to Mayview to set her mind at ease. He was already in high dudgeon by the time he arrived. "Goddammit, Mama. I'm here. Look at me. I'm not dead!" When Mimi remained unconvinced, he snatched a plastic lily out of a vase and lay down lengthwise on a couch, holding the lily erect over his chest. "Okay? Are you happy, Mama? I'm dead. I'm one dead son of a bitch." That finally made her laugh, which brought her back into the world for a while, as laughter almost always did.

That summer at the television station remains largely unmemorable except for the time that the newsroom sent me to cover a Ku Klux Klan rally in a tent on the edge of town. By then, the Klan had become an embarrassment to many white Southerners, even the ones, like my father, who still defended segregation. "They're just a bunch of crazy folks," he said, "and common as can be. It's not like it was during Reconstruction when there were gentlemen under those hoods. Plantation owners and such. They needed it then to keep the niggers and carpetbaggers in line."

I don't recall there being hoods at this rally, just a lot of overalls and blue serge suits and a smattering of robes with gaudy insignia. It felt more like a revival than anything else, and the Imperial Wizard had the leathery, rheumy-eyed look of a country preacher. Pressed for something provocative to ask, I brought up Peggy Rusk, a young woman whose wedding photo had just appeared on the cover of *Time* magazine. Peggy Rusk was the daughter of Dean Rusk, Lyndon Johnson's secretary of state, and her groom, a recent graduate of Georgetown University, was African-American. Only three months earlier the Supreme Court had struck down Virginia's ban on interracial marriage, declaring marriage to be "one of the basic civil rights."

The subject was topical, to say the least, and I figured the Wizard would have something quotable to say about it. He seemed to be composing his thoughts, so I signaled the cameraman and leaned in with the mic. This could be my first big story.

"Well," began the Wizard, "I don't think anyone should be even slightly surprised."

And how was that?

"Because Dean Rusk is a liberal. He's one of the most liberal men this country has ever seen. Naturally he would've approved of this marriage. And his daughter must have been raised to think that way. To think there was nothing wrong with it."

This was disappointingly reasonable for my purposes.

"No sir," the Wizard continued. "I think that's exactly what you should expect from the daughter of a man who's a practicing homosexual."

I stood there dumbstruck until the cameraman nudged me to indicate it was my turn to say something. I cleared my throat to buy time, then began: "You're saying that the secretary of state is . . . um—"

"Yes sir. That's exactly what I'm saying."

I drove back to the station with a racing heart, thrilled that I had a story so big that it might go national in a matter of days. Somehow, in the name of the almighty scoop, I had completely disconnected from my own reality. It's possible, I suppose, that I saw this story as a smokescreen. I had already learned the cowardly trick of mentioning homosexuality with a tone of amused and tolerant detachment.

Normally, I would have gone straight to the newsroom when I had a story to write, but I couldn't resist the urge to brag to my boss, the commentator. I spilled it out in the door of his office. He stared at me for a moment then took off his glasses and began to clean them with a tissue. He told me to come in and shut the door.

I obeyed, but I didn't sit down. He had a very grave look on his face.

"We can't run that story, son."

"Why not?"

He returned his glasses to his face. "Because it's libelous. The station can get sued from here to Kingdom Come."

"But we're not saying it. The Imperial Wizard is. I have it on film."

His mouth hitched to one side, revealing that dull pearl of froth in the corner. "Dean Rusk is a terrible, terrible fellow, I'll grant you that. But we can't say that about him. That's the worst thing you can say about anybody. It's an *abomination*."

It was awkward for him to get that long word out of his off-center mouth, but he said it more earnestly than anything I had ever heard him say.

"You understand me, don't you, Armistead?"

I understood all right. This was deeply personal to him. He cared about this subject in a way I'd never heard him care about anything. His usual response was to become red-faced in times of serious agitation, but now he had turned deathly pale. I found it disturbing in a way that I couldn't define.

What happened to him? I thought.

I'm certain he had no idea about the abomination standing right there in front of him. As far as I know he didn't learn about me until ten years later, when I finally came out in the most irrevocably public way I could manage—in *Newsweek* magazine. By then my former boss would be serving the first of five terms in the United States Senate, where he was already becoming known as the nation's most rabid opponent of gay and lesbian rights. He called us, among many other things, "weak, morally corrupt wretches." Though he never paid me the honor of naming me—that, no doubt, would have been impolite to my parents—I condemned him publicly on a number of occasions, most notably perhaps on the steps of the North Carolina State Capitol at the conclusion of Raleigh's first Gay Pride March in 1989.

Several years later I returned to WRAL-TV on a book tour. The female half of the nightly news team was one of those lazy, tell-us-about-your-book spokesmodels that touring writers come to know all too well. (In those days I never got the male anchors; they weren't comfortable being seen with men who loved men.) So, when my chirpy interviewer slipped into cookie-cutter mode about my novel, I decided to use the airtime for my own amusement and volunteered some useful information:

"You know, I used to work here."

"Really? In Raleigh, you mean?"

"No. At this very station. I was a reporter."

"Well, isn't that a hoot?"

"I worked here when Jesse Helms was here. Now he's in Washington, ranting about militant homosexuals, and I'm out running around being one."

No response.

"Life is interesting, isn't it?"

Somehow the poor thing got to the commercial without losing it completely. I was supposed to be given a full six minutes, but they showed me the door as soon as the camera was off and brought on an adoptable puppy from the Wake County SPCA—the very organization that my late mother had founded.

My mother and Mrs. Jesse Helms.

THE USS *EVERGLADES* was a destroyer tender based in Charleston, South Carolina, a graceless gray hulk whose task was to repair the destroyers tied up next to her. She rarely went to sea. Commonly known as Big Mama (presumably because a ship named after a swamp demands an effort at humanization), the *Everglades* had unsettled me from the day I'd reported on board. I had performed well enough on the USS *Buttercup*, the sinking-ship simulator at Naval Officer Candidate School in Newport, but all you had to do there was bail water and stuff a mattress into a hole to keep from drowning. Here you had to find your way back to your bunk from dinner. Big Mama was *big*—six hundred men on board—a disorienting labyrinth of ladders and passageways that often led me to asking an enlisted man for directions. And the surest way to betray yourself as the new boot ensign was to admit that you couldn't find your own room. Especially when you slipped up and called it a room.

I slept in my cabin for several months until I could find a place ashore. I remember the neophyte shock of those first swampy-hot nights on board: the sinister clanking in Big Mama's innards, the rainbow slick of oil on stagnant water, the mosquitoes buzzing through my porthole in search of blood and cleaner air. This was not *Mr. Roberts* or *South Pacific* or even *In Harm's Way*. This was a factory in the sulfurous stink of North Charleston posing as adventure on the high seas. I was the communications officer. That made me in charge of the radios and the signal flags and the decryption of encoded messages. Once a week I picked up decoding rotors in a cinderblock building on the base and brought them back to the ship in a canvas duffel bag. I was qualified to do this because of something called a Cosmic Top Secret Clearance, a designation that suggested my powers extended well into the universe and beyond. I didn't have a clue as to how those rotors worked, or the radios for that matter. The enlisted men did all that. If you were nice to them, though, they covered your ass, made it look like you knew what you were doing.

The captain of the *Everglades* was a tall, affable fellow whose pursed-lipped smile and protruding ears made him a ringer for Donald O'Connor in his "Talking Mule" movies. Captain Tidd was a good egg, and everybody knew it. He demanded professionalism, but even when he chastised me, he was decent about it. "Here's the thing, Mr. Maupin, I'm fine with sunbathing on deck. It's good for morale. But if your men are sunbathing on the starboard side, *you* should be doing it on the port side. Do you read me?" I read him all right, and began to wonder how well he read me.

There were about a dozen men in my division, all of them pretty likable. One of them, a nineteen-year-old Billy Budd of a blond named Spikes, was especially likable. He was one of our signalmen, a skill I had always found romantic, the Navy-est of all jobs. My father had learned of my birth via signal flags from another ship, when he was stationed in the South Pacific. ("Baby born. Mother and son both fine.") When Spikes worked his signal flags, every muscle in his body participated. I did my damnedest not to let my appreciation betray me but was not entirely successful.

A junior officer who joined our division told me my favoritism toward Spikes was glaringly obvious. This made me uneasy, of course, but I couldn't imagine what he had clocked, unless he meant the time that Spikes had an appendectomy and I visited him afterward at the base hospital. But that was just part of an officer's duty, wasn't it? To attend to his men in times of illness? I had read that somewhere, I'm pretty sure. At any rate, when the recovering Spikes grinned at me from his hospital bed, shirtless and golden, pushing down his pajama bottoms just enough to show me his "war wound," the moment certainly felt important enough to qualify as a duty.

Temptation lurked everywhere on Big Mama. Some of my men stood at attention during morning muster with their morning wood pressed smartly against their thirteen-button flies. They thought that was hilarious. And they were fond of grabbing each other's asses and saying, *Watch out, or I'll get me some of that.* To them such homoerotic horseplay was neither homo nor erotic, and certainly not to be taken as an invitation. At least, I don't think it was. In those days I was too filled with fear and self-loathing to read *anyone's* signals with any degree of accuracy.

EXCEPT FOR MY weekly trip to the base for the Cosmic Top Secret rotors, my duties as com officer were minimal. I kept myself busy doing other things. With the blessing of Captain Tidd, I wrote a satirical newsletter called "The Tenderloin," subtitled "Choice Cuts on the Chopping Block." (Big Mama was a destroyer tender, remember, so I considered that the height of cleverness.) The most frequent victim of my lampoons was the executive officer, the ship's second in command, a bald and introverted little martinet who was liked by absolutely no one on the ship. He was the easiest target imaginable, which made me, I realize now with a degree of shame, less of a courageous gadfly than a schoolyard bully.

Sensing my taste for the vivid, Captain Tidd put me in charge of the Welcome Home ceremonies for destroyers returning to the harbor. This usually included a "water welcome" (a tugboat or two ejaculating thick plumes of water) as well as various forms of fanfare on the dock. I enlisted a dozen cheerleaders from a local high school to shake their pom-poms as they spelled out the names of the ships ("Gimme a U! Gimme an S!"). I even arranged for a go-go girl to strip on the deck of Big Mama, where the sailors would catch sight of this sirenic hallucination upon entering the harbor, even before they saw their wives and girlfriends waiting breathlessly on the dock. I loved this scheme because it made me look like a good sport, an inarguably *straight* good sport. I had already gotten very good at using women to distract from my truth. A leer, I had learned, was as good as a lie.

Captain Tidd nixed the stripper plan, explaining to me cordially that civilian women were never allowed on Navy ships, a detail that might have occurred to me had I ever attempted to bring one aboard. The captain saw my disappointment at having missed a chance for a little showbiz and astounded me with his alternative proposal. "Get Lurch," he said. This guy, as his name suggests, was a lumbering machinist's mate who worked in the engine room. He was known to attempt pretty much anything if formally challenged. So it was Lurch who ended up stripping to that bump-and-grind tune from *Breakfast at Tiffany's*, never once violating Navy regs as he peeled off a bright-red cocktail dress and shook his hairy ass at the troops.

We deployed to the Mediterranean during the second half of my tour, six weeks in Naples, six in Malta. As usual, Big Mama stayed put, servicing destroyers in the harbor, so the men—we men—could head ashore every night. In the waterfront fleshpots of Santa Lucia, the promise of sex shared the air with the tang of garlic and charred pizza crust. I felt suddenly compromised when a tawny youth approached me on the dock, asking, "Hey, Joe, you wan' buy flying cock and balls?" until I realized he was just selling necklaces, winged phalluses like the ones on the walls of ancient Pompeii brothels. (My men thought it was a riot to hang a flying boner around their necks. For me it would have felt like a scarlet letter "H.")

Other dockside vendors offered the thrills of an "exhibeesh," a live sex show featuring a man and a woman, or, for a little bit extra, a woman and a donkey. I never went to these places, but I heard about them from my men when they returned to the radio shack late at night, drunk and jolly, and I would pretend to be worldly and amused and not at all repulsed by the thought of it. It was worth it just to feel the chianti breeze of their breath in that dim, twinkling room, or, if I got really lucky, the heat of a hand gripping my knee for emphasis.

SOMETIMES, ON MY days off, I would take a ferry across the bay to Capri. My shipmate Jim and I would wear our officer's whites to impress the tourists and spend our afternoon drinking wine on cliffs above the sparkling sea. Jim was in it for the chance of girls, but I just liked having company, someone to gab with. Once, during a Revlon festival, Jim made a feverish sighting on the terrace of the Hotel Quisisana. "Don't look now, but that's Faye Fucking Dunaway!" She was sitting two tables away, sleek as a seal in white satin pajamas and matching turban. Yes, of course, I was thrilled that Bonnie Parker had just lowered her sunglasses to check us out, but what I felt was nothing more than a brush with Hollywood glamor. I was much more taken by two youths striding through the square, tanned, feral creatures with silver-dollar nipples peeking through their fishnet T-shirts. I had never seen shirts like that. I imagined the two of them behind the closed shutters above the square, stripping each other naked in the musky twilight of their room. I could already smell them there. I was with them completely.

"She's really hot," I said to Jim, as I took another sip of my Negroni.

I THINK WE were in Malta when I was assigned my first cabin-mate as part of an officer exchange program. Giorgos was an ensign in the Greek Navy, so I was teased in the wardroom before he came on board. "You know how those Greeks are, Armistead. Better not drop the soap." No such luck, of course. Giorgos turned out to be gentle and soft-spoken and thoroughly straight. When I told him how much I loved the movie *Zorba the Greek*, he offered to teach me the *sirtaki*, so we became a chorus line of two one night on the dock in Valetta, our arms draped across each other's shoulders. Therein lay delicious freedom, since it was all right, even manly, for men to dance like this. Anthony Quinn and Alan Bates had already made it so. Years later, when both actors were dead and I learned that Bates himself had been queer, I would realize how complete an impersonation Giorgos and I had pulled off.

Malta was so ancient and monochromatic that you could barely distinguish the terra-cotta cityscape from the hills in which it lay. This was East and West, Africa and Europe, converging in a spooky sepia-toned fairy tale that set fire to my imagination. I remember a night when Jim and I took a taxi to the far end of the island where there was an isolated restaurant that had once been the actual castle of a knight. As we rounded a corner on a desolate stretch of road three widows cowled in black were caught like apparitions in the headlights of our taxi. Those cowls were not an unusual sight on Malta. Mourning seemed a permanent state there, just as longing was for me. My theme song was a haunting Gypsy tune whose bittersweet la-la-las seemed to drift from the shadows of every alleyway and door. It was a song of lost love and vanished youth, and knowing all too well that I'd never had a love to lose, I wallowed in it like an aging drunk. The words were in English, but for a while I thought "Those Were the Days" was a Maltese song, not a worldwide hit sung by a young blond Welshwoman.

When Captain Tidd appointed me editor of our Mediterranean cruise book (the Navy's version of a high school yearbook), I proposed that we call it "Those Were the Days." He loved the idea, especially that line "We'd fight and never lose," since it sounded sufficiently bold and military. I had that refrain printed on the flyleaf of the cruise book, omitting the part that comes later when the singer sees her troubled face reflected in a window and wonders: "Was that lonely woman really me?" I had not shown those lyrics to Captain Tidd, since they would have obliterated the manly flavor and revealed far too much about my state of mind. The skipper might have been able to cook up the idea of Lurch and his drag striptease, but baring my solitary heart would have been unacceptable to us both.

When the *Everglades* returned to the States, my days fell back into their usual cycle of secret rotors and water welcomes and cheerleaders on the dock. I felt listless and empty, a sorry impersonator of whatever it was I was trying to be.

Something had to change, and fast.

And I knew what it was.

SEVEN

IN THE SUMMER OF 1969, SOMEWHERE in the month between the Stonewall Rebellion and the moon landing, I finally lost my virginity. The truth is, I didn't so much lose it as dispose of it. I was twenty-five years old, woefully late by anyone's reckoning, a bargain bin of overripe produce rapidly approaching its sell-by date.

I was renting a carriage house that summer down at the tippy-end of Charleston, where, as the locals enjoyed saying, the Ashley and the Cooper Rivers flowed together to form the Atlantic Ocean. There were tall, narrow houses down there with widow's walks overlooking secret gardens. The bruised white-velvet scent of magnolia blossoms could arise out of nowhere to make me stumbling drunk in the dark. I loved all the things Charlestonians are supposed to love—the sweet-rotten stink of pluff mud, the creamy tidal taste of she-crab soup, hoppin' John on New Year's Day. I even grew accustomed to "palmetto bugs," the creepy-crawlies that skittered ahead of me down the sidewalk at night, looking a lot like common cockroaches. The neighborhood invited moonlight walks, and my carriage house, as it happened, was only steps away from a wooded waterfront park called the Battery, where, a century or so earlier, the first shots of the Civil War had been fired.

On the night in question, I was sitting on a bench by the water, probably wearing Bermuda shorts and a short-sleeved madras shirt, as I tended to do when I was off duty. I swear I had no idea about the reputation of that park. Not until then, not until that very night. The *Everglades'* Order of the Day informed us daily that a local bar called—as I remember—the Starlight Lounge was off limits to all naval personnel, but there was no mention whatsoever of the Battery. I was there for the scenery alone, the silvery spectacle of moonlight on the water.

Then a man came down the path by the seawall, stopped in front of the bench, and asked me if I had the time.

I told him no, sorry.

He shifted his weight to his other hip and asked if I had a light.

I told him no, sorry.

I had never played this game, but I knew what he was up to. His voice sounded country, a little fey, frightened; he was not especially handsome. He was wearing aftershave, but not one of the permissible manly ones like Old Spice or English Leather. He was probably new at this himself, since he seemed at a loss for what to say next. He just stood there, waiting for me to make the next move.

After a moment, I said, "Listen, I don't think I'm what you're looking for."

My impersonation of a politely affronted frat boy must have been convincing, since he looked mortified and hurried away.

I sat there on the bench for several minutes, berating myself for all the time I'd wasted running scared, the long, anemic *nothingness* of my youth.

Who was I kidding? I was *exactly* what he was looking for.

I left the bench and headed into the park, where I found him on a bench near the Confederate monument. He was already actively hitting on another man, so I interrupted them when I spoke: "I'm sorry I was so rude back there. Would you like to have a drink at my house? It's right over there. A carriage house. Not far."

He followed me without a word, leaving the other guy dumbfounded on the bench. We did not have drinks, of course. We were on each other as soon as the door was closed. I would love to make this vivid for posterity, but I recall little beyond the fact that it was poorly choreographed and lasted less than five minutes. There was no kissing, and certainly no fucking. I'm pretty sure I got a dick in my mouth, and that he did, too, but the episode was lackluster for something widely advertised as both a crime and a mental disorder. And I know it was my fault as much as his.

After he was gone, I lay there, sticky with disillusionment, and wondered if I was gay after all. I imagined Peggy Lee in the corner of the room singing her new hit single "Is That All There Is?" Then I glanced over and saw my white officer's cap on the dresser and realized this total stranger must have seen it there, too, and I was *sure* he was a blackmailer, or a naval investigator who would come to my ship the next morning to say that Ensign Maupin should get ready for his court-martial.

But the next morning, I felt no such panic. As I drove to the base with the top down on my Sunbeam Alpine, I felt like a freshly minted human being. I had finally held another man's naked body against mine and the world had not come to an end. Yes, I had passed the point of no return, but it was not at all what I'd imagined, not the death of innocence, but the birth of a giddy, wide-eyed adolescence. Even the car radio was celebrating this with a brand-new song by the Neon Philharmonic called "Morning Girl," about a no-longer-virginal young woman jubilantly greeting the day after her first night of lovemaking.

I didn't make that up. That was really playing on the radio on the first morning of my new life. It's odd to think that I was already prepared to greet the song with a sense of camp that made me chuckle on the way to the ship. Maybe that's how it works for queers. Maybe the camp comes first so we can cope more gracefully with the inevitable deed. Or maybe that's just how it worked for me.

For the record, I did not feel like a girl that morning.

As I strode up the gangway of the *Everglades* to receive my usual morning salute from the boatswain's mate on duty, I felt like a man for the very first time.

I WASN'T AN idiot about this. I knew what the consequences could be. As a junior officer I had already been required to sit in on the general-discharge proceedings for a gay sailor who'd been caught in the act. That was what they offered you: a week or so in the brig followed by a general discharge, which wasn't the full-blown disgrace of a dishonorable discharge, but wasn't an honorable one either. You were piped off the ship with a boatswain's whistle and never heard from again. It was quick and clean, so no one, including the Navy itself, suffered prolonged embarrassment.

I made up my mind to keep my sex strictly confined to the shore. There may have been off-duty sailors among the men I picked up at the Battery—there almost certainly were—but I was never aware of it. This was not the advent of unbridled bliss. Most of my trysts, in fact, qualified more as catastrophes than adventures.

A man I once followed home to his apartment fell into a violent epileptic fit as soon as we were in bed. He peed all over himself, then shooed me away in his postictal humiliation, pretending not to recognize me at all the next day when he checked my groceries at a corner market. Another trick, a married man, was blowing me in my Sunbeam behind a warehouse when the flashing lights of a cop car appeared in the rearview window. The guy was completely plastered, so I yanked my pants up and I told him to keep quiet and *let me handle this*. Climbing from the car, I approached the cop with an air of cool confidence, telling him that my friend was too drunk to drive, so I had told him to pull off the street. The cop gave me a slow once-over as he checked my ID. "Well, Ensign, make sure that you're the one who drives out of here." After he had returned to his patrol car, I saw the telltale evidence he had chosen to overlook—my long madras shirttail stuck straight out of my fly.

On another disturbing occasion I went home with a guy who had gay porn magazines scattered across his living room floor, where anyone who entered could easily have seen them. If that weren't brazen enough, he turned on his stereo to play me a song about sodomy and fellatio from a new Broadway musical in which the cast got completely naked onstage. I had never met anyone like him. He was dangerously without shame. I figured he was the one who gave me the crabs.

I had heard about crabs from the sailors in my division, who called them "skivvy crickets," but I had always thought of them as some sort of rash, not an actual living creature. When I picked one off my scrotum and watched its legs flailing wildly in the air, I realized the complexity of the situation. When my men got crabs, they made a joke about it and went to the infirmary for treatment. That wasn't an option for me. What if there was a difference between gay crabs and straight crabs? What if the medical officer, a guy I dined with daily in the wardroom, could tell that my crabs had previously resided on the balls of another man?

I decided to begin my own course of treatment. I soaked in a bath-tub, thinking the little bastards would begin to drown and swim to the surface for air. They loved the hot water, as it turned out, just as much as they loved a splash of Mennen's Skin Bracer, an aptly named product if ever there was one. My crotch became a green inferno, and the crabs just got drunk and rowdy. I had no choice but to visit a drugstore far from my neighborhood. There I bought something called A-200 for the treatment of body lice and crabs, including, pre-sumably, the gay ones.

I MIGHT HAVE played out the remainder of my naval obligation in Charleston had Captain Tidd not received an unexpected reassignment to Saigon. He'd been tapped to be the new chief of staff to the Commander of Naval Forces in Vietnam. It took me less than a day to visit him in his cabin to ask if I could serve with him. I had seen my future in a flash: a staff job in an admiral's office, the adventure of living abroad, some pretty great new uniforms. Plus, Captain Tidd liked me and wouldn't let me get killed. When I called my parents to tell them the news, that I'd decided to "ship out" to Vietnam, my mother whimpered, "Oh, darling," and my father tried to sound blustery and skeptical. I wasn't fooled in the least; he was bursting with pride, just as I had hoped he would be. He had always said that God created a war for every generation of men in our family, and this one, after all, was mine.

So, even if I was queer, I could still be the man he wanted me to be.

SHIP OUT WASN'T the right term for it. The plane that flew me to Saigon was a military charter, a Braniff airliner with a canary-yellow body and stewardesses who were grotesquely festive in their hot-pink Pucci uniforms. Everyone on board was headed for the war, so the air was charged with bursts of nervous laughter for most of the sixteen-hour flight. A lot of the guys had gotten shitfaced in the bar at Travis Air Force Base, a few hours north of San Francisco, where other servicemen, having just returned from Vietnam, had pummeled us with horror stories about what we could expect from Charlie. *You don't know, man. You got no fucking idea.* Even one of our chirpy stewardesses was working our nerves as we landed at Tan Son Nhut Air Base. "I hope you will enjoy your stay in Vietnam . . . and that I can be your stewardess again a year from now."

That's how long your war would take in those days, exactly one year.

The bus ride into Saigon had a similar flavor of grim, jocular initiation. Our military driver, whose job must have been boringly repetitive, had found his own way to spice things up. "Sit back and enjoy, folks, but stay alert. If someone on a bicycle sticks something on the side of the bus, pull it off and throw it away from the bus as hard as you can." There were bicycles everywhere, of course, jostling for space with canopied pedicabs and people toting things on poles and Dinky Toy cars that had been there since the days of the French. The low, concrete buildings along the leafy boulevards were hung with a hodgepodge of signs, some of them painted and flaking, others plastic and shiny red or gold. The familiar roman alphabet might have soothed me somewhat had it not been bristling with accents and alien squiggles.

The Navy's headquarters was on a small city block ringed with barbed wire and sandbags. It was almost bucolic once you got past the gate, a dusty courtyard made shady with lush banana plants and dau trees. On one side lay a nondescript staff building; on the other, the admiral's quarters, an old stucco villa with ceiling fans straight out of a Bogart movie. My office was on the second floor of the staff building. I shared it with the protocol officer and a plump yeoman named Cloud, whose name I remember all these years later because Judy Collins was all over the Armed Forces Vietnam Network that summer. A month after I reported for duty, the protocol officer came down with a rash that required treatment stateside, so I was able to take his desk and serenade my yeoman: "I've looked at Cloud from both sides now . . ."

Cloud and I were basically travel agents for the Navy's war effort.

We booked chopper flights across South Vietnam for visiting dignitaries: assorted military brass and congressmen, both prowar and anti-, who wanted to be able to claim firsthand knowledge of the wonderful/terrible state of things in Vietnam when they made their cases back in Washington. Though I could never have found my way on a surface road, I could tell you exactly how long it took for a Huey to fly between Binh Thuy and Cam Ranh Bay and back to the Mekong Delta, or how many generals you could comfortably fit into a "Jolly Green Giant." It was exacting, headachey work, since you did not want to piss these people off. How exactly I did this before the age of cell phones and the Internet, I can no longer remember, but I did it. I worked well past dark sometimes, finally trudging home to my sandbagged officers' hotel, four or five blocks away. I ate a late dinner for a dollar on the rooftop terrace, where, alone, with a gin and tonic, I could watch flares bleeding into the sky above the Delta.

I DID NOT see much of Captain Tidd in those early days because he worked even harder than I did. Our leader, Admiral Elmo R. Zumwalt, Jr. (understandably known as "Bud" to his intimates), was a striking, square-jawed figure with bristly caterpillar eyebrows that were almost menacing. He was not a hardass, though. At his weekly staff cocktail party he sported an embroidered white *barong* from the Philippines, through which the dark doormat of his chest was always dimly visible, like a surfacing submarine. His wife, Mouza, a willowy French-Russian brunette who resembled the actress Patricia Neal, was living in Manila for the duration but made conjugal visits to the villa in Saigon. On those occasions it was my job as assistant protocol officer to take her shopping. She called me "Ahmstodt."

I would strap on a .45 and escort her through the Chinese markets of Cholon, or out to a warehouse on the road to Tan Son Nhut for ceramic elephant coffee tables. The enlisted men who had to ship these fragile enormities back to the States referred to them as "buffies," a term Mrs. Zumwalt found endearing and promptly made her own. *Ahmstodt, I'm afraid I told Ambassador Bunker's wife about the buffies and now she wants some for herself.* I'm not sure whether Mrs. Z ever learned that the acronymic origin of that term, BUFE, stood for Big Ugly Fucking Elephant. I certainly never told her. If you're lucky enough to be assigned Patricia Neal in a war zone, you don't want to mess with it.

I adored Mrs. Z in her grace and tenderness, and she reminded me of my mother. When I told her that I would miss my little sister's wedding back in North Carolina during my tour in-country, she offered to help me have Jane's dress made in the Philippines, "where the lace is quite beautiful and not very dear," so I could feel part of the ritual. She was a strong and loving woman, so I hope I don't make her sound frivolous in this account. Her resilience as a wife and mother (her son was on a river patrol boat in the Delta) would be tested in a way she could never have imagined, long after the war was over.

MOST OF THE guys on Admiral Z's staff had something called a short-timer's calendar on their bulletin boards. Here's how it worked: each of your 365 days in country was numbered on the calendar, an outlined rendering of a naked woman usually traced off a *Playboy* centerfold. You colored in her body parts day by day, finally darkening her pubic region at the end of your tour. *They* did this, mind you; I never did. Nothing racier than an advent calendar ever crossed my bulletin board at COMNAVFORV. My efforts at looking straight were subtler and shrewder than that.

A few months into my tour, at the invitation of a fellow staffer, I went to a brothel called Mimi's Scientific Steam Bath, where a fully dressed middle-aged woman with a mouth full of gold teeth was putting two daughters through the Sorbonne by sucking off American servicemen, one right after the other. I don't know *what* I thought was going to happen with me, but it didn't. My buddy from the compound was in the neighboring cubicle, so I hoped he couldn't hear when Mimi's 14-karat labors proved futile and I murmured the pidgin word for drunk to explain my flaccid state. I had to say something; Mimi was looking *very* exasperated.

On another occasion I took a delicate Tudo Street tea girl to a Dracula movie, because I had genuinely enjoyed her company and she reminded me of Liat, the pretty Polynesian girl on Bali Hai in *South Pacific*. And, yes, I could also send home a snapshot of me and my date, knowing it would prompt a rough chuckle and an *attaboy* from my father. Daddy had once told me, man to man, about someone he called the Blue Gook, a blue-eyed Fijian girl who had serviced the sailors during *his* war. So here, with very little fuss on my part, was one more way the old man's codependent son could appear to be following in his footsteps. My tea girl had her own price, though; after our completely chaste afternoon at the movies, during which time I did my damnedest to explain why crucifixes repel bloodsuckers, the ungrateful little thing led me to a street market and demanded that I buy her a dress.

I WROTE LETTERS home on a regular basis—a few by hand on flimsy blue airmail paper, most of them on the typewriter in the protocol office. I often included personalized messages to the whole family, including Mimi and my siblings and Camilla. I had a captive audience, and I worked it a bit, being as vivid as possible in my descriptions of Saigon. I wrote about the smell of pho cooking at the curb, the lemonade made with fresh lemons and huge chucks of ice, the rainy night I felt so deliciously cozy, riding home drunk in the mildewed canvas cocoon of a pedicab. I told them about learning to use chopsticks in a floating restaurant on the Saigon River. And buying orange cellophane candle lanterns for the Vietnamese kids in the compound at the onset of Tet Trung Thu, the colorful mid-autumn festival I had mistaken for Halloween. And having my plastic name tag transliterated into Vietnamese so that the people whose country we were saving could pronounce my name properly. Our driver, the tactful Mr. Thuy, who had once assured me that Saigon would fall without the continued American presence, was the one who finally informed me that MOP-PIEN meant "crash-rim" in his language, so that the gesture of good will I wore so proudly on my uniform was not only puzzling but a little disturbing to the locals.

I didn't mind. I enjoyed being a fish out of water, getting things wrong, and laughing at myself. It made me feel like I was living in a movie, a Jack Lemmon movie, say, with a bumbling but well-intended lieutenant at an exotic foreign post. But I was beginning to wonder if it was the *right* movie for me, the one I wanted to claim for the rest of my life. That feeling grew stronger when Captain Tidd made me an escort officer and sent me out to accompany the brass whose chopper flights I'd been arranging. Tiny outposts in the Delta that had once been pins on a map in my office became achingly specific with their huddles of wood-floored tents and mascot dogs that ran out to greet the chopper with tails wagging. The guys who manned these places were no older than I was, and certainly no higher in rank, but their field greens, faded by sunlight and many river washings, were not like mine at all, where the creases made by Mamasan's iron were damningly visible on the fabric. These guys sported long mustaches and love beads, like the hippies back in the States, and sometimes, for the sake of irony, they wore medallions around their necks that said WAR in big, blocky, warlike letters.

I know how like a dilettante it sounds to say that I wanted to be one of these guys. I was a staff puke running cocktail parties in Saigon and buying buffies for Mrs. Z, but what I really craved was the instant camaraderie and freedom and, yes, the potential danger of life in the field. I had no desire to kill or be killed, but I yearned for the dusty deprivation of these far-flung riverine kingdoms. When I wrote my parents to express these feelings, my mother wrote back nervously to say that I had a Lawrence of Arabia complex, never realizing how close she had come to the truth.

The vast gulf between me and the guys in the faded field greens was made clear once again when Admiral Z's son came to Saigon on a short break from commanding a river patrol boat in the boonies. This was Elmo R. Zumwalt III, and, like his father, he had taken the nickname "Bud" to avoid the doofus-y sound of Elmo. Bud had the father's stalwart looks and already showed signs of developing the trademark Zumwalt eyebrows. He was a nice guy, too, and we liked each other immediately, so the admiral looked pleased when his son and I hit the town together that night. I think he knew that Bud the Third needed the relief of a little hellraising, and I needed the company of someone my own age and rank for once.

We got shitfaced in the bars on Tudo Street and showed up back at the compound at an unmilitary hour, noisy and stumbling. The MP who stopped us was obviously itching to kick some junior officer butt until he recognized the distinctive name on Bud's ID and sent us on our way with a salute. The admiral never spoke to us about this incident—at least not to me—but I later heard him chuckling about it with some visiting brass. I could tell he was proud of his son's service and loved him dearly. And, like his wife and son, Admiral Z was calling me by first name now. It made me feel as if I had family in this sandbagged corner of the world.

CAPTAIN TIDD'S DUTIES as chief of staff kept him buried in paperwork. I could see the toll it was taking on him, especially since he couldn't possibly unload on Admiral Z, his superior officer, or any of the staffers who were seriously career-oriented. I posed no such threat; my appalling lack of military ambition had long been evident to the captain. He could spill out his feelings with me, even reminisce a little, since we shared memories of Charleston and the Mediterranean. Assembling a few staffers, I threw a surprise birthday party for him one night at the Rex, a grand old Graham Greene–ish hotel replete with potted palms and gecko-flickering walls. I tipped the piano player to play "Those Were the Days," which was sort of our song, oddly enough, and before the evening was over he got drunk and misty-eyed telling me about the time he and his wife and young son had paddled about blissfully in a small boat on the Potomac. It did him good, I think, and I was glad to do it.

It was Captain Tidd who received my request for a transfer to the boonies. He was decent about it, considering the trouble he must have gone to bring me to Saigon. He told me he understood the instinct completely but was worried about my training, or rather, ahem, the abysmal lack of it. I had arrived in-country without the usual survival training in Vallejo, California, where roughneck naval petty officers mock-tortured the newbies in Vietcong "tiger cages." I had never been especially sorry that I'd missed that experience, but I agreed that it might be useful to learn how to fire the .45 I had worn on shopping trips with Mrs. Z.

So, while Captain Tidd cast about for a field post that might suit my limited qualifications, I spent five days in an Army training camp popularly referred to as Danger University. I was told even before the training began that I would be the first naval officer to graduate from Danger University. They called me "Navy" there, which at least offered a break from being called "Army" in Saigon by guys who felt compelled to abbreviate my first name. I learned how to wear a gas mask and shoot an M16 and set off a Claymore mine. These were all just training games, of course, but I could hear the sound of real gunfire, real war, just outside the perimeter wall, where the Vietcong were active. The letter I wrote to my family contained all this information along with the tellingly gay detail that I was getting a nice tan. I had also lost weight, I added proudly (I was 175 before I went!), thanks to plenty of marching and a deeply unappetizing VD film, in full color no less, they showed us one night before dinner in the mess hall.

There were several false starts before the Navy command settled on the right post for me. For a while Captain Tidd proposed Seafloat, a floating tactical support base that had just been built in the Cau Lon River at the southernmost tip of Vietnam. (My new friend Bud Zumwalt III was commanding a patrol boat down there.) Then there was a dusty village by the name of Moc Hoa (pronounced: *Muck Wah*) in the Mekong Delta, which seemed so certain for a while that it became my boondocks Bali Hai, the place that was calling me to my destiny, despite the unmusical sound of it.

I went so far as to set free the parrot in my Saigon hotel room, an untamed creature I had bought in a street market that had never much cared for me or the cage I had built for it. I couldn't blame her. There had originally been two parrots in that cage (Ong and Ba, meaning man and woman) but Ong had died when I was away on an escort mission in the Delta, so my mamasan had shrouded him in aluminum foil and left him on top of the air conditioner in case I wanted to conduct funeral rites. Oddly, once set loose, the widowed Ba seemed to hesitate on the windowsill, looking back at me as if to seek my permission before flying off into the muggy black night. The moment seemed so profoundly symbolic to me that I wrote home about it to my family. *I guess even parrots have their Moc Hoas,* I told them. I have no idea what that meant, but it surely ranks as one of the more embarrassing sentences I have ever written. My mother, by saving all my letters, gets points—albeit *in absentia*—for helping me remember what a posturing little popinjay I could be.

EIGHT

I ENDED UP IN A PLACE called Chau Doc, a town on the sluggish Bassac River, near the Cambodian border. It was a combat base for the boats of the Brown Water Navy, which meant that I got to wear a snappy black beret with my now-faded field greens as I manned a radio in a sandbagged communications bunker on the edge of the river. There were only three of us in this naval unit, the other two being enlisted men under my command. Our job was to keep the Army from shooting at the Navy and the Navy from shooting at the Army, and both of them from shooting at civilians.

That was not as easy as it sounds, since our jurisdiction was the Navy boats patrolling the Vinh Te Canal, a muddy trough that linked Chau Doc to the Sea of Siam, eighty-seven kilometers away. The canal delineated the border—still does, in fact—between Vietnam and Cambodia. It was narrow enough that you could yell across it. There were Vietcong on one side, constantly trying to infiltrate, and our ARVN allies on the other. Add to that the roving farmers who were pretty much everywhere and the fact that the vegetation crept down to the water's edge, and you have what was known, in the naval patois of the day, as a rat fuck. The jittery kids on the boats would see shimmering green ghosts in their night observation devices and call in for permission to fire on them, sometimes relying on convenient racist shorthand. *Hey, Sportin' Life, I got three gooks in the starlight scope crossing the ditch.*

What the hell did that mean, anyway? Were they our gooks or their gooks or farmer gooks just herding their oxen at night. It was my mission to sort that out. (Livestock was always good news, since it meant no one had to get fired upon.) I usually consulted a young

Vietnamese Army lieutenant who stood watch at another radio in the same room. He would roll his chair over to my side and firmly clamp his knees around one of mine as we discussed troop positions. This meant nothing beyond friendship, I'm sure, but it always made me catch my breath. Sure, the warmth of his legs was bliss, but I was also worried that an American might walk in and see us. Vietnamese men had no issues with being tactile. They would link pinkies while walking in the street along the river, and the sailors out on the patrol boats would spoon with each other to keep out the chill when sleeping on deck at night. I knew this because an American officer told me so, snickering and contemptuous.

Yes, our radio call sign was Sportin' Life. It was already established when I arrived, and I didn't know until after I left that it was the name of the African-American drug dealer in *Porgy and Bess*, the Gershwin opera set in Charleston, of all places. I was Sportin' Life Actual; Sportin' Life 01 was a sailor named Olynger who had already seen action in the Delta. We became fast buddies, Oly and I. He was a big-hearted guy with an infectious chuckle, and I liked making him laugh. There was plenty to laugh about, too. I had not cleaned my M16, much less fired the damned thing, since Danger University, so Oly crept into my hootch when I was on watch and broke it down for me, cleaning and oiling it thoroughly. I was the only naval officer in the compound, so he didn't want me to look sloppy. I was touched by that.

During an overnight visit to Saigon, Admiral Z asked me, over dinner at the villa, if there was anything I needed "up the river." It didn't take me long to tell him that a Jeep would be nice, thank you, sir. Three days later a Jeep arrived in Chau Doc on a barge. It looked like it had seen some action, but it meant liberation to me and Oly, since it got us out of the Army compound and gave us a prideful sense of identity as a Naval unit when we emblazoned the hood with our catchy command name (NAVLE-BCCR–III). We privately called her Nellybelle after Pat Brady's beloved Jeep on *The Roy Rogers Show*. That's what Oly remembers, anyway, so I must have called her that, too. I have a faint memory of wanting to call her Olivia Drabbe, in a nod to her Marine-green paintjob, but maybe I kept that joke to myself for fear it would sound too much like a hairpin dropping. Nellybelle was camp enough anyway.

Thanks to that Jeep, Oly and I became those guys from *Route 66*, forever blazing off in their Corvette to places of picturesque imperilment. It was an odd sensation at first, leaving Chau Doc behind without the use of a helicopter or a river vessel; it was like entering another dimension, and certainly a more dangerous one, since it made us an easier target for the VC. Now, on a whim, we could bounce down that long, elevated road through the rice paddies (with no fear whatsoever of me getting Jeeps Disease). We could stop off at Necco-colored Buddhist temples to shoot the breeze with a resident monk, or buy that roadside lemonade with the huge ice whenever we felt like it. Best of all, we could drive to the top of Nui Sam, a nearby mountain that had already excited our curiosity. We heard about it on our radio when a jovial cowboy voice we knew only as a call sign suggested we come up and visit.

Though it was known as "the highest friendly mountain in the Delta," Nui Sam wasn't very high; you could wind your way to the top in half an hour. The operative word here was *friendly*. The other, much more imposing, mountains along the Cambodian border were fully controlled by the Vietcong, but Nui Sam had an American outpost at the top. *Outpost* is the wrong word. It was a rudimentary listening station consisting of two sailors under a lean-to cobbled together from scraps of rusty corrugated iron. They monitored a device that was hooked up to electronic filaments disguised as rice stalks in the canal.

If anyone crossed the canal, the Nui Sam guys heard it and passed the word to us. To the best of my memory, they seldom detected movement, and no one ever checked up on them, apparently, since they lived there in nonregulation domesticity with their Vietnamese girlfriends. The four of them seemed quite happy in their sandbagged Shangri-La.

They greeted us with the offer of lunch, a pungent stew cooked on an open fire using local produce and "lurps," the dehydrated food made for Long-Range Recon Patrols. (Ask any old grunt and he'll tell you that lurps were far superior to those freeze-dried camping meals you buy at REI.) We gabbed merrily for several hours over Ba Moui Ba, the ubiquitous Vietnamese beer rumored to contain formaldehyde, and I fell under the spell of the whole funky Swiss Family Robinson scene. Their kitchen shelf alone captured my heart with its row of spices and tidy implements. And the view from up there! As the sun began to set, I saw the Vinh Te Canal become a fine blue pencil line across the landscape, the rice paddies a patchwork of shimmering green-gold mirrors that stretched all the way to the dark mountains in Cambodia.

I know I've said that I went to war to make my father proud, but Nui Sam was strictly for me. I returned to the mountain many times, sometimes by myself, sometimes with Oly or another friend from Chau Doc who could be entrusted with the secret of the contented logical family living up there. Once, on the way up the mountain, I left the Jeep to pose for a photo on a rocky outcrop only to find myself instantly covered in thousands of stinging fire ants. This necessitated the tearing-off of my fatigues and a zany little naked slappy-dance that did my dignity no good whatsoever. Oly, as I recall, tried his best not to smirk.

The fact that Nui Sam was a fragile Eden, doomed to evaporate like

Brigadoon when one or both of those sailors returned to the States, made it all the more romantic to me, since these people clearly loved one another. It was *Madama Butterfly* times two, twice the inevitable heartache. Nothing in my life to that point had ever invoked such a bittersweet sense of love's fleeting joy.

For a while, when I was still in-country, I imagined writing a novel about Nui Sam. I would call it *The Highest Friendly Mountain*, but in my version of the tale one of those sailors would be gay. The others would cherish his friendship, and protect his secret when he finally shared it. He would ultimately die in a rocket attack. I was still years away from publicly coming out, or, for that matter, writing anything that might be construed as a novel, gay-themed or otherwise. But Nui Sam held such sway over my imagination that it allowed me to tiptoe up to the subject in combat boots, if only in my own head. The book was never written, of course, and, in retrospect, I'm glad that my first novel was not one in which the gay character, angling for sympathy from the reader, gets conveniently bumped off at the end.

I thought I'd never see Nui Sam again. War, after all, eventually vanishes from a map. Still, TripAdvisor tells me there's now an elegant lodge on that very spot at the top of the mountain, replete with flowered terraces, a swimming pool, and canopied beds. It's a perfect place for a hotel, but the fact of it makes me melancholy. The view would still be the same, of course—I do love the idea of showing that view to my husband, Chris—but the sight of shiny brass luggage trolleys and complimentary Aveda products might remind me, soon enough, that you can't go home again.

THE ARMY COMPOUND where I lived in Chau Doc was next door to the Seabee hut, where the naval construction team was quartered. This was a reddish-brown stucco building from the French

Foreign Legion days, a crumbling relic of earlier wars, earlier occupa-
tions. The Seabees were famously good at living well. They brought
in steaks from a ship in the river and had a full-service lighted bar,
with a bartender named Madame Snow. I watched movies there at
night, first-run movies like *The Prime of Miss Jean Brodie*, or chestnuts
like *Gone With the Wind*. I remember, too, the bats in that building,
hundreds of them, who usually stayed folded under the arches but
would swoop toward the movie projector as soon as it lit up. Their
vampire shadows would appear on the screen, flapping toward the
white columns of Tara or down the streets of Edinburgh with young
Maggie Smith.

I liked the Seabees—what's *not* to like about a cross between sailors
and construction workers?—so I was thrilled when they invited me
and an Army lieutenant to become Honorary Seabees. The ritual went
like this: we were told to take off the tops of our fatigues and kneel
before a pair of wooden chopping blocks with hatchets in our hands.
The goal was to pulverize a piece of paper as completely as possible in
the course of a minute. They let us practice this several times before
we were blindfolded and the competition began for real. Can you see
it coming? I couldn't. When the blindfolds were removed, we discovered that we had axed our shirts into ribbons, so there was much
hooting and hollering all around. To show we were good sports, the
lieutenant and I wore the ragged shirts for the rest of the night, or at
least until we got drunk and tore the tatters off each other at the bar.

Just innocent horseplay between men at war.

Unless you know that the Army officer invited the naval officer
back to his hootch at midnight to show him some "cool stuff" a friend
had sent him from home.

One of those items was an audiotape his friend had secretly recorded in a movie theater. The movie was *The Boys in the Band*.

The other item was a magazine called *Avant Garde* with a poem by W. H. Auden called "A Day for a Lay," a graphic account of a man-on-man blowjob.

The lieutenant was dropping hairpins like hand grenades.

This was certainly as literate an invitation as I had ever received, and probably the most obvious, as well. I didn't take him up on it. I went back to my own hootch and jerked off on my cot before sleep. Had I been a little less terrified of a court-martial—and the lieutenant had been a little more irresistible, I suppose—there's no telling what would have happened.

At the very least, we could have listened to the movie.

I HAD A friend in Chau Doc named Giles Whitcomb. As that suave name connotes, he was both a Harvard man and a spy. He worked in naval intelligence and often showed up at the morning briefings when the Army commandant, Colonel Horatio Hunter (another name I might have invented but didn't), would bloviate at length while waving his baton at a map of the region. Giles and I would swap grins across the room whenever the colonel was interrupted by the fuck-you lizard that sometimes hid behind the map. The fuck-you lizard was named for its distinctive cry, a passable replication of someone shouting *Fuck you*. The first word was short and emphatic, the second drawn out to the point of becoming personal. *Fuck yooooo*. Giles and I found this hilarious; the colonel did not.

One day Giles wasn't there anymore. This didn't surprise me, since his official duties, unlike mine, didn't seem to adhere to a routine of any kind. He was practically James Bond, complete with the silky good looks and an unflappable demeanor. When I heard from him again, he radioed to say that he was in Cambodia and would I mind bringing him his three-piece gray suit. He could meet me in a town called Neak Luong on the Mekong River, twenty-seven miles from the border. It would take me only a few hours to get there by Swift boat, and I would have a place to stay.

I knew better than to ask him what he needed with a three-piece gray suit in Cambodia. American and South Vietnamese troops had invaded that country a few weeks earlier, so intelligence was no doubt required. Maybe he needed business attire for Phnom Penh; maybe it wouldn't be safe to look like an American GI.

At any rate, I went. I folded his suit into a duffel bag and headed up the river, past dusty villages so unused to the new American presence that young women bathing in the river saw no need to cover their breasts as they waved at the boats. Little children ran to the water's edge repeatedly shouting something that sounded like Ah-Pa-Lo, which baffled me until I realized the word was *Apollo*. The moon landing was still our greatest ambassador there. They didn't know to distrust us yet.

Meanwhile, back in the States, four students at Kent State University had just been shot dead by members of the Ohio National Guard. Those students, and the nine others who were wounded, had been protesting the Cambodian invasion. Nixon had actually announced the invasion on television, and half of all Americans polled had expressed support for it. They believed, as I still believe, that we were helping the South Vietnamese by cutting off the flow of Vietcong troops into their homeland.

America is always helping *someone* when it invades another country.

GILES GOT HIS suit when we docked in Neak Luong, and I got a new assignment: working the radio on a fifty-foot Tango boat moored on the Mekong River. Oly had kindly agreed to take my watches in Chau Doc, where things were relatively quiet. I stayed in Neak Luong for the duration of the Cambodian campaign. Radios are the last thing to go when military operations finally shut down.

There were thirteen of us on this little boat, a snub-nosed shoe box designed for landing troops. It was oppressively hot, so we wore cut-off fatigues most of the time. The locals wore sarongs, bright-hued, block-printed loops of cotton that set them vividly apart from the Vietnamese thirty miles down the river. Toward the end of our stay, we decided to make this fashion statement our own, so we swapped C-rats for sarongs in the village markets and wore them around the boat as we pleased. We thought we looked good in them, and I suppose we did.

We led a lazy, Huck Finn–ish existence there in Neak Luong. The river was the color of tea with milk, which meant it handily concealed a variety of swimming snakes, but that didn't stop us from splashing around in it when the heat became intolerable. The radio was below deck, an airless, olive-drab sweatbox hung with short-timer calendars, most of them a lot more gynecological than the *Playboy*-based calendars back in Saigon. Naturally, I lived for the moment when my watch would end and I could enjoy a change of scenery on deck again. All of us lived for the weekly arrival of the mail boat and the ice boat. We would chip ice into our canteens and mix it with a packaged powder for a simulation of orange juice. (For the record, it wasn't Tang, but something much tastier that my mother could buy at the Piggly Wiggly and mail to us. She was thrilled for a chance to help with the war effort.)

We saw nothing of battle, just the sound of it on the radio sometimes. During our stay, we fired a total of three shots, all of them at George, our mascot dog, who had suffered a seizure and was drowning in the river, too far away from us to be rescued. It broke our hearts, but we returned soon enough to the mundanity of waiting for a war to end. We reread letters from home and trimmed our Bostons.

A Boston, in case you're wondering, was a haircut popular with the men of the Brown Water Navy. You grew your hair out in back and trimmed it straight across at the nape of your neck, forgoing the usual military taper. You could do this because there was no one around to check on you. I have no idea why it was called a Boston. The only hitch—though I can hardly call it that myself—was that someone else had to help you, standing behind you with scissors to make sure the line was straight.

We did this on the fantail of the boat. There was a shower back there, nothing more than a length of black hose that pumped water directly from the river. We were both naked, my buddy and I, having just showered at the end of the day with a bar of spicy, paper-wrapped Chinese soap I had bought at a stall in the village. I don't remember his name all these years later; I can just barely remember his narrow, vulpine face. What does come back to me, time and again, is the soft mushroom kiss of his cock against my butt cheeks as he leaned in to trim my neck.

That I'll remember forever.

ONE DAY TOWARD the end of June word came from a command post down the river that our boat was about to become the last American naval vessel to withdraw from Cambodia. That was made official a few days later when an ABC correspondent named Steve Bell (later to become an anchorman at that network) showed up at the riverside with a film crew and two crates of beer and told us he was going to make us "heroes on the six-o'clock news." Even then, we didn't really buy that line, since what we were doing amounted to a retreat. Americans had had enough of Nixon's Cambodian adventure, and this would merely be the visual proof it had happened. Still, we were seduced by the beer and, let's face it, the chance to be on TV.

So off came the sarongs and the frayed cutoffs and out came the camouflage fatigues festooned with grenades and jungle knives. As the cameras captured our historic withdrawal, a dozen men were shamelessly John Wayne–ing around the deck. I was not one of them. Please don't give me credit for shame or modesty or anything like that. I wanted to be there, too, but I was stuck down below on radio watch, suffocating under an arbor of paper pussies still waiting to be colored in.

Meanwhile, the guys up on deck withdrew from Cambodia. Twice they withdrew. That is to say they pulled away from the riverbank twice, so that the cameramen could get the right angle on our war-torn vessel. There would have been plenty of chances for me to be seen had I actually been there. Before the watch schedule had fucked me over, I had imagined my father at home in front of the TV with his Triscuits and his martinis, yelling, *Goddammit, Diana, come look! It's Teddy!*

We had been under way for less than half an hour when the boat ahead of us—the one bearing the ABC television team and the public affairs officer from Delta Headquarters—radioed that she had just taken a B-40 rocket over the bow. To complicate matters, the public affairs officer had been wounded by a sniper bullet that had passed, somewhat unceremoniously, through a beer can in his right hand.

Our boat, less than a kilometer behind them, went to general quarters, which involved little more than becoming officially nervous. There was nothing else we could do. In the heat of that moment, the idea came to me. It was so idiotically simple, so solidly foolproof that I marveled it had not occurred to me before. I might have missed the big photo op, but the chance to claim my moment in history had not passed. The last American sailor to withdraw from Cambodia would be the man who was standing on the fantail when this boat crossed the border into Vietnam.

The border was an hour away, plainly marked by a flagpole flying the Vietnamese colors. I would get off watch in thirty minutes, leaving plenty of time to position myself. The only problem was how to hang out on the fantail without attracting attention, since I didn't relish being caught in the act of self-glorification. The solution was to take a shower—that black hose back aft, where we trimmed our Bostons. So, when my watch was over and the shooting had stopped, I took off my clothes and strolled to the fantail, where I turned on the hose, soaped up, and sang "Raindrops Keep Falling on My Head," certain that victory was within easy reach.

The flagpole was less than two minutes away when something catastrophic happened. The ranking officer on the boat, a commander, appeared out of nowhere and walked aft of me, dawdling around the stern. I knew immediately that he was going for the title of Last Man Out. And he knew that I knew. Apparently he had no issues with self-glorification. He wanted his own story to tell back in the States.

There was no time to waste, so I dropped the soap (yes, I dropped the soap) and strode purposefully to the anchor winch, a metal structure extending rearward over the wake of the boat. As I passed the commander, I offered him a crisp salute, a courtesy he did not return. *Son of a bitch* was what he muttered as I mounted the winch and cantilevered my body over the churning brown water. My grip on the oily metal was perilously unsure. The commander, refusing to surrender, grabbed a nearby line, secured it with a sheepshank (or something) and began to lower himself off the stern. He was gaining on me, so I inched out even further on the slippery steel.

For one gruesome moment, I was sure I was about to fall.

I wondered in that moment how the Navy would phrase the letter to my parents. *Dear Mr. and Mrs. Maupin: Your son died the way he would have wanted: stark naked and covered in soapsuds and desperately seeking attention.*

I did not fall, however. As the flagpole at the border slid abeam of the boat I arched my back and flung my left leg in the direction of Cambodia. I must have looked something like a figurehead installed by a ship fitter on acid.

The commander left the fantail and never spoke to me again.

THERE WAS A name for what I was in Vietnam: straphanger. That term was coined by the Airborne troops, and it meant someone who wasn't really part of a unit, someone who was just along for the ride. I don't think I'm being hard on myself here. I did my job well enough when called upon, but I was mostly in it for the stories. That's why I had volunteered for Christmas Eve duty on the canal—so I could write home about the red and green flares bursting over the rice paddies, and the choppers overhead blaring a grotesquely mangled "Silent Night." That's why I had asked my hootchmate, Lieutenant Flash Blackman (yes, real name), to take me on a mission along the border in his two-seater fixed-wing aircraft—so I could make jokes about "strafing the enemy" after I got airsick and vomited out the window.

While never a straphanger, Giles Whitcomb had a similar hunger for new adventures. I never saw him again after I left Cambodia. I know now that he died in 2003 after two decades of quiet humanitarian service with the United Nations, a job that took him to the aftermath of ethnic cleansing in Kosovo, to the eruption of the Galunggung Volcano in Java, to the bloody interethnic massacres in Rwanda. His widow said he didn't talk much about his service in Vietnam. He felt bad about it, she said, because he didn't have nightmares like other people. I know exactly how he felt, though that war has, so far, never exacted from me the toll that Giles eventually had to pay.

Giles died of non-Hodgkin's lymphoma, a cancer attributable to Agent Orange, the "rainbow herbicide" that American forces sprayed across the jungles and rivers of Vietnam to obliterate hiding places for the VC. We know about that stuff now. Forty years later, there are still babies in Vietnam being born without eyes, babies with their thin limbs twisted like pretzels. When Giles died, Senator John Kerry, our former secretary of state, wrote a letter in support of full veteran's benefits for Giles's widow, saying that all Navy men in the Delta had been exposed to Agent Orange. Kerry had known Giles when they were training for the Brown Water Navy in Coronado. He remembers bicycling to the base with him, just the two of them, on bright-blue San Diego mornings. He seems to have loved Giles the way I did.

Here's the kicker: the official who had authorized the use of Agent Orange, believing it would save the lives of American servicemen, was the very man who had sent me to Chau Doc, the man who had shipped that Jeep up the river, my beloved Admiral Zumwalt. His own son, Bud III, my drinking buddy on Tudo Street, had been doused with Agent Orange when commanding his patrol boat on the Ca Mau Peninsula. He died of lymphoma in 1988, by then a middle-aged North Carolina lawyer. Both he and his father had publicly attributed his cancer to Agent Orange. His father, nobly, had taken responsibility for his son's illness, though his son had never blamed him for it. They had even written a heartbreaking book about it, which included the fact that Bud Zumwalt IV, the admiral's grandson, had been born with a birth defect that made it difficult for him to concentrate.

My life was quite different by then. When I read about Bud's death, I was in England on a book tour, speaking out on radio shows about Clause 28, Margaret Thatcher's sinister effort to silence homosexuality. I felt heartsick for the whole Zumwalt family, especially Mouza, so I phoned my father in Raleigh, who had met the admiral at a Washington dinner in the early seventies when Zumwalt was serving as chief of naval operations. Pap had been tickled about the dinner, since the admiral had remembered me affectionately, but he had since grown disgruntled with Zumwalt's efforts at modernizing the Navy, liberal measures that had put him on the cover of *Time* magazine. He had ordered an end to racial discrimination and championed issues like spousal benefits and updated enlisted uniforms. As far as my father was concerned, that goddamn *tempus* was *fugiting* all over again. I should have guessed how he would spin the news of Bud's death.

"That's very sad," he said. "I'm sure he was a fine fella, and I know you liked him. But his old man was a damn fool."

"For authorizing Agent Orange, you mean?"

I knew he didn't mean that, but I wanted to make him spell it out.

"Hell, no! For taking the goddamn blame for it. What kind of a military leader is that? He was playing right into the hands of the enemy."

"Jesus, Pap, they're not even our enemy anymore. The war has been over for fifteen years. He just wanted to clear the record. His son was dying. It was an act of love."

"That's the silliest goddamn thing I've ever heard. War is hell, always has been. If you start getting softhearted every time there's—"

"So that's what you would have done?"

"What the hell are you talking about?"

"If I were dying and you had authorized the chemical that had killed me? Would you have covered that up for the sake of duty or the country or something?"

"Don't twist my words!"

"How am I twisting them?"

In truth, I *was* twisting them, because I wanted to pick a fight with him. Not about that old fiasco of American imperialism, but about a horrendous new war he had so far refused to notice, despite my own very public words on the subject. My friends had been dying of AIDS for four years, ignored by Reagan, and shunned on a daily basis because of a horror they had never seen coming. The shamer-in-chief was Senator Jesse Helms, whose fund-raising and propagandizing arm, the National Congressional Club, was operated out of my father's law firm by one of his partners. Thousands of direct-mail flyers flew out of that office every week. Helms had most recently tried to destroy a Senate bill meant to provide desperately needed funding for New York's Gay Men's Health Crisis. "We have got to call a spade a spade," Helms said, "and a perverted human being is a perverted human being."

Had my father thought of his own son, even briefly, when he heard those words?

Did it bother him that he never came to my defense, never told ol' Jesse that enough was enough? Was he at all ashamed about that?

Maybe he cringed at Zumwalt's candor about Agent Orange because it suggested that a father's love for his son was more important than anything else.

WHEN I GOT back to Chau Doc from Cambodia, Oly had already returned to the States. He had been standing twelve-hour watches in the radio bunker in my absence. I wrote him up for several medals, since he certainly deserved them. I didn't see him for another thirty years, when he showed up at the start of a new millennium with his pretty wife at a northern California book-signing for *The Night Listener*. He looked much the same—round-faced and smiling and blond, or at least silver reminiscing as blond. He ran a food brokerage company, which I took to be successful, since he lived in a gated community in the East Bay. I was stunned to see him again, and all the more so when he reached into his pocket and pulled out a couple of ribboned medals, holding them out to me with a sheepish smile.

"They arrived when I was already back in the States. You never got to pin them on me, sir. It's not official until your officer pins them on you."

I knew where this was heading, but I couldn't find the words. The sound of "sir" was what had floored me, a gesture of respect that took me back thirty years, before I had found my calling as a writer and an LGBT activist, before I had finally stopped believing in God and country and war itself. America had yet to make things right with gay people who had served in the military—the repeal of "Don't Ask, Don't Tell" was still a decade away—but here stood Oly, calling me sir, honoring me unilaterally.

My eyes were damp when I stood up from the book-signing table to pin the medals on my old friend. I struggled far too long with the latches, while Oly stood patiently at attention, but there was nothing not to cherish about that awkward moment: the rush of recovered memories, the salutes we exchanged at the end, the utter confusion on the faces of the customers waiting in line for my autograph.

NINE

HARLAN GREENE, A LIBRARIAN AT THE College of Charleston, recently created an interactive map called "The Real Rainbow Row: Charleston's Queer History." I remember and admire Greene for a landmark gay novel he wrote in the early eighties called *Why We Never Danced the Charleston*, so I was tickled to find my old apartment at 38½ Tradd Street depicted on his map in the Number Two position. Number One, understandably, was the Battery, that cruising ground on the waterfront where so many of us found one another. My own digs were merely where I lived for a while, hardly the site of a social revolution, unless you count—and I suppose I must—the moment when I learned how it felt to fall in love.

I moved into Tradd Street when I returned from Vietnam and started work as a reporter for the Charleston morning newspaper, the *News and Courier*. As the address makes clear, it was smaller than small, a furnished nook in the attic of an eighteenth-century brick townhouse. It was easy for me to call it a garret because an artist displayed her work downstairs. Elizabeth O'Neill Verner—Miss Beth to her friends—was a stately old white woman whose etchings and pastels of African-American women—flower sellers mostly—reflected her respect for her subjects.

My little aerie (sometimes I called it that, too) overlooked the gardens and rooftops of Cabbage Row, a street that was celebrated as Catfish Row in DuBose Heyward's novel *Porgy*, the source material for Gershwin's opera. Miss Beth did the etchings for that book. (It occurred to me, of course, that Sportin' Life, the fictional inspiration for my radio call sign in Chau Doc, had somehow led me to the neighborhood where he had peddled cocaine.) Since I've always chosen theme music for moments in my life, I would lie in bed in a big four-poster and sing myself to sleep with "Summertime." There was a thick manila rope tied around one leg of that bed that Miss Beth said I was to throw out the window in case of fire.

I covered the military and academic beats for the newspaper. What I loved, though, were the oddball Southern Gothic feature pieces that sashayed my way. I reported on the Spanish moss blight that threatened to wipe out one of the Low Country's most beloved features. (It never did.) I covered the Chitlin Strut in Salley, South Carolina (pop. 415), where politicians and proletarians alike gathered to affirm their allegiance to fried hog intestines. I was told not to arrive early, since the chitlins were cleaned in hot water, and the odor of parboiled pig shit could linger in the humid air like Woolworth's perfume. Senator Strom Thurmond came to that event and posed offering a forkful of deep-fried guts to his ex–beauty queen wife, the latter of the two Miss South Carolinas he married over the course of his lifetime.

My favorite story was an exposé I did of Boone Hall, a plantation house ten miles out of town, where tour guides were telling gullible Yankee tourists that this was where *Gone With the Wind* had been filmed. They got quite specific with the lie on the day that I took the tour. *This was the room where Scarlett threw the vase and almost hit Rhett. And out back is where poor little Bonnie Blue fell off her horse and died.* It took no more than a phone call to Hollywood—oh, how I loved having a reason to do that—to establish the fact that nothing in *Gone With the Wind*, with the exception of a long shot of the Mississippi River, had been filmed outside of Culver City, California. (Boone Hall still attracts tourists with its slave quarters and its avenue of oaks, but there is no more loose talk of *Gone With the Wind*.)

Another assignment that lingers in memory, since it let me creep even closer to Hollywood, was an interview with Victoria Vetri, a

Playboy Playmate whose most notable film role had been that of the satanically doomed woman that Mia Farrow meets in her basement laundry room in *Rosemary's Baby*. Ms. Vetri was on a press junket promoting a film called *When Dinosaurs Ruled the Earth*, in which she was clad in skimpy animal hides like Raquel Welch in her much more famous prehistoric movie. I don't remember what I wrote, but the photo that accompanied the story showed Miss Vetri dog-paddling in a lake, holding a fish in her mouth.

My stories were playful and oddball, so they began to get noticed by the sort of people who paid attention to bylines. Even my former boss, Jesse Helms, who was already preparing for his first Senate campaign, wrote me a generous fan letter from Raleigh: "I've been seeing your fine hand at work in the pages of the News and Courier, so obviously my wish for your success has come true."

That, as it happened, was the last time I ever heard from him.

ONE STORY UNFOLDING in Charleston at the time affected my career profoundly, though I never got to write about it in the *News and Courier*. A slim, bow-tied English writer named Gordon Langley Hall renovated an antebellum house on Society Street and soon became the darling of, well, society. Hall, after all, had some stories to tell. He had grown up at Sissinghurst, the family seat of the Bloomsbury set, the illegitimate son of two of Vita Sackville-West's servants. He had known a Whitney in New York, an old lady who left him her house and her fortune. He'd written a few novels, too, as well as paperback biographies of such women as Princess Margaret and Lady Bird Johnson. The people he regaled at SOB (South of Broad Street) parties were intrigued to learn that he had been adopted by Dame Margaret Rutherford, the dewlappy old detective in the "Miss Marple" films. Folks realized, of course, that Gordon was a little eccentric, maybe even "that way," since his dogs were sometimes seen wearing pearls on their afternoon walks, but that sort of thing was largely ignored until the day he returned from the Gender Identity Clinic at Johns Hopkins and, in an effort to inaugurate his new life, began wearing angora sweaters around town.

The genteel whispers grew into an indignant uproar when the Englishman fully transitioned to female, renamed herself Dawn Pepita Langley Hall, and married a young African-American garage mechanic named John-Paul Simmons in her drawing room on Society Street while the groom's father played "The Battle Hymn of the Republic" on the Victrola. According to Dawn, wedding gifts delivered to the home were firebombed in the garden. Though this was South Carolina's first legal interracial marriage, only a bare-bones notice of the nuptials appeared in the *News and Courier*—and on the obituary page, at that. Dawn Simmons became a local outcast and an international tabloid celebrity, one of America's first open transsexuals. When a reporter had the temerity to ask Dame Margaret what she thought of her son becoming a woman and marrying a Negro, she was said to have remarked, "I do wish Gordon hadn't picked a Baptist."

I saw Dawn only once, buying popcorn in the lobby of a movie theater. Her frumpy clothes and sharp features and penetrating brown eyes made her a little off-putting, like a spiky bird of prey to be approached with caution. I'll always be sorry I didn't say hello, given the difference she eventually made in my life by her mere example, her brave singularity. It was a singularity far greater than anyone had imagined. Dawn became visibly pregnant, left town for a few months, and returned to push a beautiful light-brown daughter around the Battery in a baby carriage. This was written off as delusional at the time, or a "publicity stunt," or an elaborate hoax designed to torment her tormentors.

Can he do that? they asked.

Is that even possible?

It is, if you've been a woman all along. Dawn insisted she had been born intersexual, so the procedure at the hospital had merely corrected the condition that had kept her from having children. She had always been female, she said. Her husband, to whom she remained devoted despite his bouts of schizophrenia and spousal abuse, later confessed that the baby had been his by another relationship. Dawn died in 2000, with her loving daughter, Nastasha, by her side. The story slipped into the realm of fable in Charleston, as so many stories do in that place, changing a little with each new retelling of it.

Readers of *Tales of the City* will wonder if Dawn Simmons had in some way served as inspiration for Anna Madrigal, the transgender landlady at 28 Barbary Lane. Yes and no. Dawn had certainly opened my writer's imagination to the possibility of gender fluidity, an idea that still bordered on the fantastic back then. But Anna's generous, expansive, mystical spirit—her voice, if you will—would eventually come from somewhere else entirely. Somewhere much closer to home.

THERE WAS A legend in Charleston at the time—and still is, I presume—that Edgar Allan Poe's last completed poem, "Annabel Lee," was inspired by a beautiful Sullivan's Island girl named Annabel Lee Ravenel who had stolen Poe's heart when he was an enlisted man stationed at Fort Moultrie in the 1820s. "I was a child and she was a child, / In this kingdom by the sea." Annabel Lee, however, had a serious case of consumption and a disapproving father, so it ended badly. "Her highborn kinsmen came / And bore her away from me, / To shut her up in a sepulcher / In this kingdom by the sea." That was all it took for me to head out to Sullivan's Island, a community of aristocratic beach cottages, to poke around in the palmettos in search of Annabel's final resting place. I don't know why I thought I'd find a "sepulcher" that no one else had noticed in the past 150 years, but that's the kind of romantic I was.

And that's the kind of romantic who spotted his dream man from the staircase at Miss Beth's studio one balmy spring day in 1971. The shop was full of browsing tourists. He was flipping through etchings in a box, when his eyes swept upward and pinned me on the staircase like the clean blue beam of a spotlight. I don't remember where I was heading that afternoon, but I stopped heading there immediately. I went down to the shop and made brazen small talk about Miss Beth's pastels with him. He was one of those leonine blonds with five-o'clock shadow and furred forearms, but I realized, with a rapidly deflating heart, that he was there with a beautiful woman. She was roughly his age—thirtyish I guessed—with sleek dark hair and a bourbon-and-honey voice. She touched his arm as she spoke to me.

"Do you live in this marvelous place?"

I told her, somewhat proudly, that I did. Just upstairs.

She exchanged a look with the man. *Lucky boy.*

They struck me as the most sophisticated people I had ever met. They may well have been at that point. They were New Yorkers, actors who had driven up from Atlanta where they were rehearsing a Chekhov play at the Alliance Theatre. Even their names evoked glamor: Curt Dawson and Barbara Caruso, the cowboy and the heiress. We chattered away at length about things I don't remember now, but the end result was an invitation to join them on a tour of Middleton Plantation.

Middleton is on the upper reaches of the Ashley River and boasts the oldest landscaped gardens in America. Its stately brick manor house and rolling terraced lawns lent a distinctly theatrical air to our outing. We were a jolly threesome for most of the afternoon, except for a moment when we entered a boxwood maze and Barbara was briefly separated from us. It was then that Curt turned and gave me a private smile, leaving me with the distinct impression that I was about to be kissed. (I just did a search and found there is no such maze at Middleton Plantation today. Maybe it was removed in the last forty years, or maybe my memory, a theatrical beast in itself, had constructed the perfect set for my first love story. That happens a fair amount. I can say for sure that Curt and I were alone amid some greenery and that his faded-denim eyes seemed, ever so briefly, to be asking me something.)

I was still unkissed when they headed back to Atlanta. Curt and Barbara seemed intimate in the way that only a couple would be, so I doused my hopes and said goodbye to them. Anyway, wasn't it supposed to be hard to tell the sexuality of actors? You could make the wrong assumption based on their openness, their dramatic demeanor. I might have been downhearted if Barbara hadn't said something in a (seemingly) offhanded way just before they drove off down Tradd Street.

"Did Curt tell you he played Donald in *Boys in the Band*?"

THREE DAYS LATER a letter arrived from Curt. It was easily the most exciting letter I had ever received. His stationery was the color and texture of a brown paper bag, and his name—that studly cowboy name—was boldly printed at the top in black military stenciling. It was masculinity itself. He said that he and Barbara had enjoyed their time with me in Charleston and would like to invite me to the opening night of *Three Sisters* in Atlanta. I could stay with him at his apartment, he said.

His apartment. Not *our* apartment.

I asked the city desk editor for a long weekend and drove down to

Atlanta in a state of giddy anticipation. Curt's place was in an apartment house on the edge of Piedmont Park, standard-issue digs for itinerant actors. The building was the color of dried blood, a charmless brick hulk from the forties, but spring was exploding across the street in a riot of pale-green buds and pink dogwoods. (Were they actually pink? I don't remember for sure. They felt pink.) The moment needed theme music, so I found some on the radio: "If" by Bread, a love song so bubbly it might have been carbonated.

Curt gave me those blue eyes and a hug as soon as I arrived, then hustled me down the hallway to Barbara's apartment. *Look who's here, darling.* There was another hug and some laughter and a few cups of tea before they left together for last-minute business at the theater. The next time I saw them they were onstage, looking supernaturally gorgeous in costume. She wore a dark tailored satin gown that gleamed as she moved. He was in a brown flannel uniform with two rows of brass buttons that rose along the V of his torso—or, at least, helped to create it. I remember how it felt to watch Curt striding across the stage in shiny black boots that reached almost to his knees.

There was a cast party in Curt's apartment after the play. I remember that party with more clarity than the lovemaking that finally took place when the last of the revelers had said good night. There was everything in that room: young and old, male and female, gay and straight and who-knows-what, and they all seemed to adore one another as they slouched on sofas and passed the warm wine and made rueful jokes about their romantic disasters. And every one of them, the beautiful Barbara included, seemed to accept, without a scrap of discernible judgment, that I belonged in that room with Curt. It was then that I saw how life could be if you let it happen. It was a revelation to me, though I was hardly the first queerling to find his heart in the midst of a theater troupe. My fellow San Franciscan Harvey

Milk, who, like me, had served as an officer in the Navy and voted for Barry Goldwater for president, was said to have thrown off his uptight shackles when he toured as a producer with the cast of *Hair*. That would certainly do the job nicely.

When Curt and I were alone after the party, I asked him about the page he had torn from a glossy magazine and taped to the wall of his bathroom. It was an advertisement that featured a man shaving.

"Why do you have it there?" I asked.

He held my chin in his hand and gave me a don't-be-silly look. "Because he's beautiful."

Then he took my hand and led me into the bedroom.

THE HARDEST THING to grasp about this new adventure was that a woman could approve of it. Most of the women I had known in the South were prone to referring to homosexuality as "such a waste." Barbara not only knew what was happening between me and Curt but gave it her wholehearted blessing. The three of us drove to the mountains of North Georgia and rented a little cabin in the woods. Barbara had her own bedroom, of course, but the rest of the time we were a jolly threesome, and it was glorious to have a witness to our bliss. Sometimes she and Curt would exchange brief, knowing glances that I took to be rooted in old jokes and shared memories. Once, when gathering fallen branches for our fireplace, Barbara skipped ahead of us chanting merrily, "Gather ye faggots while ye may." She was teasing him about me, but it wasn't at all malicious. She wanted her old friend to find love.

At least that's how I read it, because I wanted that, too, so badly. I had decided that Curt was perfect for me, the ideal companion I had always needed. I'm pretty sure he had not decided that about me, but he was gentle and funny and made me feel like the only other person in the world. That Bread song had now become *our* song whenever I wanted to summon that weekend in the woods.

Before spring was over he wrote me from New York on that sexy stationery and told me about the new play he was doing, the new soap. I combed his words for some tiny clue that he couldn't live without me, but I sensed a de-escalation of ardor, the breezy banter of one friend writing another. Which is terrifying when you're determined to be in love. I had no choice but to call him in New York and feel him out on the subject. "Oh darling," he said. "I promise you'll get over this. You're just a young queer and I'm an old one." That made no sense to me whatsoever, since I was twenty-seven and he was just thirty-two. "We're going to be chums forever," he added.

Ouch.

We *were* chums forever, or as close as we could get. I visited him in New York, and he visited me later in my new home in San Francisco. I remember how proud I felt when I discovered him in a copy of *After Dark* magazine in my Russian Hill laundromat and showed off his steely gaze and cupid's-bow lips to all my friends. Once, on a visit to his hometown of Russell, Kansas, he sent me a comically dreary black-and-white postcard of a grain silo and a couple of pickup trucks. On the back he had written: *Drove the Chevy to the levee, but the levee was dry. Love, Curt.*

On another visit to San Francisco in the early eighties we drove up Highway 1 to Manka's Inverness Lodge, which was still just a funky Czech restaurant, not the Craftsman foodie destination it is today. After our order had been taken by a lethargic Czech waiter with unusually long arms, Curt was prompted to remark under his breath: "Manka see, Manka do." His wit, I noticed, had grown more trenchant and tinged with world-weariness. Or maybe I was finally noticing the man himself, now that he was no longer my high-booted

Russian soldier and we could just be friends heading up the highway together to explore the cruisy shrubbery of the Russian River.

Curt died of AIDS in 1985. By then, because of AIDS, I was a fierce foe of the closet, so it bothered me when his *New York Times* obituary reported that he had died of "complications resulting from cancer." I suspect that was done for the folks back in Kansas. I was glad to know, however, that it was Barbara Caruso—the beautiful, enduring Barbara—who had kept things light and loving when she scooped him off the floor of his apartment for his last trip to the hospital.

"C'mon, darling, time for us to go."

CURT WAS NOT particularly famous when he died. He had done a few soaps and *Sleuth* and *Absurd Person Singular* on Broadway, but he had been in the second cast of *The Boys in the Band*, not the original. Still, he never stopped being a star to me.

He once invited me to visit him on the set of *The Guiding Light*, where, buzzed on my first-ever toot of cocaine, I made the captivating discovery that a soap-opera set looks like a Macy's furniture show-room with a camera whirling frenetically in the middle. Such memories are all I have of Curt. I searched for him recently on YouTube to no avail. He endures mostly in the hearts of those who received his particular magic at a particular time, but he endures nonetheless.

In 1993 I flew to New York for the Gay Games and the twenty-fifth anniversary of Stonewall. I made a speech about the heroes of AIDS from the pitcher's mound at Yankee Stadium before an audience of 50,000 people. My friend Ian was also there that night, charming the audience with a typically self-effacing opening joke: *My name is Sir Ian McKellen, but you may call me Serena.* Afterward, in the batter's box, he let me know that he planned to read "Letter to Mama" the following night in his new one-man show, *A Knight Out*.

This was the letter I had written not long before my mother died.

The letter I had so hoped would fix things between us.

The letter I thought I had thrown down a well.

To hear my own words spoken in a Broadway theater by one of the world's greatest actors had me weeping buckets. I wept for my long-gone mother, for all the friends I'd seen die in the previous decade, for my youthful inability to bare my heart completely without hiding behind the veil of fiction.

And then something astonishing happened: there onstage Ian began to pay tribute to his first significant love, an actor he had met in 1961, when he was fresh out of Cambridge and appearing in an amateur production with graduates of the Royal Academy of Dramatic Arts. The actor had won Ian's heart one night in London when they had gorged on each other and Sara Lee apple pie and the new Broadway soundtrack of *Gypsy*. This golden-haired twenty-year-old from Kansas had struck Ian as quintessentially all-American with his incandescent smile, his baggy Army pants, and scuffed sneakers. The romance had been brief, but they had kept up for years, as actors do—one of them on Broadway, the other in the West End.

Curt had been the first of Ian's friends to die of AIDS.

Yes, Curt. *That* Curt.

Ian and I had fallen in love with the same man, ten years apart. I went backstage afterward to tell him as much, and we were both gobsmacked. The playwright Terrence McNally, standing nearby and hearing our conversation, said that he himself, as a matter of fact, had once had a thing for Curt. We laughed about that, all three of us, conjuring Curt like a hologram in our midst, recognizing the secret of his appeal: when he was with you he paid complete attention, and sometimes, when you needed it most, that could feel like forever.

TEN

I MISSED VIETNAM, AS STRANGE AS that sounds. I missed that rough-hewn fellowship of men and the allure of those dusty villages. Most of all, I missed the sense of purpose, however delusional, that I had found there. So, when my friend Mel called me in Charleston to ask if I wanted to go back to Vietnam as a civilian, I told him yes without a moment's hesitation. Mel and I had been friends when he worked as a staffer for Admiral Zumwalt in Saigon. Now he was working at the White House and had an interesting scheme up his well-starched sleeve. How would I like to organize some Vietnam veterans who would return to the war to do good works in the name of "Vietnamization"? (That was Nixon's term for leaving the war in the hands of the South Vietnamese, without losing face or appearing to surrender.) He would be up for reelection in a year, so he needed a distraction from the hordes of antiwar veterans spreading like crabgrass on the mall behind the White House. He despised those long-haired peaceniks, obsessed over them, especially a cocky Yalie named John Kerry, late of the Brown Water Navy, who had created the Vietnam Veterans Against the War and was getting press for it.

That's where Mel's scheme came in. What Nixon needed, Mel felt, was a counterpropaganda force of veterans who were not ashamed of their role in the war and were willing to talk about it to the press. But such an entity had to be organized, and it should not, under any circumstances, appear to come from the White House.

And so the Cat Lai Commune was invented. I named it that to give it a hip, countercultural ring, though no one seemed fooled, since most of the group were good ol' boys recruited from conservative veterans' organizations. After a month of preparation, ten of us boarded a chilly

C-140 transport plane, flying out of Alaska for Vietnam with a load of helicopter parts and a ton of blood. Once in Cat Lai, a port town in the lower Mekong Delta, our job was to build a twenty-unit housing complex for disabled Vietnamese naval veterans. It looked less like a complex than a motel, and a crappy one at that, since only a few of us knew how to lay cinderblock or install windows. I earned my keep by writing inspirational pieces about our experience, one of which was published by William F. Buckley Jr.'s *National Review*. Though there were Vietcong nearby, we worked without guns or uniforms, unless you count the royal-blue nylon T-shirts we wore to identify ourselves to the locals. For two sweltering months we were a high-profile, right-wing Habitat for Humanity.

Our main job, of course, was to talk to the press. Both the Associated Press and the *New York Times* drove out from Saigon to meet these odd-duck veterans who had returned to the war as civilians because they believed so deeply in the cause. Gloria Emerson, the celebrated *Times* correspondent, seemed to smell a rat but decided, incorrectly, that we'd come back as an act of penance, having committed atrocities of one sort or another during our time in-country. My usual rap was that most veterans weren't like John Kerry and his followers: we were proud of our military service and had not ended up as "potheads and radicals." No one guessed we were doing the work of the White House, specifically the team of Chuck Colson, Bob Haldeman, and John Erlichman, the infamous Dirty Tricks Department that would eventually cost Nixon the presidency with the Watergate burglary.

Back in Charleston, I kept in touch with Holger Jensen, the AP correspondent I had met in Cat Lai. I was already longing to escape the closet-sized steam bath of South Carolina, so I asked him if he could set me up for a job interview at the AP. I arrived at the bureau in New York with my cumbersome reporter's scrapbook under my arm—all my greatest hits: the Spanish moss blight, the Chitlin Strut, the *Gone With the Wind* hoax—but they refused to look at it. They said they wanted to see how well I worked under pressure, so they put me in a glass isolation booth that looked like a discard from a fifties quiz show. There, in less than half an hour, I arranged the pertinent facts of Lucille Ball's 1961 wedding to comedian Gary Morton into a plausible AP story. *Thousands jammed the sidewalk outside of New York's Marble Collegiate Church as America's favorite redhead blah, blah, blah . . .*

Three days later I got a call at the *News and Courier*, saying that I had passed the AP test, and that, luckily, there was an opening in the bureau in Buffalo. I didn't say no on the spot, for fear of sabotaging the offer, but back at Tradd Street, Miss Beth, in a rare moment of lucidity, confirmed my suspicions. "Honey, from what I hear tell, Buffalo is one place you do not want to shuffle off to." I put off answering the AP for several more days when, to my mortification, they called me back. They'd just had an opening in the San Francisco bureau. Would that be preferable to Buffalo?

I had seen San Francisco on my way to and from Vietnam. I had stayed at the Powell Hotel off Market Street and taken a cable car into the hills. A Gray Line tour bus had taken me to the gravesite of my favorite nonexistent person, Carlotta Valdes from Alfred Hitchcock's *Vertigo*. My friend Peggy Knickerbocker, then the wife of fellow Navyman and Chapel Hillian Jay Hanan, had pointed out the Chinese movie theater in North Beach where the Cockettes performed (*What did she just say?*) and taken me to a party in Sea Cliff, where one of her friends, a straight guy I didn't personally know, embraced me with alarming tenderness when he learned I'd just returned from the war. (Southern men, in my experience, never did such things for fear of instant emasculation.) When I processed out of the Navy on Treasure Island, I had stared across the crystalline blue bay at the shining white towers of the city and wondered, ever so idly, if I could see myself living there.

It had certainly *seemed* preferable to Buffalo.

I MADE TWO significant purchases before I drove west to California: a white Opel GT and an Irish setter–colored houndstooth tweed suit I had seen advertised in *Playboy* magazine. The Opel GT, if you remember, was a sort of low-slung mini-Corvette. You practically had to lie down to drive it. You yanked a crank near the gearbox to make the headlights rise out its sleek, featureless nose. It had no trunk whatsoever, or even a hatchback, so there was barely enough space behind the seat to stuff my new houndstooth suit and my framed ancestral portrait of Grandpa Branch. That suit, by the way, came with a pair of matching knickers as an alternative to the trousers. Clearly, I thought I would be someone considerably more debonair by the time I arrived in California.

I mentioned my new job to a trick I'd picked up at the Battery. "Oh, you're gonna love San Francisco, honey. They have fifty gay bars there." My response was as primly aghast as you might expect from a young Republican with a white Opel GT and a knickers suit. "No way. I would never go into one of those." Needless to say, I was in one of *those* on my first night in town. But I'm getting ahead of myself.

I felt a tinge of melancholy when I broke the news to Miss Beth. She was becoming foggier all the time—and more than a little infirm, so I worried, probably without warrant, that my absence from her house would be difficult for her. I knelt by her chair in the shop and shared my excitement about having a chance to live in San Francisco. She understood completely. *That city is just as lovely as Charleston, and the people are so elegant. The ladies put on gray suits and white gloves just to go shopping.* To me, this sounded suspiciously like Kim Novak in *Vertigo*, but I let it go. Maybe San Francisco had actually been that way, once upon a time; maybe Miss Beth was remembering that time and not the Hitchcock movie. I chatted with her a few minutes longer before she cut short our conversation by asking me my name. I told her my name, though she had known it very well for several years.

Well, you're a very nice young man. You should meet the young man who lives upstairs. I think you'd like each other very much.

In her genteel senility, Miss Beth had just fixed me up with myself.

It was the perfect benediction for my road trip west, since, after a lifetime of stifling pretense, I would finally get to meet myself in San Francisco.

I HAD DRIVEN as far as Clinton, Iowa (pop. 26,000), when an unimaginable phone call interrupted the trip. My friend Tom, an artist and a fellow member of the Cat Lai Commune, had invited me to stay in his houseboat on the Mississippi River. We were having dinner in town that night in his parents' dining room, a quaintly antimacassared scene out of Norman Rockwell. Tom's mother took the call in another room. We could hear a succession of polite murmurs before she brought the phone to the table, yanking the cord behind her like a torch singer with an obstinate mic. She looked like she'd just won the Publishers Clearing House Sweepstakes.

"It's the White House," she whispered to her son, covering the receiver with her hand. "A Mr. Holderman . . . Holleran . . . something. They want you in the Oval Office on Tuesday. President Nixon wants to see you, Tom! They've been trying to reach Armistead, too! Should I tell them you're here?"

It occurs to me now that I could have missed this moment completely. I'd been on the road for four or five days, with five more to go, and I wasn't checking in with anyone along the way. Had I not been invited to stay at Tom's houseboat, had Bob Haldeman not called at suppertime, I would have been unreachable on my cross-country odyssey, thereby missing out on one of the more surreal episodes of my life.

The president wanted to "recognize" us for our volunteer efforts in Vietnam. The urgent necessity that this happen on a particular day—this Tuesday!—should have been a red flag. I wasn't thinking about that at the time, though. I was thinking about how much fun it would be to call the AP in San Francisco and tell the bureau chief I'd be a few days late for work because the president wanted to see me in the Oval Office.

All was revealed on a crisp blue morning in October, when our limousines nosed through a crowd of protesters at the White House gates. Nixon's nemesis, John Kerry, had been planning this demonstration for weeks, so we were there to show the world that Nixon cared about veterans. It also gave him a good excuse to stay indoors during the protest. But even from the Oval Office you could hear them, a rolling surf-roar of outrage led by a charismatic young Turk who would one day seem as stiff as Nixon himself in his unblinking defense of unpopular foreign wars.

When the ten of us entered the Oval Office, I recognized the niche by the door, those three little shelves with a scallop-shell cap whose contents have changed with each new president. Nixon—or, more likely, his wife, Pat—had chosen half a dozen ceramic pheasants for that spot. I had already seen those birds in a magazine when Elvis Presley came here to be made a "Special Agent-at-Large for the Bureau of Narcotics and Dangerous Drugs." There was no such position, of course, but Nixon, having received an earnest letter from the King, had agreed to the meeting in the belief it would make him look cool with "the kids." Elvis, we are told, wanted desperately to atone for having inspired the Beatles, whom he regarded as a deeply degenerate influence on the youth of the nation.

I myself witnessed Nixon's burning need to be accepted by the young. There were beads of sweat on his upper lip when he stepped forward to shake our hands, and his body language suggested nothing so much as a jittery freshman at a fraternity rush party. We were just a bunch of twentysomethings, and he was president of the United States, yet he hadn't a clue as to how to be natural with us. It didn't help that he was using a dry professorial tone that might have succeeded as a speech but failed utterly as conversation. ("Now, let's see what would happen if we were to get out just a bit too soon . . . a month too soon, three months too soon, four . . .") It sounds strange to say that I was suffering for him, but I was. His discomfort was palpable.

So, as leader of the group, I made a little speech of my own, trying to inject a lighter note as I told the president about our lack of experience at building houses and the way that Gloria Emerson, the *Times* journalist, had grilled us about the atrocities that might have secretly motivated our return to Vietnam. That got a rise out of him, if not exactly the rueful chuckle I had imagined. "Yeah, of course," he muttered with the darkest of scowls. "She is a total bitch." She was already on his Enemies List, I realized, and there was a whiff of brimstone in the air that made me decide to drop the subject. (When I saw Emerson again at a booksellers' convention in the nineties, I couldn't resist telling her about Nixon's response. She loved it as I much as I thought she would, and said she would wear that designation as a badge of honor.)

The president, as it turned out, saw only one chance to be one of the guys, and he took it when we were talking about our affection for the Vietnamese people. One of us pointed out that our mamasan, the middle-aged woman who cooked our meals in Cat Lai, had always warned us when the Vietcong were around.

"And those little girls," said Nixon, looking directly at me. "When they're riding down the street on their bicycles with the tails of their silk *ao dais* blowing in the wind . . . they look like little butterflies." This observation might have sounded sweet had it been made, say, by Mrs. Zumwalt, but coming from a man with jowls and five-o'clock shadow, it seemed drenched in drool. I realized, to my horror, that Nixon was trying to talk sex with us—a little wink wink, nudge nudge with the troops—but, as his lousy luck would have it, he had chosen to do so with the only cocksucker in sight.

I told this story to the noted historian Douglas Brinkley in 2002 when he was writing a book called *Tour of Duty: John Kerry and the Vietnam War.* (In those days Kerry was energetically preparing to run for president in 2004.) The next time Brinkley called me in San Francisco he said that he had just checked out my account of those twenty squirm-inducing minutes with Nixon in the Oval Office.

"Checked it out? How?"

"You're on the tapes," he said.

The tapes. *The* tapes. From the tape recorder Nixon had secretly installed in the Oval Office. I was on them?

For a moment I thought I'd been caught red-handed. Storytellers have a way of improving their stories over the years, and I am certainly no exception.

"Did I remember it correctly?" I asked nervously.

"Actually," he replied, "it's better than you remembered."

This is how Brinkley put it in his book: "As fine a humor writer as Armistead Maupin turned out to be, the transcript of the White House tape recording of this meeting reads even funnier than does his remembrance of Nixon's small talk." As proof of this, Brinkley offers this word-for-word comment from the president after he made that remark about the little butterflies: "It's quite a sight. They told me when I was there in '56 that a Vietnamese mother tells her daughter that she is to carry herself like a swan. And I don't mind saying, just among our . . . and I'm no expert on this thing, but the Vietnamese women are actually not all that attractive. But I have never seen clothing that does more in, shall we say, a spectacular way than it does for the Vietnamese. But you all know that!"

I SAW NIXON one last time when I returned to Washington the following year for his inauguration. I spent most of that time loitering in bunting-hung ballrooms with other blazered young men, but the event that lingers in memory was the night I sat in the Presidential Box for the Inaugural Youth Concert. There was a blue velvet rope between me and the First Family, but they were all just a yard away: Pat and Dick, Julie and David Eisenhower, Tricia and her new husband, Edward Cox, and old Mamie Eisenhower herself, the former first lady, now a fragile seventy-five. Toward the end of the evening a self-confessed Republican rock band performed an atonal update of "If You Don't Want My Peaches, Don't Shake My Tree." I could tell that Mamie was jarred by all those pounding decibels, but she kept on smiling gamely as she plugged her gloved fingers into her ears.

When the audience began to clap along, Nixon tried to be a good sport and join in the fun with "the kids." I could see him clapping from where I sat, and it was a pitiful sight. Somehow he missed the beat every time.

For at least a year after I moved to San Francisco I proudly displayed a framed photo of Nixon and me shaking hands in the Oval Office. I figured it would start conversation, and indeed it did when

I brought guys home from the bars on Polk Street. Almost to a man, they reacted with looks of revulsion and mild panic, as if they had just realized they had been picked up by Jeffrey Dahmer.

After Nixon's resignation I took the picture down and never displayed it again.

ON MY FIRST night in San Francisco I slept at the Press Club, a fusty old residence on Post Street with frayed chenille bedspreads and clanging pipes. I was staying there as a guest of the AP bureau chief until I could find a permanent place to live. The club was for journalists, as the name implies, but in 1971 women in the profession were still refused full membership because men swam naked in its pool. That sounds promising, I know, but the place was not even remotely gay. For that, I had to walk a block uphill to Sutter Street to a club called the Rendezvous. How I knew that, I couldn't say for sure; I may have stumbled across a stray copy of the *Bay Area Reporter*, a gay handout whose initials conveniently spelled out the word *bar*.

It took commitment to visit this place. You couldn't just look both ways and slip in off the street to check out the crowd. Once past the door you were faced with a dauntingly steep staircase that offered no clue as to what awaited you at the top. There would be no easy escape. It would be like that scene in *Advise & Consent* when all those shadowy faces at the bar turn to cruise the anxious newcomer. I was on the verge of bolting when, somewhere above me, the voice of Barbra Streisand reminded me that we're just all children, needing other children, and yet letting our grown-up pride hide all the need inside. So I took a deep breath and began to climb.

It was worse than I thought. They were *slow dancing* with each other, all those men on the dance floor, slow dancing to Streisand under twirling colored lights, as if that were the most normal thing in the world. There was a DJ on one side spinning records in a glass booth that looked like a radio station. The call letters on his mic were KYKY. I didn't get it. I thought it was a real station, in fact.

Tacky doesn't scare me anymore, but it did back then. I didn't stay long at the Rendezvous, and I don't recall a single face from my first-ever visit to a gay bar. I wasn't recoiling from pickup sex; I was already beginning to get the knack of that. On my way to San Francisco, after that surreal audience with Nixon, I got stranded in a snowstorm in Laramie, where I had picked up the desk clerk at the Wyo Motel. I had chatted him up so long that he finally invited me behind the desk to watch a TV movie, a remake of *Death Takes a Holiday* with Yvette Mimieux and Bert Convy, which I had endured in its entirety before working up the nerve to invite him to my room. He told me he would meet me there. When he finally showed up at my door, fat snowflakes caught in his flaxen hair, he was holding a six-pack of beer I'd never seen before. This would welcome me to the West, he said, since it was made with Rocky Mountain springwater. I didn't like the tinny taste of it, but even Coors, a brew I would later boycott for its antigay policies, paired well enough with a plump, pink penis on a snowy Wyoming night. And I did feel welcomed to the West.

So it wasn't the prospect of sex that had rattled me at the Rendez-vous but a sudden vision of institutionalized queerness. Was this how I wanted to do it, after all—with the twirling dancehall lights and the slow dancing and an overall air of lurid tattiness? Nowadays I would relish the chance to be in such a place, a room wiped clean of techno music and video screens that didn't look like some chrome-trimmed sports bar in the Indianapolis airport. For that matter, I would love to be able to slow dance with my husband without feeling the least bit silly.

But I've never been quite in sync with the times.

THE AP BUREAU was located on Market Street, in the Fox Plaza building, a looming concrete tombstone that marked the grave of the grand old Fox movie theater. The work of a wire service, I soon learned, was a never-ending treadmill of words—not unlike the Internet—since the news was never "put to bed" the way it was with newspapers. There was always the other wire service, the UPI, running neck and neck with you. Even worse, you were rarely offered a byline to inspire you to do your best work. I was told by more than one person that the AP doesn't make stars, and that seemed true enough, with the exception of the blandly named Bob Thomas, who worked at the bureau in Los Angeles and covered movies.

For my first assignment I was told to follow a four-mile peace march through Golden Gate Park to the Great Highway. I'm sure this had everything to do with that detour I made through the Oval Office a fortnight earlier but no one at the bureau was ungracious enough to rub it in, or even mention the warmonger Nixon. That march gave me my first taste of San Francisco Values, not to mention jubilant public nudity, so I collected wacky details and shared them with my coworkers back at the bureau. I liked most of those people, and they seemed to like me. One experienced and chipper young woman who sometimes ran the desk at night was especially helpful. She would whisper to me what the sport was ("That's basketball") when I had to take scores over the phone, thereby sparing me the humiliation of having to ask the gruff-sounding guy on the other end of the line.

Others were not so kind. When I reported to work one evening, a disgruntled veteran of the bureau, clearly resigned to never becoming chief, poked his finger in my face and said: "Listen, bud, I've got my eye on you. People tell me you're lazy and you talk too much and you waste too much time polishing your stories. That shit doesn't cut it around here, so just watch your step. Understand?"

I did understand, depressingly enough. I had spent far too much time working on a feature piece about the king of the Gypsies in the East Bay. But that story was fascinating and full of rich details, and never before told, so I wanted to make it sparkle. And if I was a little talkative sometimes it was only to allay the grim gulag atmosphere of that room. But I wasn't lazy, dammit. Who were the "people" who were saying that? And why had they left it up to this asshole to tell me?

I was sure I was about to be fired, so I fell into a crippling depression for the rest of the night. On the way home, in the sickly green twilight of a Muni bus, I resolved to think of nothing else for the rest of the ride. It's an old trick of mine: banish every thought from your head except the one that's tormenting you and you'll soon grow weary of it. It's a sort of meditation on misery. You'll be forced to stop torturing yourself. It worked that night, and it was still working the next morning when it occurred to me that I wasn't important enough to be fired. I could keep this job forever, doing grunt work ad nauseam, like this bitterly unhappy man who had just tried to break my spirit. I could do that, but I would not.

I resigned a month later. My delicately worded letter to the bureau chief explained that I wanted to look for something "more creative." The chief said he was disappointed to see me go and warned that it would be hard to get work as a feature writer at the local newspapers. He proved to be dead right about that.

Flash forward to a new millennium and a book signing in a large California city. An older man has been in the line for my autograph for at least an hour, so I tell him I'm sorry about the wait. He brushes it off with a wave of his hand.

"Do you remember me?" he asks.

I don't remember him, so I say what I usually say when someone puts me on the spot like this: "Help me out here, would you?"

He tells me his name and says that we worked together at the AP.

I recognize him instantly as my tormentor on that demoralizing night. "Well, I'll be damned," I say, wondering if he remembers how he treated me. He doesn't seem to remember a thing, so I don't bring it up. He thinks we were good buddies. I sign his book *Thanks for the memories*, keeping the last laugh to myself.

MY FIRST APARTMENT in the city was a furnished front room in a yellow Victorian house on Sacramento Street. It had flocked wallpaper in a vibrant shade of whorehouse red, like most of the fern bars in town; I loved that about it. I would be living alone, so, for company, I bought a mynah bird at a pet shop on Fillmore Street. He had impressed me when he said HOW ARE YA? in the shop, but unfortunately that proved to be his only impersonation beyond an ear-piercing whistle that suggested someone had left a tea kettle on too often in his presence.

The apartment was a block from Lafayette Park, so I soon discovered how busy the bushes were at night. It was a Pacific Heights sweater-and-slacks crowd, which struck me at the time as sort of hot, and I could invite guys back to my place after checking out the goods. Most of my fellow bushmen, however, wanted to get off right there on the spot, despite (or maybe because of) the threat of the police. Squad cars would make the loop at the crest of the park, flashing their high beams to flush us out of the brush like so many quail at a Dick Cheney shooting camp. As soon as we saw those beams, we would scatter and go bounding down the steep open lawn to Gough Street, yelping like pups. Or at least I did, on more than one occasion. The one time I went to another guy's place—where I had naturally *presumed* he lived alone—his lover came home and saw us and pulled a full Jacqueline

Susann on me, shouting *SLUT* as I grabbed my clothes and stumbled down the hall. I was laughing when I got to the elevator. I *was* a slut. And beginning to enjoy it immensely.

I had several subsequent hookups with one of the guys I met in the park. It never got serious, but I really took to his friend, Nancy McDoniel, a young actress from Missouri who played Nurse Ratched in a Little Fox Theatre production of *One Flew Over the Cuckoo's Nest*. Though she brought an icy hauteur to that role, she was kind and warm and elegant offstage, and we were good friends in the seventies until she moved to New York for acting work. Our friendship informed the one I would eventually create for Michael Tolliver and Mary Ann Singleton—a naive gay man feigning sophistication with a slightly more naive young straight woman. Nancy, like Mary Ann, also had a "good-time Charlene" roommate, a United Airlines stewardess, as we called them back then, who kept bottles of Jade East and Old Spice in her bathroom cabinet for the convenience of the men who would sleep over. Nancy and I would giggle about "the friendly skies" of that bed down the hall.

So it was that guy I picked up in the park, Nancy's friend, whose name I have long since forgotten, who answered a question I put to him nervously one night.

"What does it mean when your pee turns the color of bourbon?"

It meant I had hepatitis, of course. My liver had been kicked to shit, and I had been dragging around listlessly for days, and every time I came home the damned mynah bird would yell HOW ARE YA? HOW ARE YA? HOW ARE YA? and it wouldn't make a bit of difference if I covered his cage with a towel, since he would only turn into a screaming tea kettle in retaliation. The doctor who treated me told me I needed bed rest. That meant, in the end, giving up my apartment and returning the mynah bird to the pet shop and flying back to North Carolina for a mother's care. It meant that my golden California Dream had come to a screeching stop.

Back in Raleigh, I would lie in bed all day, staring up at the stained-glass window I had designed as a teenager starved for a little color. My mother was very sweet, thrilled to be taking care of me, as I knew she would be. Only once or twice did she approach the subject of how I had acquired the hepatitis. "There are lots of ways to get it apparently." She was laying a breakfast tray on my bed, French toast with eggy crenellated edges, the way I like it. Her tone was both breezy and forced. "I hear you can even get it from a toilet seat," she added. She could talk herself into anything.

A case in point: in those days she and my father were riding to the hounds with a fox hunting club out in the country. They wore the traditional scarlet jackets (though I had learned to call them pink, in the British manner), and I loved how they looked when they came home on Sunday afternoon, mud flecked and pink-cheeked, exhilarated by the chase, a couple straight out of *Auntie Mame*. They had not been chasing a fox, however. My mother, as founder of the Wake Country SPCA, would never have agreed to that. This was a "drag hunt," so called because they were chasing the bedding of a fox, a rag that was dragged through the woods prior to the hunt. That gave the hounds the scent trail they needed, but no fox was killed in the process.

Only, one day one was. My mother rode into a clearing and found the hounds in a huddle going wild with bloodlust. Bits of red fur were flying everywhere like dandelion pods on the wind. The hounds, it seemed, had flushed out a real fox, so they were delirious. My mother fled the scene on horseback, sobbing. She was inconsolable when the master of the hounds approached and told her that these things happened sometimes in spite of their best intentions. That was not enough for her. She would never hunt again, she said, not if sweet little animals were going to be killed. The master of the hounds hesitated for a moment, then offered to share a secret with her if she promised not to tell the other members of the hunt.

That fox had already been dead, he told her, when the dogs got to him. The hunt organizers had found its corpse on the side of the highway that morning and placed it at the end of the drag to satisfy the appetites of the dogs—and, presumably, some of the humans who longed for a taste of the real thing. This explanation struck me as pure malarkey, but my mother had chosen to buy it. If she felt, as I did, that faked savagery was every bit as life-demeaning as actual savagery, she did not say so. She needed this explanation to endure the unendurable. In that way, it was not unlike the case of hepatitis her son had picked up off a toilet seat in San Francisco.

Three years later, when my mother's breast was removed, I sent her a stuffed animal that I'd bought in New York City at F.A.O. Schwartz. It was a little red fox, soft and squeezable, and she took it with her to the hospital every time she went back.

MY TWO-MONTH RECOVERY seemed to take forever. At night, down in the Chimney Room, with its used brick fireplace and Confederate flag and oiled chintz café curtains, my childhood lurched back like the Creature from the Black Lagoon, threatening to drag me under. In my early youth I had wanted to live in this house forever (or maybe next door, in Miss Lillian's little house, after she died) but that dream was gone now that I'd become one of Tennyson's lotos-eaters. My brother and sister were already married and living away, so

I would sit with my parents in the blue light of television, annotating scenes from *The Streets of San Francisco*.

"That's the cable car I take to work!"

"That's Russian Hill, where I want to live next!"

"Look! Angel Island! I went there last summer!"

And thus I held tight to the paradise that had almost been lost.

ELEVEN

I DID FIND A PLACE ON Russian Hill—that "pentshack" I mentioned earlier—a tiny studio perched on the roof of an old yellow-brick
house at the crest of Union Street. The address was 1138½, a satisfying
echo of 38½ Tradd Street, my storybook aerie in Charleston. To get
to it you had to climb dozens of steps, some through the steep front
garden, still more through the side of the house until you reached
the roof. The moment I saw the view I knew I was home. There was
a sliding glass door that opened on to a painted plywood deck that
opened on to the full pageantry of San Francisco Bay and the distant
mountains of Marin. At night the beacon on Alcatraz pulsed softly
against the wall, so softly that I didn't notice it for weeks.

The main room was only big enough to contain an armchair and
a bed, a problem discussed at length when my parents visited and
found me sleeping on a mattress on the floor. My mother suggested
that what I needed was one of those captain's beds with drawers beneath it, so I could at least have a little storage space. So my father
measured the room with his conveniently foot-long feet and we drove
out to an unpainted furniture store in Mill Valley. There, as any idiot
could have predicted, the choice of a bed took on embarrassing di-
mensions.

"A single bed will give you more space in the room," my mother
insisted.

I told her I didn't need to move around. I could put a table and
chairs out on the deck and eat meals out there when the spirit
moved me.

"That's silly, darling. There's only one of you, and the single bed is
plenty roomy."

I told her there was more storage in the double bed.

"You'll be way too cramped in that room," she insisted. "You'll have to squeeze around the bed just to get to the kitchen."

"I like a big bed," I said feebly.

My father was the one who put an end to this. "For God's sake, Diana, he's a grown man. He might wanna have company some night."

Did he know what sort of company? Certainly not.

Did my mother know?

Maybe. No, probably.

Did she really think that a smaller bed might keep it from happening?

I NAMED THE pentshack Little Cat Feet after that line in the Carl Sandburg poem. "The fog comes / on little cat feet." It didn't really *need* a name, but I've always enjoyed naming places, and the fog was so full of mystery when it rolled over my deck at night and blurred the Deco buildings on either side, leaving only the random yellow rectangles of their windows. Sometimes it got so thick that all I could see from my deck was the pink neon fish above a restaurant down at Fisherman's Wharf. There was something insistently symbolic about that fish, like the billboard with the big eyeglasses in *The Great Gatsby*. For someone once steeped in Anglican mythology it was tempting to think of the fish as an early Christian *ichthus*, but I knew in my fledgling pagan heart that San Francisco was a place where myths could flourish just fine without the help of Jesus. Little Cat Feet already felt steeped in its own secret history, which is why I eventually plopped it on the roof of my fictitious 28 Barbary Lane and made it the apartment of my creepiest villain.

In 1993 when *Tales of the City* was filmed for television, the pentshack was meticulously re-created on the roof of a parking garage in North Beach. The fact that there was a police station downstairs made it all the more titillating to smoke a joint behind the camera as I watched a scene come to life in a replica of my first real San Francisco home. Nothing would have been sweeter than to share that moment with my best friend, Steve Beery, who lived just a few blocks away in his own little studio on the leafy crest of Telegraph Hill. ("In the pubic hair of Coit Tower" was how he always put it.)

Steve had been my biggest booster and confidant for fifteen years. My muse, really. We had been lovers briefly, but friendship was what truly agreed with us. We had been cabinmates on cruises to Alaska and Mexico, fellow travelers to London and the Cotswolds and the Isle of Lesbos—adventures that had all sparked plot turns in "Tales of the City." We became real-life Hardy Boys as we searched Nob Hill's Grace Cathedral for an elevator that would lift us to a catwalk hundreds of feet above the floor. *What if?* had been our constant marching song as I spun a tale that was never allowed to end. What if that shed in the park is where the mysterious hermit named Luke lives? What if he turns out to be someone long presumed dead? What if that society columnist somehow falls in love with the hermit? *Of course* I wanted Steve with me that day. The story was still going on.

The phone rang at least eight times before he answered. I knew what that meant.

"Sorry, sweetie, were you asleep?"

"More or less," he said.

"Do you feel like a little trip? I'm down at the pentshack set. It's fucking amazing and you have to see it."

"I dunno, bud."

"I could send a cab to Coit Tower. You wouldn't have far to walk. I've saved a director's chair for you."

He was thirty-nine years old and too weak to get out of bed. He never made it to the pentshack set—or, for that matter, more than a fortnight past forty.

Remember his name: Steve Beery.

When the time is right, I'll tell you how we met.

It's something I might have made up myself.

THE PENTSHACK—THE ORIGINAL one—cost me $175 a month. That sum will bring bitter tears to the eyes of modern renters, but even back then, the money had to come from somewhere. Having quit my post at the AP, I was desperate for cash, and I wasn't too proud to take any job that let me stay longer in San Francisco. Both local newspapers, as predicted, had already turned me down, so I signed up with Kelly Girl, an employment agency so accustomed to its flunkies being female that they mailed me a form letter advising me to wear "a conservative skirt" when I reported for work. That might have been interesting on my first assignment: handing out flyers for a roommate-finder service on a street corner in the Financial District. For another day job they sent me to a warehouse in Daly City, where I loaded department store mannequins into a truck. My coworker was a gentle, feebleminded giant who reminded me of Lenny in *Of Mice and Men* and insisted on honking the boobs of every mannequin we handled that day. Later, I found work as a clerk in a Thai import shop on Union Street called Fabulous Things. Bored socialites from Pacific Heights, always on the prowl for something Fabulous, would unroll whole bolts of shimmering silk, wrap it around themselves for a quick pose in the mirror, and dump it in a heap before they left for their vodka lunches in little French courtyards down the street. I lasted a week.

Another job seemed to have dropped from heaven. I was making one last effort at religiosity by attending an Episcopal Church not far from Little Cat Feet. I had already abandoned the effort it had always taken to believe in God, but the little Craftsman church was charming, and I thought it might do me some good to volunteer at its suicide hotline. The rector, a stalwart Redfordesque guy with a wife and kids, who was secretly called "God's gift" by the women of the parish, took note of my jobless state one Sunday morning after the sermon and offered to pay me by the hour as a part-time assistant, drafting occasional letters for him. That had a nice Dickensian ring to it—a vicar's amanuensis—and it was, after all, a form of writing, the very thing I wanted to do. I enjoyed the time I spent with this liberal-hearted man, though there proved to be very few letters to compose. There were even fewer suicides to prevent in my volunteer job. I would sit there alone at night, waiting for the phone to ring, hoping against hope that someone would at least get depressed. (An ill-attended suicide hotline appears in several scenes of *Tales of the City*.)

I wasn't at a loss, however, for how to spend my nights. I could amble down Russian Hill to the hubbub of North Beach, sometimes taking a longer, more scenic route through the leafy canyon of Macondray Lane, just so I could descend the rickety wooden stairway leading down to Taylor Street. There were several such pedestrian byways hidden in the crevices of Russian Hill, but this was the one that inspired the Barbary Lane in my books. I was deliberate in the juxtaposition of those words. *Barbary* to connote the raw-boned frontier wildness of the city; *Lane* to suggest the peace of an English village. Seemingly contradictory, yet anyone could sample both sensations in the course of a twenty-minute stroll down to North Beach. Once you hit Columbus and passed the bustling Italian cafés, you had only to take a left at Carol Doda's blinking nipples on the sign in front of Big Al's. The last few blocks were the hardest, since aggressive barkers, and sometimes the girls themselves, would try to drag you into clubs for what was known then as a "nude encounter." I would pick up my pace here with a smile plastered on my face. My own nude encounters awaited me at the foot of Broadway, where a faceless, signless, four-story concrete building stood beneath a freeway off-ramp that has long since been torn down. The building is still there, considerably altered. A quick online search reveals that the bones of its high-ceilinged front room can still be glimpsed in the shared office space it offers millennials with laptops and dreams of a start-up.

This was Dave's Baths. Even those two words suggest an unlikely duality. The term *Baths* conjures up a bacchanal in Roman times: add the word *Dave's* to the front and, *voilà*, you have a folksy barbershop in Toledo. Both masculine moods were invoked, each in its own nourishing way, once you got inside.

You had to sign in at the desk. I'm assuming that most guys gave a fake name. I certainly did, since they never checked IDs, and I was still worrying about whether or not this was actually legal. I used the name Elloughby Branch, grandly enough, though it may help to know that this was a jokey spin on my Confederate ancestor's name: Lawrence O'Brian Branch—LO'B Branch. Okay, right, makes it even worse.

The hardest thing about confronting your past is the pinch of the overlapping parts, when you are no longer one thing and not quite the other. It makes you squirm to face yourself in transition, foolish and floundering. But it has to be said that if anything delivered me from the privileged white elitism of my youth it was the red-lit cubicles and darkened hallways and even darker mazes of Dave's Baths. Everyone went there, pilgrims united on a quest for cock; and even a rejection, if delivered kindly enough, could reveal the difference between a bastard and a nice guy in the dark. My tastes in those days were largely vanilla and oral (it was still such a novelty to have one of those wonders in my mouth), and only afterward, when I lay spent and happy in the arms of a stranger, another tender man-child like me, did I even begin to notice the secondary matters of race, creed, and national origin. It was a deeply democratizing place.

I more or less abandoned Dave's when I discovered the other baths across town, the Ritch Street Baths and the Club Baths, which we called Eighth and Howard in the interest of discretion. It was a much longer walk, and I did have to walk, having totaled my Opel GT in a head-on collision on Russian Hill, but it was always worth the effort. Even the walk itself past the denim-dense alleyways south of Market could offer its own *alfresco* entertainments. Once you got to Ritch Street you could sink into a huge Jacuzzi with a dozen of your brothers. *It's like a Minoan temple,* I had gushed to my new friend, Jan, though I didn't know exactly what that meant, since I had merely read the phrase "Minoan Lounge" on a poster. Afterward, on the other side of that room, you could order a nine-grain turkey sandwich with sprouts and enjoy it while lolling on a velvet beanbag with others taking a break from their revels. How strange to remember that there was once a culinary aspect to the baths. Even stranger to remember that I did not find it repellent in the least. The lights in those places were kept low for more than one reason.

Jan, by the way, was the sister of a friend from my Chapel Hill and Navy days. She was the person I took to see *The Boys in the Band* and *Cabaret* to show her what gay life was (sort of) like. A vivacious redhead with a husband and two small kids, she loved hearing every juicy detail of my nocturnal rambles. I had decided, early on, that San Francisco would mean a brand-new life for me; there would be no lying about myself to her or to anyone else. So, one evening after a long day at the AP, I had thrown back a couple of stiff mai tais at a Polynesian restaurant in Fox Plaza and made my way to Jan's upper-floor Victorian flat in Cow Hollow. She was washing her children in the tub at the time. Seeing the stricken look on my face, she dried the kids and put them to bed, finally joining me in the living room, where I sat with lowered head on the edge of an armchair. She sat on the sofa across from me, frowning with concern. "What is it, babycakes?"

She used that term of endearment with almost everyone, I would discover, but I had never heard it before that night. It would end up as the title of one of my novels.

Fumbling with an awkward preamble (including the shameful and already inaccurate assurance that I would change it if I could), I finally said: "I'm homosexual."

She absorbed that for a moment then left the sofa and knelt in front of me, taking my hands in hers. "Big fucking deal," she said with the loveliest little smile.

That's all it took. I started coming out to everyone. Friends. Coworkers. Cabdrivers. Anyone who would listen. It was so exhilarating. Once, as a reason for quitting a boring office job, I confessed to the employer that I was gay. "So what?" he said with a shrug. "I'm married and I'm fucking my secretary. That's no excuse."

I was more than ready for the next level when a reporter for *San Francisco* magazine approached me about a photo feature she was writing called "The Ten Sexiest Men in Town." She wanted to include an out gay man and wondered if I would be willing to, um, be him. I jumped at it, recognizing an easy way to clear the Etch A Sketch tablet of my make-believe life and start afresh in the city, free of secrets. (The "sexiest" part was embarrassing—and hyperbole, to say the least—but this was 1973, and the notion of an "eligible bachelor" list in a mainstream lifestyle magazine was already sounding passé.) Here was my chance to utter my own "big fucking deal" in a way that was public but not so public as to make it all the way back to Raleigh. I would be in good company, too. Among the other men on the list were respected local cultural figures like the actor Peter Donat and the Reverend Cecil Williams of Glide Memorial Church. I was photographed striding across the crest of Russian Hill in Levi's 501s and a plaid flannel shirt, a breeze ruffling my hair. They described me as a Vietnam veteran and an aspiring writer who "ekes out a living doing odd jobs and writing letters for an Episcopal minister." The fact that I was "homosexual" was mentioned, very matter-of-factly, in the last sentence. All in all, quite gracefully done, I thought.

The rector thought otherwise. When I showed him the magazine in his office, feeling—yes—rather proud of myself, he read the pertinent caption slowly then looked at me with an unreadable expression. What was he feeling? Shock? Pity? Disbelief? I was flummoxed. He had given every impression of being an open-minded man. I had honestly expected him to congratulate me on my courage.

He got up from the desk and closed the door. "I'm so sorry about this, Armistead. I'm going to have to let you go."

I just stood there gaping at him.

"It's not what you think. I'm not prejudiced. I'm not one of those people. It just wouldn't look right for you to be working here."

I asked him without a trace of anger: "Then what sort of person are you?"

The answer came, but not from the rector, from me, because it was suddenly oh-so-blazingly obvious. "Oh . . . a gay person."

"I'm so sorry," he said again. "I know you understand."

I did understand. Coming out makes you dangerous to those around you who believe they have to stay in the closet at any cost. Especially if they work with you. Especially if being with you might not *look right*. Especially if, from the beginning, they had secretly hoped for a little more than someone to write their letters.

I left his office without a word, in no mood for absolutions.

AS IT HAPPENED, I would not be the last person to be dismissed from that church for being openly queer. Five years later, the assistant rector, Father William Barcus, came out of the closet—in the pulpit, no less, in the presence of that very rector, with TV cameras rolling—when he preached against the Briggs Initiative, the ballot measure that would have outlawed gay and lesbian teachers in California. Supervisor Harvey Milk, who led the battle against Briggs, was also in the church that day, and we were swapping Cheshire Cat grins over what we knew was about to happen. Bill Barcus had already used that pulpit to decry the homophobic murder of a local gardener, Robert Hillsborough, who had been stabbed to death by four men yelling, "Faggot! Faggot!" Hillsborough's death had awakened everyone to the escalating violence against gay people in the city. But Bill, following the established rules of the ecclesiastical closet, had voiced his indignation as a compassionate outsider. Now he was ready to make it personal and "join his people in the fight."

To hear him tell it—which I did, on a video released after his death from AIDS in 1992—all hell broke loose after his announcement. His coming-out had been a landmark moment that stirred the excitement of the national press and sent many closeted priests running for cover, as he put it, "skirts a-twirling." And that tape reminded me how Harvey and I came to be in church that day.

> One day Armistead Maupin came to me at [the church] and said, "When are you going to stop preaching about *them* and start preaching as *us*?" And I said, "Armistead, it would just ruin my career. You don't understand." [He] looked at me and said, "You were not ordained for a career, you were ordained for a vocation. Can we not find one honest man in

the church? Just one?" So I went to my friend Harvey Milk, and he said, "Can we not find one honest man?" And I said, "You got him."

Bill Barcus did find his vocation. He was eventually *released* from his parish (the sardonic italics are clear on the videotape) by the rector he had embarrassed. When he was transferred across town to Grace Cathedral, he served as canon to the bishop and established the church's first program for the homeless. At one point there were as many as three hundred people sleeping in the cathedral at night, so Canon Barcus looked for more permanent housing and secured the Club Baths when it was ordered shut by the city as a response to AIDS. Those little rooms at Eighth and Howard—so familiar to me in the sex-fueled days of my youth—became the city's first dedicated housing for the homeless. Bill was especially proud that there were armed guards to keep residents safe, and that pets were permitted on the premises. This new Episcopal Sanctuary spawned several others over the years, the most recent of which, a newly built five-story, forty-eight-unit building, opened in 2002.

It's called Canon Barcus Community House.

EVERY ASPIRING WRITER knows the drill: you take a lackluster office job because you need to eat and pay the rent, but the writing you do at work (if you're lucky enough even to be doing that) drains you so much that you don't feel like writing at night. So you quit after a few months and fully commit to freelancing. There is freedom in that, at least, and the chance to stretch as an artist, and it's better to struggle financially than to live under the heel of a boring master. Only it isn't, really. Struggling means living in a state of perpetual panic, and you can't be creative when you're feeling like that. So you nail down another steady paycheck, deeply relieved but hating yourself a little bit more, and so the cycle repeats itself.

I had several writing-adjacent jobs in the early seventies. I worked as a mail boy at an ad agency in Jackson Square. The boss there was a retired admiral who had hired me because of my service in the Navy—and, like Mary Ann Singleton in *Tales*, part of my job entailed raising the American flag every morning on the front of the building. Then I would push my cart from office to office, dispensing mail and free cans of Shasta soda, one of the agency's top clients. I got to know the whole building that way, so I mined their gossip and jokes for a snappy newsletter that I published once a week. People loved it, but it tipped off the admiral that I might have a few ambitions beyond the mailroom. I was not, he informed me nicely, the mail boy in *How to Succeed in Business Without Really Trying*. It wasn't like that here. There would be no meteoric rise to the top.

Another agency, a PR firm in the same neighborhood, lured me in with the title of account executive. There I worked with World Airways in Oakland when it was promoting a tricked-out 747 for private charters. It was intended for rock stars and millionaires, so it was Peter Maxed to the max with pink and orange velvet. On the day of the photo shoot for the campaign, when a male model was needed to go with the female one they had hired, I rushed home for a dinner jacket and obligingly posed with her, a glass of champagne in my hand. I remember that gig because it was the most interesting. I remember, too, the one that made me quit. One of the partners had come into my office (I had my own office!) with a pamphlet from a pharmaceutical company we were representing. "Put this into layman's terms," he said. "The language is very technical." When he returned, he asked if I had figured it out. "Yes," I said, "it's a pill you stick up a dog's ass to keep him from farting." He nodded with a dim, defeated smile and left.

What discouraged me most, really, was the talk of retirement plans. These guys were dead serious about this. Their intention was to stay for the next thirty years, beneath these very fluorescent lights, arriving at eight and ducking out at noon for lunch, then trudging home at six, but they would be handsomely paid if they just stuck it out. I could think of nothing more terrifying, so I quit before it started sounding like a good idea. To bolster my resolve after I'd abandoned that paycheck, I had cards printed bearing my phone number and six words:

Armistead Maupin writes for a living.

This was my declaration of independence, my commitment, in writing, to a writer's life, even in the face of penury. I handed the card out mostly in bars, or to guys I wouldn't mind seeing again after a night at the Glory Holes on Sixth Street. The freelance jobs I managed to snag were interesting but seldom produced the cash I needed each month for Little Cat Feet. I expanded my old king of the Gypsies piece from the AP for a feature in *Coast* magazine. I wrote feature stories for *Pacific Sun*, a weekly newspaper in Marin County, where I described the backstage life of a Nude Encounter girl, and, later, a Levi's denim jacket art contest at which one of the judges, Rudi Gernreich, the "inventor" of the topless swimsuit, greeted each vividly embroidered entry with an arched eyebrow, foreshadowing the high camp drama of *Project Runway*. Though I was clueless about it then, Gernreich and his lover, Harry Hay, had, over twenty years earlier in Los Angeles, founded the Mattachine Society, one of the country's first gay rights organizations. Because of the vital need for secrecy, the group had been modeled on a Communist cell, which may have accounted for Gernreich's silence on the subject once he got famous as a designer.

Another local happening that grabbed my attention was a benefit being thrown at California Hall on Polk Street by a Union Street hairdresser named Kenneth Marlowe. He was about to embark on a sex change, so he had hired the seventies remnants of a big-band orchestra (Tommy Dorsey? Benny Goodman?) and invited *tout* San Francisco to come dance the old-fashioned way and pay for his surgery. He called it "the ball to end all balls." That was certainly more than enough to entice me, but Marlowe had also persuaded Sally Rand, the legendary fan dancer from the 1939 World's Fair on Treasure Island, to perform at the event. The room was full of spry seventy-somethings, largely straight couples, as nearly as I could tell, twirling deliriously around the dance floor, while Marlowe performed as a brassy but warm MC. Sally danced, teasingly, with her fluffy white ostrich-feather fans, under what had to have been a fifteen-watt blue bulb. Kenneth Marlowe, now on his way to becoming Kate, had given himself a send-off like few have ever seen in the city.

The next day I had lunch with both Kate and Sally at a restaurant on the Russian Hill end of Polk Street. It was Sally's seventieth birthday, so I ordered a cake. She blew out the candles with gusto and proceeded to tell raunchy stories about her stripper days at the Music Box (now the Great American Music Hall). Kate, not to be outdone, told us that she—Kenneth, that is—had grown up in a whorehouse in Winnemucca, Nevada, where his mother had been the madam. I was fascinated by the thought of that all-female setting for a boy who felt like a girl, so I later borrowed it for Anna Madrigal's backstory. When it came to her essence, however, Anna was not in the least like Kate, any more than Dawn Simmons had been back in Charleston.

Some years later, to my confusion, I read a memoir by Kate Marlowe in which she described a tough childhood in Chicago, where her mother had been a gangster's moll. Her history had a way of changing, it seemed, depending on her mood and audience. Much as I would later do with Anna Madrigal, she would grab bits from here and there, anything that caught her fancy, in her construction of a vivid life.

NONE OF THIS paid the rent, of course, so I started borrowing money from my father. It was never very much—just a hundred or two from time to time—but the old man, predictably, got more and more apoplectic, telling me I'd been a goddamn fool for quitting a real job that had a future. I was starting to think he was right. More than ever, though, the prospect of a nine-to-five job was abhorrent to me.

"Don't ask him again," my mother told me one night on the phone. "I'll see what I can do." Not long after that she mailed me a cashier's check for a thousand dollars. "It's my mad money," she said mysteriously, "and I expect you to pay me back."

Mad money? In high school that's what a girl kept in her purse in case she had trouble with her date and had to get home on her own. Why would my mother need mad money? And how long had she been stashing it, anyway? I knew not to ask. She had given me treasured presents before—antiques mostly, like a shiny brass coal pail I kept magazines in for years, and an English miner's lantern with red glass that still sits on our dresser at Diamond Street—but nothing could compare to the gift of a mother's mad money to keep my reckless dreams afloat.

MOST OF US don't know when our Moment comes. We don't feel it at all. It's just a passing whim, or a phone call or a snippet of conversation that leads to one thing and another and you end up with a life you would never have had at all had it not been for that first thing, that first random thing. Mine was just a funny lead I had followed up on. A young woman of Spanish land-grant heritage (her middle name was Vallejo) told me at a cocktail party about a strange heterosexual mating ritual at the Marina Safeway, so I decided on the spot to write about it for the *Pacific Sun*. Everything—and I mean everything—flowed from that decision. Journalism more or less failed me in that endeavor—or, really, I failed it—but a fictional entity was born who would live in me for the rest of my life.

I had no choice but to make up Mary Ann Singleton. None of the single women down at the Marina Safeway—a swooping manta ray of a sixties supermarket whose style became the template for scores of others around the country—would admit to a reporter that she was loitering in the vegetable department in her rhinestone-studded brushed denim pantsuit for the sole purpose of a little male company that night. I could see it all happening before my eyes, the circling predators, the forced titters when carts bumped carts, the not-that-subtle discussion of zucchini and cucumbers—but it was nothing that anyone, male or female, would discuss.

So I took a few notes for color (the chain's slogan back then was *Since We're Neighbors, Let's Be Friends*) and went home and made up a story, finally freed from the tiresome bonds of journalism. The young woman I invented was a bright, but decidedly naive, escapee from Cleveland—enough like me, in other words, that I could put words into her mouth with a degree of confidence. Mary Ann's friend Connie Bradshaw, who had brought her to the Safeway to cruise, was a stewardess who fancied herself a pickup artist but inevitably failed with men. Mary Ann is approached by a creep in a white belt who asks her about snow peas but ends up calling her a bitch when she rebuffs him. She is consoled by another man who has overheard them. Mary Ann likes him. A lot. She thinks he might be the man of her dreams, in fact, until she discovers that he's there with the man of *his* dreams.

The story struck a nerve with readers of this Marin newspaper (especially the women), so the editor asked me if I would consider following Mary Ann's adventures from week to week. He was launching a new San Francisco edition of the paper and thought this would work nicely in the city. I agreed on the grounds that I could follow other characters as well, including the winsome boyfriend of the gay man Mary Ann had met at the supermarket. (He was Michael Huxtable back then; in his second incarnation his last name became Tolliver.) I named this new venture "The Serial" and had pancake-sized promo stickers made that I personally slapped on every light pole on the cruisy blocks of Polk Street. I was filled with hope.

That came crashing down five weeks later when the San Francisco edition of the *Pacific Sun* folded. The editor told me that "The Serial" had easily been their most popular feature, and proved it by bestowing the title on another writer, Cyra McFadden, who created her own hilarious and acerbic (and eventually best-selling) satire about yuppies in Marin County. I fell into a funk, realizing that I was flat broke again. Somehow I managed to land another paycheck at the San Francisco Opera, where I wrote press releases and diva profiles in a windowless room. My boss was Maestro Kurt Herbert Adler, a blustering Austrian-born tyrant who commanded a backstage brigade of nervous, scurrying women. I knew nothing, and cared less, about opera. I faked a lot of it with an encyclopedic book on the subject that my mother sent me at Christmas. She had inscribed it: "For Teddy, our new 'Opera Star.'" She was understandably elated that I had found steady employment.

Maestro Adler was an unrelenting homophobe—no small achievement when you've run an opera company for two decades. On Christmas

Eve he summoned half a dozen staffers to his office while he made decisions about casting the fall season. For part of this time he was on the phone with Leontyne Price, one of the great sopranos of the day, on whom he unleashed a torrent of gooey Viennese charm, the likes of which we had never seen. He even blew kisses to her dogs. I'm not sure why the rest of us had to be there for this moment, except perhaps to hear that the maestro actually knew the *names* of her dogs. Then Adler pored over a long list of proposed singers. One of them, a famous tenor, really raised his ire. "No!" he yelled, slamming his hand down on his desk. "I vill not knowingly hire another fehrrry in this house." It was unnerving, to say the least, since I realized he must talk this way all the time, and that no one here would dream of calling him on it. I don't think he meant the fairy in the room. He had not hired me, after all, knowingly or otherwise, and I was far less worthy of his attention than Leontyne Price's dogs.

At some point in that scrambling rat race of an opera season, I received a phone call at my desk from Virginia Westover, a society columnist at the *San Francisco Chronicle*, whom I had come to know casually at opera fund-raisers.

"Listen," she said. "I was at a party last night, and Charles McCabe was going on and on about your serial in the *Pacific Sun*."

Charles McCabe was a senior columnist at the *Chronicle*, a crusty, hard-drinking Irishman with a roadmap of a nose to show for it. He wrote essays about shaving and other manly pursuits, like his love of Ranier Ale, which he called Green Death. Some people found him misogynistic and homophobic. I was one of them.

"He must've hated it," I said to Ginnie.

"No, no. He thinks they should have something like that in the *Chronicle*. I don't know if it was just loose talk, but I thought you should know."

I wasted no time in contacting McCabe. He wrote back to say that the paper needed young blood, since the columnists were nothing but "a bunch of old farts about to fall off the hooks" and I was "just vulgar enough" to fit in at the *Chronicle*. He arranged a meeting with the editor, Charles deYoung Thieriot, whose great-grandfather had founded the paper in 1865, when it was called the *Daily Dramatic Chronicle* and covered the various "entertainments," fleshly and otherwise, of the Barbary Coast. When it came to the newspaper's contents, Charlie Thieriot's chief concerns were said to be society parties and duck hunting, since that was how he spent his own time. He had personally designed the masthead for the "Social Scene" column, a sophomoric effort in every way, since its crude curlicue lettering looked like something from a 1935 high school yearbook.

I dug out a blazer and a tie for the interview. The editor proved to be a gentleman, a little reserved but kind. He was nervous about running fiction in his newspaper (make your own joke here), so the title of the serial would have to indicate that it wasn't actual news. And he wanted to be clear about one other thing:

"This will have to run five days a week. Eight hundred words a day. Not weekly, the way you did it before."

"I understand."

"You can write a story that will just . . . keep on going?"

"Absolutely."

"Forever?"

"Yes sir."

My heart was in my throat. How the fuck was I going to do that?

TWELVE

She's 25, Single And Mad for S.F.

MARY ANN SINGLETON was 25 years old when she saw San Francisco for the first time.

She came to the city alone for an eight-day vacation. On the fifth night she drank three Irish coffees at the Buena Vista, realized that' her Mood Ring was blue, and decided to phone her mother in Cleveland.

"Hi, Mom, it's me."

"Oh, darling. Your Daddy and I were just talking about you. There was this crazy man on 'McMillan and Wife' who was strangling all these nice, young secretaries, and I just couldn't help thinking ..."

"Mom ..."

"I know. It's just your silly, old mother, worrying herself sick over nothing. But you never can tell about those things. I mean, look at that poor Patty Hearst, locked up in that closet with all those awful ..."

"Mom, this is long distance."

"I'm sorry, sugar. I'm such an old worry-wart. You must be having a grand time!"

"Oh, Mom, you wouldn't believe it! The people here are so friendly. I feel like I've ..."

"Have you been to the Top of the Mark like I told you?"

"Not yet, but ..."

"Well, don't you miss that. You know, your Daddy took me there when he got back from the South Pacific. I remember he slipped the bandleader five dollars, so we could dance to Moonlight Serenade and I spilled Tom Collins all over his beautiful, white Navy ..."

"Mom, I called to tell you something."

"Of course, dear. Just listen to me rambling on. Oh, one thing, before I forget it. I ran into Mr. Lassiter yesterday at the Ridgemont Mall, and he said the office is just falling apart with you gone. They don't get many good secretaries at Lassiter Fertilizers."

"Mom, that's sort of why I called."

"What do you mean, honey?"

"I want you to call Mr. Lassiter and tell him I

won't be in on Monday morning."

"Oh, Mary Ann, I'm not sure you should ask for an extension on your vacation."

"It's not an extension, Mom."

"What? I don't ..."

"I'm not coming home, Mom."

For a moment, the line seemed to go dead. Then, dimly in the distance, a television announcer began to tell Mary Ann's father about the temporary relief of hemorrhoids. Finally, her mother spoke: "Now you're being silly, darling."

Mary Ann tried to stay calm. "I'm not being

silly, Mom. I really feel comfortable here. I mean, it seems like home to me already."

More silence.

"Mom, I've thought about this for a long time."

"You've only been out there five days."

"I know, Mom, but I'm really sure about this. It's got nothing to do with you and Daddy. I just want to start making my own life, have my own apartment ..."

"Oh, that. Well, of course you can, darling. As a matter of fact, your Daddy and I thought those new apartments out at Ridgemont might be just perfect for you. They take lots of young people, and they've got a swimming pool and one of those sauna things, and I could make some of those darling curtains like I made for Sonny and Vicki when they got married. You could have all the privacy you ..."

Mary Ann's voice was gentle but firm. "Mom, you aren't listening to me. It isn't the privacy or living with you and Daddy or ... any of that. It's just me. I love it here. I'm grown up now and ..."

"Well, you certainly aren't acting like it! I've never heard such a thing! You can't just run away from your family and friends *to* go live with a bunch of hippies and mass murderers!"

"Oh, Mom, that's just a lot of TV *crap!*"

Her mother lowered her voice reproachfully. "Don't you talk nasty to your mother, Mary Ann ... and it's not a lot of TV ... stuff. What about those Giraffe Killers?"

"Zebra."

"Well, whatever. And what about those earthquakes! Your daddy took me to see that awful movie, and I nearly had a heart attack when Ava Gardner ..."

"Mom, I've made up my mind about this. Will you just call Mr. Lassiter for me?"

Her mother began to cry. "Something terrible is going to happen to you. I know it."

"Now who's being silly? What could possibly happen to me, Mom? San Francisco is a lot safer than Cleveland, and the people here are so mellow."

Her mother stopped sobbing for a moment. "What *does* that mean?" she asked suspiciously.

* * *

WHEN IT WAS OVER, Mary Ann left the Buena Vista and walked through Aquatic Park to the bay. For several minutes, she stared at the Alcatraz beacon, drunk with the prospect of an undefined future.

"What could possibly happen to me, Mom?" The words came back to her on a chill wind, nibbling uncertainty on a corner of her mind.

Back at the Fisherman's Wharf Holiday Inn she looked up Connie Bradshaw's phone number. Connie was the only person she knew in San Francisco. Mary Ann had heard that she was a stewardess for United, but hadn't spoken to her old high school friend since 1968.

"Oh, God, I can't believe it!" squealed Connie, when Mary Ann identified herself. "How long are you here for?"

"For good," said Mary Ann, savoring the words.

"Oh, super! Have you found an apartment yet?"

Mary Ann decided to be direct. "Not yet. I was wondering if I might be able to crash at your place for a couple of days. My savings account isn't holding out too well."

"Sure," said Connie, without hesitation. "No sweat. That is, if you don't mind an occasional sleep-in."

Mary Ann was thrown for a moment. "Oh ... you mean guys?"

Connie uttered a throaty laugh. "Do I ever, honey!"

Tomorrow: The friendly skies of Connie

WHEN I WAS FOURTEEN AND GETTING good at masturbation, I went on a cross-country bus trip that could not have been more charged with erotic stimuli. My Explorer troop was headed to Philmont Scout Ranch in northern New Mexico, and, along the way, we slept at Army bases where uniformed privates with a buddy-buddy air and bulging muscles would lead us to the mess hall and show us our cots before taps. One night at Fort Campbell, Kentucky, they took us to a movie in a Quonset hut. It was *Twilight for the Gods*, starring Rock Hudson. I had seen the actor before in *Giant* and *Written on the Wind*, but my libido had yet to rise to the occasion. Here, however, Hudson played a sea captain in the South Pacific who was always shouting and climbing rope ladders in a storm. He was taller than anyone in the movie, maybe even the world. His Adam's apple was the size of an apple.

By the time I was grown up and living in San Francisco, I had heard about the size of other parts as well. Hudson frequented the baths and had a legendary sex life, and the lucky guys who had a shot at him tended not to keep the information to themselves. So, when someone I picked up at the Lion Pub invited me to a gallery opening in Palm Springs that counted Rock Hudson among the hosts, I was seriously tempted. The other host, he added, was someone called Prince Umberto de Poliolo, who ran the gallery and consorted with one of the lesser Gabors—Magda, as I recall.

But was this really the right time to be leaving town? The *Chronicle* had approved "Tales of the City" in principle but had wisely requested six weeks' worth of episodes to establish a safe backlog before they started to run it. I had submitted thirty installments for their approval, keeping the gay content limited to Michael Tolliver's appearance in the Marina Safeway, for fear of scaring them off. Even then, though, they were dragging their feet, refusing to set a firm start date. I was a wreck for months. I just sat around at Little Cat Feet, waiting and worrying.

So maybe a little getaway was just what I needed.

WE WERE GREETED at the Palm Springs airport by a friend of the guy from the Lion. This man had hazmat-yellow hair and the tightest, tannest face I had ever seen on someone his age, whatever that was. He drove a powder-blue Lincoln Continental convertible, with the top down. As we cruised through the balmy desert afternoon, he would look over his shoulder at me and speak with casual affection of his good friend Lee ("Lee always says . . . Lee hates it when I . . . Lee almost bought that house"). I finally took the hint and asked if he meant Liberace, having suspected as much when he pulled off the road twice to change his rings. He had a lock box in the trunk full of hideous diamond rings and, apparently, liked to keep them rotating.

The gallery, disappointingly, was not the high-ceilinged salon I'd conjured up from Ross Hunter movies. It was just a storefront on the main drag packed with shiny, pastel people drinking white wine out of plastic glasses. I don't remember what the art was. If Magda's prince was there, I never knew it, since there was no telltale regalia in the room. Rock Hudson certainly wasn't there. It was mostly a gathering of merry gay men and a few old ladies with architectural hair.

One of the people in that crowd was a guy named Jack, who told me in the course of an animated conversation that he had once been Rock Hudson's live-in lover. His unspectacular looks didn't immediately suggest that. He was balding and in his early thirties (exactly my age to the day, we would later discover), though he emanated a certain feral charisma on which his confidence seemed to ride. Rock wasn't there that night, he said, wasn't even in town, in fact, but I was welcome to join him—Jack—and a few others for a party afterward at a house in Indio. I had no idea where Indio was, but it sounded like a workable plan. My friend from the Lion had already left with the guy with the rotating diamond rings, so I was free and easy.

THERE WERE A dozen people in that house in Indio. All men. Many of them seemed to have some connection to Rock Hudson—a gardener, a trainer, an optometrist. It was just a tract house without a tract, sitting alone in the midst of a moonlit plain. There were sodas and snacks on a butcher-block island in the kitchen. I was offered a drug by our host—a pill, as I recall, or maybe a tab—so I asked Jack what it did. *It's TT1*, he told me. *A relaxant that's given to women during childbirth*. That was all the information I needed. In those days if something had a name you took it.

And just like that I rose on gossamer wings into a realm of unimaginable contentment where my heart was open and the stars hung low as fireflies and bare male flesh caressed me like a soft tropical tide. If there had been a baby to have, I would have had it on the spot. It was not like any orgy I have ever known. It was a conversation of spirits, a silent glider flight into the sweet possibility of everything.

I found an old fox fur coat in the bedroom and was inspired to put it on. The satin lining felt smooth and cool against my bare skin. I wandered out into the desert with the coat hanging open, like some tipsy dowager looking for her driver. *Florence of Arabia*, I remember thinking. Every time I glanced back, the house was smaller, finally reduced to a golden ingot against the black, black mountains.

I stopped and stood perfectly still.

I tried to take in everything, the here-ness and now-ness of it all. I inhaled the spicy desert night and thought of my faraway mother and how she would have disapproved of this coat—my avidly fox-hunting mother who wanted no foxes harmed, ever. I apologized to the creatures on the coat, petting their patchy fur, though they looked like they hadn't been up and about since the forties. It came to me then, in the clarifying light of a gibbous moon, that my mother, despite her occasional contradictions, should have always been my guide. I had wasted my youth trying to be my father.

I turned my gaze away from the house and the mountains until I was facing a ghostly huddle of Joshua trees and the desert beyond. Somehow I had done this without turning my body at all. My head had apparently rotated 360 degrees, taking in everything along the way. I knew this had to be a hallucination—*had* to be—so I tried it again, going the other way this time with the same astonishing results.

Remember how to do this, I thought. *Now that you know it's possible.*

I found Jack in one of the bedrooms, sprawled across a rumpled comforter. He made room for my head on his chest, where silky brown hair swirled in purposeful patterns, like the lines on a topographical map. His cock, though soft, was a marvel of beauty and girth. I wondered how I could ever have thought of him as less than extraordinary. If I were a movie star I would have wanted him in bed with me, too.

THE HIGH WORE off by morning, but the afterglow lasted for two days. The twelve of us wandered the desert in cars, like apostles in no need of a messiah. When we passed a dilapidated wooden billboard that bore only the words DESERT LIGHTING, I laughed with sheer delight, because, you see, it was no longer about a local lamp store but the very sunset that was gilding the desert and casting mystic blue shadows on the mountains. Later, we stopped at a date shake stand, my first-ever experience of that drink. Its cold, creamy, Mediterranean sweetness struck me as nothing less than an elixir of the gods. After that, just because we could, Jack and I went down on each other in a palm grove behind the date shake stand.

A woman joined us on the second day, a fiftyish socialite in a caftan, who seemed smitten with Jack. Everyone, in fact, seemed smitten with Jack, but I was the one by his side on this nomadic adventure. As proof of the moment he gave me one of his treasures, the corroded iron chassis of a toy car he had found in the desert years before. It was a magical object, rough and sculptural, and I clung to it like a trophy I'd won in a dream that might not be there in the morning. After we'd had sex for the third time, Jack told me about his current lover, a nineteen-year-old towhead on the Berkeley diving team. That could have bothered me just a little, but it didn't. Jack said I would love him just as much as he did. In fact, he said we would make a perfect triad, so the three of us could meet again in the desert, where he knew of a special secret oasis with a spring. We could cover the sand with Persian rugs and wear loose linen drawstring pants like sultans and make love under the stars.

That sounded perfectly doable to me.

I was a little loony by the time I got back to Little Cat Feet, already pining for the seamless dream I had left behind. I decided to put it all in writing, so I sent a five-page letter to my sister about my desert awakening. I had already told Jane I was gay—she was the first person in the family I had told. We had been close for a long time in the way that a gay boy and his little sister can be in a fiercely patriarchal family. Approaching puberty, Jane was already tall for her age and very pretty, so I made up my mind (with only the tiniest bit of transference) that she would become a world-famous model. I named her Erika Thane (many years before there was a character named Erica Kane on *All My Children*). I thought that distinctive "k" in her new name would be crucial to her career. I took snaps of her down by the creek, posing her next to a bank of red azaleas. I have no memory whatsoever of approaching a talent agency, but to this day Jane sometimes signs her letters "Erika."

She had been a lot bolder than I had in claiming young love. As a teenager I was still brewing vegetable dyes in the kitchen and burning incense in my bedroom. Jane, at that age, was creeping out her bedroom window to be with a stunning Paul Newman–esque boy whom my father considered "common." A boyfriend with a funny Greek name did not jibe with our parents' plans for Jane to lead the debutante ball. When I came out to my sister, it did not come as a surprise to her. She told me, in fact, that my mother already knew and the topic had been on the table in Raleigh ever since a young woman they both knew came to visit me in San Francisco hoping for a proposal, only to be taken to the end of the pier at Aquatic Park and told about the wonderful man I was dating. The three of them had agreed that my father must never know. Ever. Southern women keep secrets to protect their delicate men.

I spared no detail in my letter to Jane about my Palm Springs transformation.

I even wrote it with carbon paper, so I could keep a copy for myself and have a permanent record for the ages. I looked for it recently and couldn't find it—no surprise, really, considering the tragic state of the cardboard boxes a university recently referred to as my "papers." I called Jane at her home in Portland and asked if she had kept the original, but she didn't even remember it. I wouldn't have blamed her if she had tossed it on the spot, since, even for her, it must have been a bit much. But for all the silliness and false profundity of a first-time drug epiphany, I knew that something had changed in me. There had been a letting-go, a cracking-open that had finally made a fulfilling life imaginable.

And fiction. It made fiction imaginable.

JACK CALLED A month or so later and suggested a reunion of the TT1 gang. Rock Hudson was fulfilling a long-held dream of appearing onstage and had taken a role in *John Brown's Body* at the San Bernardino Playhouse. Jack told me he had a block of tickets, and Rock needed lots of moral support. So I traveled south again, realizing that this time I would finally get to meet the tortured sea captain I had fallen for at fourteen in *Twilight for the Gods*. Not to mention the rancher who had courted Elizabeth Taylor in *Giant* and the big-city womanizer who had caused Doris Day to blow her bangs in exasperation in three wildly popular comedies.

John Brown's Body was not suited to Rock's talents. Based on an epic poem about slavery by Stephen Vincent Benét, it was essentially a glorified reading in which the actors stood soberly at attention like trees in a forest. While Rock was certainly the most imposing of the trees, that only complicated matters during his big death scene, since he hit the stage with the resounding boom of a felled redwood. It was funny, and shouldn't have been, though the audience had the decency not to laugh.

The dressing rooms, as I recall, were subterranean, and the line of people waiting to see the movie star wove through a labyrinth. When it was finally my turn, Jack did the introductions, but as soon as Rock's enormous hand was grasping mine, there was a power failure in the building, and the room went completely black for at least fifteen seconds. There we stood, in the dark, still holding on, saying nothing.

"Well," I said at last, "this is certainly the opportunity of a lifetime."

He laughed, to my great relief, and the lights came back on.

THE *CHRONICLE* FINALLY set a date for the launch of "Tales of the City"—May 24, 1976—a Monday morning that would inaugurate the five-days-a-week routine. As it happened, Rock was in San Francisco the weekend before, so he invited a group of mostly younger men to join him and his lover Tom Clark for a long Sunday brunch at Mama's on Nob Hill. Somewhere in the course of the afternoon I told him—bragged to him, that is—about the start of my new serial in tomorrow's newspaper.

Rock invited us all back to his suite—the Diplomat Suite of the Fairmont Hotel—where he showed up a few minutes later than the rest of us and announced that he would like to do a little reading. With the help of a desk clerk he had secured an early copy of the next day's paper (what they used to call the Bulldog Edition), so he opened it with a dramatic (if slightly drunken) flourish and began to read aloud:

"Mary Ann Singleton was twenty-five years old when she saw San Francisco for the first time."

That would have been thrilling enough in itself—that a legendary movie star was performing the first chapter of my new work—but there was something else that made the moment deliciously *meta*, as we like to say today. This is the scene in which the vacationing Mary Ann Singleton is on the phone with her mother in Cleveland, breaking the news that she plans to stay in San Francisco for good. Mom hates the idea and warns her daughter against all the "hippies and mass murderers" for which the city is notorious. "Your daddy and I were just talking about you. There was this crazy man on *McMillan & Wife* who was strangling all these secretaries . . ."

And who played Commissioner McMillan in that long-ago television series? None other than the man who was reading this passage to an audience of young men in his suite. And I had written it some months before I had ever imagined I'd meet him. *Meta* was the word, all right. The reading may have been a bit slurry, and more than a little calculated on the movie star's part, but it charmed the pants off me.

The very next night.

ROCK AND HIS lover Tom had invited me to dinner at La Bourgogne, a chichi French restaurant in an alley cul-de-sac off Mason Street. We sat in a tufted beige banquette under a crystal chandelier. Rock ordered bullshots, the cocktail made of vodka and bouillon that he and Tom swore by. Tom was almost as tall as Rock but looked more like an accountant than a movie star. He had once been Rock's PR man, in fact, and still identified himself that way when they wanted to avert suspicion. There were four people in their circle: Rock, Tom, the actor George Nader, and George's lover Mark Miller, who functioned as Rock's secretary. They were very close, the four of them, but they were rarely seen together in public, for fear of betraying what they were: two couples. Rock and Tom told me that night that they always went out in groups of three and carried briefcases, so they would look like they were headed to a business meeting. They were proud of this ruse, and seemed to think I'd find it amusing. It was just sad to me, though, a hangover from the past, and I wondered suddenly if that's what I was at this very moment: the third man.

The bullshots had emboldened me. I suggested to Rock it might be time for him to come out. I said he had always been an icon of American masculinity, so his honesty about being gay would be a revelation to the world, a historic moment that would change the lives of millions of people like himself. And, best of all, he would finally be free to be himself. No longer hiding his love and moving about in threes. No more threats from tabloids. He would be a hero, not a source of secret gossip. He would finally be running his own life. The world would never forget him.

The actor gave me slow, sleepy smile, a smile I recognized from his screen performances. "I've always talked about writing a book someday."

"Then write it!" I said. "I'd be happy to help if you need someone."

He seemed to consider that, or maybe just pretended to consider it. Tom's face had suddenly hardened. He shot a look at Rock.

"Not until my mother dies," he said.

I laughed, because there was truth in it. We queers can be so afraid of losing our mother's love. But, privately, I was thinking: *You gotta be kidding me! If I were married to Rock Hudson, I'd be calling my mother tomorrow!*

AFTER DINNER ROCK suggested we hike up the hill for a nightcap at the Fairmont. Tom, who was already blitzed and irritable, flaked out as soon as we reached the alpine challenge of Powell Street and hailed a cab. "Aw, you're a big wuss," said Rock, waving him away in mock contempt. "We're not wusses, are we, Armistead?" I wasn't about to admit to as much, so I tried to keep pace with the giant striding ahead of me, his coat thrown over his arm, his fifty-year-old glutes dancing under the dark sheen of his gabardine pants. I was relieved when he stopped to catch his breath and attempted, with a jauntily extended thumb, to hitch a ride on a cable car. It didn't work, of course—the incline was too steep—but the gesture had the desired effect: the tourists hanging on to the cable car went nuts, one even shouting *Commissioner McMillan!* as they passed us with bells a-clanging. I could tell Rock was tickled, and I was proud to be seen with him, though no one at all would have recognized me.

When we reached the Diplomat Suite, Tom was already passed out and snoring in the bedroom. Rock closed the door and led the way into the living room. Did he make us drinks? I don't recall, but we ended up sitting across the room from each other, two guys in suits and ties, making talk too small to be remembered.

Then Rock said: "Well, I should be over there, or you should be over here."

I wondered how often that line had worked for him, since it was certainly working now. One of us joined the other. (Again, I don't remember which, since my mind at that point had slipped from its mooring and was levitating out of body, like souls are expected to do above the dying.) We kissed for a while, loosening ties and fumbling at buttons. Then he stood up and pushed down those gabardine pants. He was wearing cotton boxer shorts, gray and brown stripes on white. I remember *that*, of course, because I was *focused* now, and I remember the suspense of a grand unveiling because of all I'd ever heard, and for very good reason, about this man.

So why the hell couldn't I keep my hard-on? Sure, he was older than most of the guys I went for, but he was easily more magnificent than any of them. If I had met him in a cubicle at the Glory Holes, I would have been on him like a puppy on a chew stick. He himself was hard as . . . all right . . . a rock, making him perfect for an act of objectification. Except, he wasn't. The disconnect was just impossible. And he understood this all too well. This wasn't his first time at the lost boner rodeo.

He got up off the floor and sat next to me on the sofa, laying his arm across my shoulder.

"You know," he said quietly, "I'm just like any other guy."

I gazed down at a little leather pouch on the floor. This was where he kept his poppers, his real medicinal amyl nitrate. His initials were monogrammed in gold: RH.

"No you're not," I said. "And I'm Doris Day."

He smiled wistfully, as if he might've heard that one before.

THIRTEEN

IT TOOK A WHILE FOR "Tales of the City" to catch fire. Readers of the *Chronicle* were initially baffled. There hadn't been fiction in a daily newspaper for at least a century. What the hell was that thing doing there, anyway, floating on an inside page of the People section? Some of the fault, I knew, was in the plotting. Those early episodes were as bland as a hospital meal—The New Girl goes to the disco, The New Girl looks for a job, The New Girl dumps her old high school friend. I was still being way too guarded about my own truth, and, even worse, I had yet to figure out how a compelling cast could evolve from this sequence. "I love your new writer," someone wrote in a letter to the editor. "What high school does he attend?"

Things picked up when I found a place for Mary Ann to live, a rickety old house at the top of some rickety wooden stairs on a street that wasn't a street at all but a wooded footpath. That gave me a dollhouse to play with, but I had to populate it and fast. I chose a straight guy named Brian Hawkins (a surname in my family) who was exactly my age, and a failed lawyer to boot, and was exorcising the radical ideals of his youth with nightly doses of stranger sex, much the way I was offing my conservatism. Then came Mona Ramsey (also my age, and a family surname) who works as a copywriter at an ad agency having failed at her dream of being Lillian Hellman. She was one of those hippies who was still around in the Bicentennial Year, still dressing the part and owning her mantra, if somewhat cynically. She's the only person in the house who knows about the secret past of its landlady, Mrs. Madrigal.

"So what's her secret?" the managing editor asked one day. As a

ARMISTEAD MAUPIN

senior suit from the front office, he was tasked with keeping an eye on the plot.

"She used to be a man," I told him.

He blinked at me for a moment. "What do you mean, 'used to be a man'?"

"She's transsexual. She had a sex change twelve years ago."

He took off his glasses and rubbed his eyes in weary exasperation. "You can't say that, Armistead. You'll lose them before it's even started."

"Lose who?"

"The readers. The people in the Sunset."

It was the common conceit of the front office that folks who lived in the Sunset District, that treeless grid of stucco cracker boxes on the edge of the ocean, were not as sophisticated as the rest of us. They were more easily offended and prone to canceling subscriptions. They were often cited when critical decisions were made. *The people in the Sunset* . . . To me, it sounded like zombies on the march.

"Just hold off for a year or so," said the managing editor. "Just keep her mysterious for a while." Though it was firmly rooted in what we know today as transphobia, the managing editor's panic proved useful. By keeping Anna mysterious I could build suspense and keep readers coming back for more every day. It also gave me a chance to establish Anna Madrigal's humanity, before readers—or some of them, anyway—could dismiss her as a freak show. This was 1976, the year Bruce Jenner was racking up gold medals at the Olympics and being celebrated as Male Athlete of the Year. Caitlyn Jenner would have been unimaginable back then, and Anna Madrigal, while just a creature of newsprint, would have invoked similar disbelief. So I waited a year before breaking the news to the people in the Sunset, and by then they were so hooked they had no choice but to keep on loving the landlady. Now, without question, Anna Madrigal is my proudest achievement. Christopher Bram's *Eminent Outlaws*, a critical study of "gay male writers who changed America," published in 2012, called Anna "literature's first nonthreatening, nonsuffering, three-dimensional androgyne." But her full humanity might not have developed as it did without the nervousness of the *Chronicle*'s front office.

Not that they weren't concerned about the proliferation of garden-variety gay characters. Michael had picked up a hunky gynecologist at the roller rink and enjoyed a long chat with him in bed. (The bed was merely implied by the mention of sheets.) Mona, apparently, had once had a live-in girlfriend, who was now back in town. Even Beauchamp, DeDe's philandering husband, seemed to be logging time at the baths. Almost overnight the serial had gone gay as a goose.

The poor managing editor had to call me into his office and show me, with some mortification, a wall chart he had made. There were two columns on the chart; one was headed Heterosexual; the other, Homosexual. He would enter the names and "preferences" of characters as soon as they appeared in the serial. The idea was that at no time should the gay people in "Tales" number more than one-third of the total population and thereby, presumably, disrupt the course of Western Civilization. I couldn't help wondering if the managing editor had cooked this up on his own or if Charlie Thieriot himself had told him to bring me in line pronto.

I went back to my desk and wrote an episode in which Frannie Halcyon, the society matron from Hillsborough, returns from a long, drunken luncheon with her friends and passes out in her herb garden, only to wake and find her beloved Great Dane, Faust, vigorously humping her leg. The next time I saw the managing editor I told him the dog should go in the Heterosexual column. He conceded defeat with a curdled smile and never brought out the chart again. (You won't find that episode in the finished novel, since my editor at Harper & Row found it distasteful and urged me not to use it. I regret that decision. It's a funny bit, I think, and rather poignant, since Frannie refuses to reveal Faust's misconduct to her family. "It's okay, baby," she says to the dog at the end. "Mama knows you didn't mean it.")

I usually wrote in the early afternoon at the *Chronicle* office at Fifth and Mission. The six-week backlog I was supposed to maintain got gobbled up quickly by an active nightlife and a tendency to shoot the shit with the women in the People section, where I found that telling stories was a lot more fun than writing them. I would also take a lunch break sometimes and walk down to the Glory Holes, where the cheap daytime entry fee was called the Businessman's Special. (After one such lunch break, I was called into the editor's office for a reason I've long since forgotten. A minute into our meeting I glanced down and saw a glob of pink bubblegum on the knee of my Levi's. I covered it with my hand, trying not to smile. Quite the businessman.)

All this procrastination made the People editor very nervous, since sometimes I was writing Wednesday's column on a Monday afternoon. I got a little nervous myself, wondering where this saga would end (or, rather, where it was heading, since it was never supposed to end). I snatched stories from the night before—if, for instance, some preppie guy had taken me home from the Twin Peaks because of his unbridled lust for my Weejuns, the collegiate loafers that betrayed (or, perhaps, in this case, exploited) my Southern-boy origins. Sometimes, at a loss for personal yarns, I would arbitrarily force two of my characters to talk to each other across Anna Madrigal's kitchen table, thereby letting them take the reins of the plot and veer off wildly into the unknown. That's when I began to find out who they were. Or, more to the point, who *I* was. The pressure of the deadline made it impossible to overthink things. There was, in fact, a lot of underthinking going on, which unconsciously revealed all sorts of embarrassing truths about the author himself.

My parents were subscribing to the *Chronicle* by mail. That meant they would get four or five episodes in a single mailing. There were encouraging words from them at first, when "Tales" was all Mary Ann and her landlady and the handsome rogue who lived upstairs. When the plot threads grew more sexually diverse, my mother began making nervous jokes on the telephone: "Your father wants to know how an Eagle Scout knows these things."

I laughed and told her that I lived in this crazy town, after all, and that I noticed things. I reminded her that a writer must empathize, so my story would unfold from all its characters, whether I was writing about an alcoholic matron or a dying businessman or a disillusioned hippie. (I could hide behind all those people, I assured myself, because I was all of them, and none of them.)

My mother was silent for a moment. "Well, I love the story. And your dialogue is very believable."

She was not buying it, but never mind.

We were used to avoiding that subject.

THE PUBLIC WAS hooked on "Tales" before the year was out. I heard this from readers in bars and restaurants, and even at the baths sometimes, where other patrons would often express amazement (or outright ire) that I was exposing our secret gay world. One guy was outraged that I had written about Gay Night at the Grand Arena roller rink, since everyone in his law office knew he always went skating on Tuesdays, and now, goddammit, they knew why he had chosen that night. I thought that was hilarious and told him so. I was losing all respect for the closet by then, including, of course, my own.

People began to speculate about who I might be. No one, after all, could be named Armistead Maupin. The smarter ones cited *Mademoiselle de Maupin*, Théophile Gautier's novel about a lusty, cross-dressing woman, in support of their claim that my name was a pseudonym. Others thought I might be Herb Caen, the newspaper's beloved "three-dot columnist" (so named for the ellipses that peppered his daily entries), a theory that irked me, since I was already feeling competitive with Herb for the reader-bestowed title of "the first thing I read in the morning." Caen was already King of the *Chronicle*. Why should he get credit for what I was doing? My favorite speculation came in an anonymous letter: "You're not fooling me, Armistead Maupin! I know for a fact that you're a lesbian collective in Marin County."

Well, I was certainly doing the *work* of a lesbian collective in Marin County, and my dutiful labors at the loom of story were beginning to get to me. The more intricate the tapestry became, the more I worried about eventually having to unravel it. Why the hell hadn't I mapped this thing out before I began? My cast of characters was relentlessly lily-white, for one thing, so I decided to introduce a major African-American character, that former lover of Mona's who arrives unexpectedly to rekindle their relationship. D'Orothea, as I named her, is a New York model, a sophisticated beauty not unlike women I'd met while working as a mail boy at the ad agency. I could write about such a woman, and convincingly. So that's what I did.

One of my readers wasn't buying it, though. "Shame on you," she wrote. "Up until now your characters have rung true, but D'Orothea is nothing but a white woman in black skin." I found this completely demoralizing. My Southern white-boy bones had been laid bare for all to see. And, if one reader felt this way, there must be others in a readership of half a million who were thinking the same thing.

I was despondent for an afternoon, until I saw the way to make lemonade from this unconvincing lemon. What if D'Orothea really *was* a white woman in black skin? What if she had curled her hair and darkened her pigment (like the white author of *Black Like Me*) to secure a job as an "Afro model"? What if Mona, a dyed-in-the-wool liberal, had loved D'Orothea's blackness at least as much as she had loved D'Orothea, and D'Orothea was fearful of letting the truth be known at last. That would give me a whole new closet to explore, a whole new source of humor and absurdity. (Forty years after I wrote my way out of this literary corner, I saw just such a comedy play out in real life when Rachel Dolezal, a civil rights activist for the NAACP, was revealed to be a white woman posing as an African-American. Folks on Twitter gave me far too much credit for predicting Ms. Dolezal.)

DID I MENTION that during these days of desperate invention I had a night job as well? I worked down at Club Fugazi, in North Beach, where I tore tickets and pushed scenery and wrote corny dialogue for a brand-new musical revue called *Beach Blanket Babylon Goes Bananas*. This homegrown phenomenon, featuring a zany Carmen Miranda piled with fruit and an operatic Glinda the Good Witch (both played by the hilarious, saucer-eyed Nancy Bleiweiss) today holds the record as the world's longest-running musical revue. No, I did not get a piece of the action—I've never been clever about business. What I got was the nightly thrill of standing in back of that old Italian meeting hall while the lights dimmed and the curtain went up and a four-man band dressed as French poodles played the opening bars of "San Francisco." This was one of those times when you say to yourself: This is it, kiddo. These are your glory days. Remember them when you're old. I was so proud to bring out-of-towners to the show, among them Rock Hudson, whose towering, laughing presence near the front of the stage added to the joy of the room that night.

After that first debacle of a tryst at the Fairmont, Rock and I had become buddies with occasional benefits. We cruised some of the raunchier San Francisco clubs together, including the Glory Holes and a leather bar called the Black and Blue, where a slab of corrugated iron hung in one corner to form a triangular orgy room. It was packed, and Rock wasn't exactly dressed for it. The biker wannabes writhing in the darkness around us all but ignored the tall, touristy-looking guy with a slight paunch under his red alpaca sweater. *If you only knew what you're missing,* I thought. Since Rock was looking left out, I reached over and gave his butt a friendly pinch.

He looked baffled, then turned to me.

"Was that you?"

"Yep."

"Just checking."

His smile could light up the darkest corner.

ON SEVERAL OCCASIONS Rock invited me and some friends to stay in his home in Beverly Hills, a tile-roofed ranch house on Beverly Crest Drive his circle referred to facetiously as "The Castle." Everything there, in fact, had a whimsical name. The guest room, a relentlessly red space often reeking of poppers from previous visitors, was referred to as "Tijuana." Rock himself had been dubbed "the Matinee Idol" by his lover Tom, who uttered the words more often in contempt than in affection. Rock's other private nickname was Trixie, presumably because of his extracurricular sex life. He was a good sport about such teasing when he wasn't drunk himself. He loved being a host, perhaps because it offered him respite from Tom's sniping. The image that lives in memory is Rock in his sunlit kitchen, sporting the world's longest nightshirt as he scrambled eggs for his guests in a big iron skillet.

Rock had a deep groove on one of his thumbnails—a deformity

really—that made me curious enough to ask about it one day. "Just an old war wound," he said, and I believed him, because I knew of his naval service and remembered how he had heard Doris Day, his lovely costar-in-waiting, singing "Sentimental Journey" on his ship's speaker system as they passed under the Golden Gate on their way home. It was Rock's assistant Mark Miller who set me straight about that thumb. "That's not a war wound," he said. "He does that to himself. Watch him."

Sure enough, Rock was digging that groove with his own forefinger, incessantly gouging away at the nail in a quiet act of self-flagellation. He had spent decades being someone he was not—an illusion that was successful outside of the gay grapevine—but that mangled thumb betrayed the pain of his repression.

So did the booze. He was horrified to see that I smoked grass (and asked me not to do so at the Castle), but he went on vodka benders that left him angry and sobbing. When I watched him stagger across the courtyard and collapse into a hot tub full of young men, forcing them to break his fall, it wasn't nearly as charming as he seemed to think. Things got even worse when Rock and Tom were hammered at the same time. Their George-and-Martha bitchery, so witless as to be unworthy of that term, sometimes drove me into another room.

Still, Rock seemed genuinely to believe in coupledom. When he realized I was still single, he made it his business to fix that. "Everybody needs a husband," he told me. He was more excited than anyone I knew when I told him I was going on a *Love Boat* cruise to Mexico with a guy I had met in Minneapolis. When the ship returned to San Pedro, Rock was there to greet us, waving up from the crowd on the dock like a doting aunt with hopes for a wedding. (The chatty passenger standing next to me at the rail gasped when she recognized him.)

That should have been the consummate blessing for a new romance, but my shy, collie-dog of a Minnesotan met someone he liked better right after he moved to San Francisco to live with me. I was still on deadline, of course, so there was no way I could skulk off to lick my wounds. I chose instead to suffer publicly, in my column, believing then, as I did for far too many years, that fictionalizing pain is the best way to make it go away. I walked to the newspaper office and wrote a melancholy monologue for Michael Tolliver in which he says that you must never show your need for love lest you doom yourself to never having it at all.

Lordy. I might as well have been Miss Alma in *Summer and Smoke*. My public *tristesse* didn't last for long, though. It couldn't. Not when a group of self-described Mary Anns found their way to my house and wanted my autograph for a scavenger hunt. Not when a straight bar in the Financial District threw a "Tales"-themed party at which a signature drink was created for Anna Madrigal, and half the room came dressed as her. And certainly not when I dragged myself out of the Glory Holes at four o'clock one morning to find a box of *Advocate*s with this headline on the cover: ARMISTEAD MAUPIN IS SAN FRANCISCO'S NEWEST CELEBRITY.

I was having so much fun. The personal and the political had merged for the first time in my life. The most frivolous act imaginable could be part of this new revolution. When I auctioned off jockstraps in a rabbit suit at a Folsom Street bar, I was doing it to benefit lawyers who were fighting for our rights.

MY GROWING VISIBILITY as an openly gay man had a downside: it made it harder to maintain a friendship with Rock. I had really just been part of his sexual sublife, the part he didn't show to the world, and now that I was finally the master of my own soul, it felt demeaning, even insulting, to cooperate with the closet, just for the sake of hanging out with a movie star. It was nothing dramatic;

I just stopped going to the Castle. Rock was used to others organizing his life, so I doubt that he even noticed. In many ways I was glad to be free of the poisonous alcoholic atmosphere of the house. It smelled of mendacity—an old Tennessee Williams word that is more than adequate for a nest of harpies living out a lie at the bitter end of the seventies.

I wrote about Rock in "Tales" in 1981, using Michael Tolliver as my stand-in at an all-boy pool party. In the Victorian storytelling tradition, I put blanks in place of Rock's name, and changed telling details to blur his identity. I consider it an affectionate portrait of a man who wants to be "just another guy like you" but is too suffocated by the Hollywood closet to find his way into the light.

In 1985, when Rock's AIDS diagnosis was made public, I was as jolted as the rest of the world. I was heartsick, of course, because he was suffering the fate of so many of my friends, and I knew what lay ahead. But then I got angry when I read pathetic lies being spun by the people who ran his life. Rock didn't have AIDS; they claimed in some accounts he had anorexia. Or, even more preposterously, they claimed he was on a watermelon diet. Ross Hunter, the gay man who had produced so many of Rock's movies, said he had never known the actor to be gay. Hollywood was used to lying about that subject, and they kept right on doing it.

Then my friend Randy Shilts, a reporter for the *Chronicle*, called and asked if I would speak on the record with another reporter about my friendship with Rock. (Randy would write *And the Band Played On*, the definitive study of the AIDS epidemic, and eventually die of the disease himself.) I knew what he was up to. The tabloids were already having a field day with the "secret shame" of Rock Hudson and his "deadly kiss" with Linda Evans on the set of *Dynasty*, so it was time for the mainstream press to treat the story with dignity. When the *Chronicle* reporter called, I kept it simple: I said yes, of course, Rock was widely known within the industry to be gay, so there was no scandal at all here beyond the fact that it had taken this horrendous disease to demolish the charade that had made Rock's life miserable for so long. The word *outing* had yet to be invented (by a reporter at *Time* magazine, when brave gay activist/journalists like Michelangelo Signorile started telling the truth in print), but that, in effect, was what I had done.

Some people were unhappy with me. A columnist for the *Bay Area Reporter*, San Francisco's gay newspaper, wondered in print what sort of "friend" I could be if I was willing to spill the beans so freely. Gay people were supposed to keep that secret, weren't they? The old man who ran the sidewalk flower stand on Castro Street clucked his tongue at me as I passed. Rock's old lover Jack, the very person who had introduced me to Rock, called up drunk one night to yell, "How could you do that to that beautiful man?" It stung to have my motives misunderstood, especially by gay people, and I wondered if Rock was among them. I hated to think that he might feel that way, especially as he was suffering. I did not call the Castle, however, in fear that similar vitriol awaited me there.

Still, I've never regretted taking that heat. Once the press could talk about Rock's homosexuality, a whole new dialogue could open about AIDS and the people whose suffering had been ignored. Within the week, *People* magazine had published what had to have been its first sympathetic cover story about a gay Hollywood star. Rock's hospital room received 35,000 letters of support from fans saying they loved him just the way he was.

And Rock finally commissioned The Book—the one we had talked about nine years earlier at the restaurant in San Francisco, the book where he could reveal the true stories he'd always wanted to share. To my great relief, he told his biographer, Sara Davidson, that I was the first person she should talk to.

FOURTEEN

ORTON PLANTATION WAS EVERYTHING AN ANTEBELLUM
Southern mansion was supposed to be: white-bricked, white-columned, lazing in idle elegance on the banks of the Cape Fear River. Nothing else in North Carolina came close to it, which was why, when I was still a boy, we made pilgrimages there to import its azaleas to our suburban Raleigh backyard. We bought tickets like everyone else, even though my parents knew the owners, who threw garden parties there sometimes for the Society of the Cincinnati, a hereditary society that George Washington had founded to keep aristocracy alive in the absence of royalty. By the 1970s, my father had risen to the august position of President General in that fraternity, a job that came with a diamond eagle pendent that Washington himself had worn, and all sorts of chances to wear it. Among them: an invitation to an over-night stay at Orton.

Mummie liked fancy-dress parties as much as Daddy did, and Orton would have been a lovely setting for her hazel-eyed English beauty. By then she was letting strategic streaks of gray appear in her dark hair, knowing they worked to soften the lines in her face. My guess is she had driven to Durham to find a gown at Montaldo's, North Carolina's temple of high couture. She had once excitedly shown me a dress from Montaldo's she said was "just like one worn by Suzy Parker."

So there she is at that MGM plantation house, soaking in an old-fashioned clawfoot tub, soaping her body with luxurious deliberation as she meditates on the night ahead. Her gown is laid out on the bed in the other room. She can hear the tinkling of crystal as tables are prepared downstairs for the grand soiree. She touches her breast once, then a second time, then frowns. There it is.

I think it's safe to guess that she didn't tell Daddy right away, knowing it would sour his antebellum weekend. More than likely she had slapped a brave Melanie Wilkes smile on her face and waited until her doctor in Raleigh could confirm her self-diagnosis. That's the way she was when it came to bad news.

She had deserved a better life from this point forward. She had grown up in relative austerity, despite a father whose pretensions of aristocracy had foretold her husband's. As a teenager during the Depression she had canned apricots in a factory in Georgia to pay her way at the Martha Berry School for Girls. She remembered how the velvety pulp had scalded her hands. At twenty she had saved her brother Richie's life by authorizing the amputation of his left leg after a car accident. She stood by him for six hours, holding his hand, watching everything, and at one point he begged her for a gun, so he could end his pain right there. Her first child, me, had been a difficult breach birth, kicking his way out of her like a Rockette when her husband was away at war. As an adult, she had endured my father's whiskey-driven tantrums and spent years as the lone caregiver to his increasingly feeble and addled mother. But Mimi had died in her room out at Mayview and joined her husband at Oakwood Cemetery, and the three children were grown and gone. She was still in her fifties, still considered lovely. She must have thought, at least for a while, that she had a shot at a happy ending.

I don't remember how I first learned about the cancer, but I remember the forced jollity with which my mother spoke of the mastectomy on the phone. "I told them they could have one breast as long as I was allowed to tattoo the other one." That was so unlike her that it made me cry. I said, "Good for you," trying to match her jauntiness. She made the same remark to a reporter with the *Triangle Pointer*, a local Raleigh tourist guide, of all things, that had once interviewed her about fox hunting. She referred to her illness as "The Big C"—

just the way Daddy's hero John Wayne had done several years earlier. Folks in Raleigh thought her candor was very brave, and of course it was, especially then, but I suspect Mummie knew there was no way she could endure the loneliness of *that* secret. I think she wanted this out there in the world, marshaling the love and support of her friends, beyond my father's ability to squelch discussion. Our journeys were uncannily similar, my mother's and mine, at this point in our separately lived lives. We were both escaping from secrecy, unilaterally claiming our truths, and both using the media to do it.

For me, it was *Newsweek*, which identified me, in the summer of 1977, as a "homosexual columnist" in a cover story about Anita Bryant and the new surge in gay activism. Like so many queers of my generation, I had received Anita Bryant like a punch in the gut—and earlier than most, I suppose, since I had seen the story about her "crusade" on the wire service as soon as it arrived at the *Chronicle*. This former Miss America runner-up and gospel singer, the current spokesperson for Florida orange juice, was so enraged by a new ordinance protecting gay people from discrimination in South Florida that she vowed to repeal it through an organization she called "Save Our Children." Gay people could not reproduce, she argued, so they were forced to "recruit children" for their lifestyle. They must never be protected by laws of any kind; they must be stopped, in fact, in the name of the children, in the name of Jesus.

Bryant's campaign and a new nationwide demand for gay rights brought *Newsweek* to San Francisco for its cover story. They asked my permission to call me homosexual, which I granted freely, joyfully, in fact. (You had to ask permission back then, since the mere suggestion that someone was gay was seen by the law as a libelous act. Liberace—Libe-fuckin'-race—was infamously awarded a million-dollar libel settlement after a British columnist described him as "fruit-flavored." As late as 1981, when I described my activist friend Vito Russo as a "gay film historian" in an op-ed piece for the *New York Times*, I was met with editorial squeamishness. Vito, author of *The Celluloid Closet*, had been out for many years and writing about it, but the *Times* required an affidavit from him before I could call him gay in print. I never saw that affidavit, but I'm sure Vito had enormous fun composing it.)

Like Vito, I was proud of my role in this revolution and welcomed any recognition for it. I knew that my mother had known I was gay for years, but I was never sure if she'd discussed it with my father. A heads-up was in order, so I wrote my parents to alert them about the upcoming *Newsweek* article and how it would describe me. They never wrote back, but forty years later I've learned how they dealt with it—a solution that seems downright quaint in an age when media disgrace is instant and inescapable. They simply left town for a week, riding horses up at Cataloochee Ranch in Maggie Valley until *Newsweek* was off the stands and my father could safely face the gaze of his fellow lawyers on the Fayetteville Street Mall.

That can't have been an easy week for my mother, since the old man, by long-established custom, used her as a sounding board for his rage. I can only hope that she had a few moments to herself on horseback in the hills. Her mastectomy had not stopped the relentless march of the cancer in her body. It had found its way into her lymph nodes and was already hell-bent for her bones. She didn't talk about it anymore. She was worried about how it would trouble him. She knew he couldn't face the thought of losing her, so why make it difficult for him?

IT'S IMPOSSIBLE TO overstate how thoroughly Bryant's pious eye-batting bigotry galvanized the queers of my generation. From the moment I read the wire story, I had set about plotting ways to address it in "Tales of the City." As freakish fate would have it, I had already established Michael Tolliver as the son of Florida orange growers. (I had figured this would make him a working-class boy, someone not immediately identifiable as me, and place him a safe distance from my folks in North Carolina.) It was completely plausible that Michael, a gay man still closeted to his family, might get a letter from his church-going mother in Orlando, proudly telling him that she had just signed up with the Save Our Children campaign. It would finally force the issue between mother and son in a way that neither one of them could ever have anticipated.

I wrote Michael's reply to that letter in forty-five minutes at my desk at the *Chronicle*. Nothing had ever taken less time to write, since I'd been collecting my thoughts on the subject for more than fifteen years. My mother had not actually joined Save Our Children; though, with my father's goading, she had embraced a new archconservative Republican movement that would demonize LGBT people in one way or another to this very day. (With the notable exception of my sister, my biological family continued to vote for Jesse Helms for the remainder of his career.)

The *Chronicle*, typically, didn't get it at first. The editor who had kept the hetero/homo chart in his office said I was moving drastically off topic and was sure to lose readers. "Why should people in San Francisco care about something that's happening in Miami?" He had his answer in a matter of days when the city erupted in anti-Anita rallies and heated press conferences. Harvey Milk, the gay candidate for supervisor, was as quick on the draw as I was. There were no memes in those Web-free days, but there might as well have been. Oranges were suddenly everywhere, sprouting on lampposts and bulletin boards in bars with slogans attached: ANITA BRYANT SUCKS ORANGES.

A DAY WITHOUT TOLERANCE IS LIKE A DAY WITHOUT SUNSHINE. When a nationwide boycott of Florida orange juice was launched, gay bars no longer served screwdrivers but a drink made of vodka and apple juice called an Anita Bryant. At the annual Cops vs. Queers softball game in San Francisco, I was invited to throw out "the first orange," a predictable fiasco since the fruit fell far short of the plate.

"Letter to Mama" was set to be published on a Monday. That weekend there was a midnight benefit at the Castro Theatre for the Miami Gay Support Committee. With typical homo sass, the event was titled "Moon Over Miami." The performers included a group called the Sometime Sondheim Singers, the comedy team of Brown & Coffey, Bobby Kent at the Mighty Organ, and someone identified at the top of the bill as Armistead *tales of the city* Maupin. I was nervous. I was just going to *read* something, after all. The conceit was that the audience would be privy to Monday's "Tales" column before anyone else in town, but that seemed a little flimsy the more I thought about it. And not all that entertaining.

The Castro is one of those great old Deco movie palaces, a Bedouin's tent of gilded plaster draped histrionically from the highest point. Though it holds 1,500 people, its "stage" is just a movie-theater stage, a thin strip of darkness upon which it's awfully easy to feel small. I don't remember whom I followed that night or how I introduced the letter. I remember only that moments after I began reading, the piece had stopped being about Michael at all and become something much more excruciatingly personal. There I was, alone, with a manifesto shaking in my hands, fighting to keep my balance. I felt in danger of toppling onto the Mighty Organ.

An unnerving silence settled over the room when I was done. It took me a while to realize that people were crying. I noticed my own tears as I made my wobbly way to the steps at the end of the stage. I sank into an empty seat in the front row of the theater as the applause began. It was a primeval sound, a rumbling that grew from a few hands clapping into a stadium-style foot-stomping frenzy as the audience rose to its feet.

"I thought the fucking roof would come down," was how my friend Cleve Jones put it recently when we shared memories about that long-ago evening. Cleve had been Harvey Milk's curly locked young lieutenant in those days. He had personally flyered the Castro to draw a crowd for the midnight event when ticket sales were flagging. He and Harvey were both weeping over the letter, he said. As for me, I was too shaken to stand, and it felt inappropriate somehow to take a bow for something we were all sharing at that moment. I stayed in my seat, where I felt a sort of laying-on-of-hands, dozens of my brothers and sisters touching me in benediction.

The letter met with a similar response when it appeared in the *Chronicle* on Monday morning. Readers wrote to tell me that they had cut out the column, deleting Michael's name and substituting their own before mailing it to their parents. Others had used it as a template for their own coming-out letter. Nothing I've ever written has had such an impact. "Letter to Mama" has been set to music three times: as an art song by composer Glen Roven, as a solo number in the *Tales of the City* musical by Jake Shears and John Garden, and, perhaps most enduringly, as a choral piece by David Maddux that has become a standard for gay men's choruses around the world. Actor Paul Hopkins performed it in the Showtime miniseries of *More Tales of the City*. Ian McKellen and Stephen Fry have both read the letter to audiences in Britain and America. Embarrassingly enough, reading it myself can still make me cry.

I WAITED FOR a response from my parents, the smallest sign that they had seen "Letter to Mama" and been moved by it. It had been a love letter to them, after all.

The only response came from my father several weeks later. He had scribbled it, as usual, on a yellow legal pad:

—

> Dear Teddy,
> As you know your mother is very ill, so any additional stress can only exacerbate the situation.
> *Love*,
> Daddy

In others words: Shut up before you kill her.

I knew my mother didn't feel that way herself. We talked enough on the phone for me to understand that I had not broken her heart. We talked about the plush toy fox I had sent her, about her beloved horse, Pegasus, and how she wanted to start looking for a good home for him, you know, just in case. She was thrilled about an offer I'd received from Harper & Row in New York to collect my columns into two novels, for which I would be paid the staggering sum of five thousand dollars.

But one day, out of the blue, she said: "You know, I'm glad that you're happy, sweetheart. I just don't think you should talk about your . . . lifestyle . . . so much."

I couldn't blame her for using that ridiculous word, since it was all over the place in those days. It was everyone's convenient substitute for the Great Ickiness, the Lifestyle That Dare Not Speak Its Name, and with it came the implication that it was chosen—a style, not a life. Only straight people got to have lives.

"Why?" I asked pleasantly. "Why should I not talk about it?"

I knew already that my family was talking about it. All of them. My younger brother, Tony, upon hearing the news, had minced no words and called me a cocksucker, which at least favored accuracy over euphemism.

"I'm just afraid," said my mother, "that it'll hurt your career."

"Mummie . . . it *is* my career." I explained to her that this was my chance to make a difference in the world, that I had found my voice as a writer, and that I could mine my own life for completely fresh material. There would be readers who could relate to that, too, if I remained honest and wrote from the heart. Being openly gay would work completely to my advantage. It could make me famous, I told her. There simply wasn't a downside.

She wasn't buying it. Her voice was quavering, like we were in a car heading toward a cliff. "Do the people at Harper & Row know about . . . your intentions?"

"Of course! Why do you think they bought it?"

Okay, that was stretching it. Harper & Row (now HarperCollins, and still my publisher after forty years) was angling for a stylish *New York Times* bestseller along the lines of Cyra McFadden's *The Serial*, the franchise I had originated when I was still at the *Pacific Sun*. They even had plans to mimic that book by binding *Tales* in glossy cardboard with a spiral ring. That proved not to be cost effective, thank heavens, since I could never have looked Cyra in the face again. We ended up with a whimsical map of San Francisco on the cover (by Sausalito cartoonist Phil Frank) that was linked to a key on the back identifying various locales in the book. There were no other words at all—nothing so bold as to say it was a novel. Many bookstores, out of confusion, ending up shelving *Tales* in the travel section.

And, despite my assurances to my mother, Harper & Row did not have big plans for me as a queer. Many of its executives, still tiptoeing

around their own sexuality, or denying it outright, had squirmed no-
ticeably when I sailed into the offices at East Fifty-Third Street full of
my recent liberation—Scarlett O'Hara arriving at the ball in her red
dress. My own editor, a bow-tied, old-world bachelor, was so vague
about his life after work that he seemed not to have one at all beyond
a weekly card game with friends. I told him I wasn't asking for a naked
male torso on the cover—a cliché the publishing world would eventually employ ad nauseam once it realized there was a market out there—
just some tiny bit of text to indicate that this was a novel that could
appeal to people like me and their friends. He gave me the weariest of
Old World New York sighs and said, "Oh, Armistead . . . *toujours gai,
toujours gai!*"

I had had high hopes for that first of the *Tales* novels. Rock Hudson had lent me his modest gravel-roofed getaway house in Bermuda
Dunes, so I could work for a week on reassembling and, in some
cases, reimagining the first year's worth of columns. At one point I
put them all on the living room floor and rearranged them like
a Rubik's Cube, discovering new ways to heighten suspense and de-
velop themes. How could this not be a bestseller? To get on the *New
York Times* list all you needed (I had heard) were book sales of roughly
fifty thousand; "Tales" had grabbed ten times that many readers in
the *Chronicle*. Surely, some of them would want the story in permanent form, or would at least tell their friends about it.

Not nearly enough of them did. They thought they knew the story
already. Harper & Row took 25,000 returns on that mysterious map-
covered book. It was as if *Tales of the City* had entered the Witness
Protection Program and successfully disappeared. I would eventually
build a readership for the subsequent books through the pioneering
LGBT bookstores that were popping up across America in the 1970s,
among them Unicorn Books and A Different Light in Los Angeles,

Walt Whitman Books in San Francisco, Oscar Wilde Memorial Book-shop in New York City, Giovanni's Room in Philadelphia, White Rabbit in Raleigh, Glad Day Bookshop in Boston, and Lambda Rising in Washington, D.C. When Gay's the Word in London imported the books they were seized in 1984 by Maggie Thatcher's customs agents as part of "a conspiracy to import indecent material."

That's when I knew I was on my way.

FIFTEEN

"I'VE BEEN THINKING," MY MOTHER SAID on the phone one day. "How would you like to have Grandpa's Branch's bed?"

It took me a moment to realize she meant that old mahogany sleigh bed, the one built by "slaves in our family." The one Mimi had cried herself to sleep in.

"For good, you mean?"

"Of course for good. Tony and Jane both got family furniture as wedding presents, and you'll never be married, so . . . you should have something. We can ship it out to you. Will it work in your new place?"

My new place was a Hobbity garden apartment set amid the roses and tree ferns of the lower Filbert Steps. The ceiling was low, but the bed would certainly fit, and its curvy lines and glossy wood would lend charm to the unembellished dry-walled room. The bed I was currently using was just a mattress on a frame.

"It would look great here," I said. "I'd love it."

It occurred to me that I had slept in this bed for the first time on a recent Christmas visit to Raleigh. I knew it could comfortably accommodate two, since I picked up the son of a local sheriff at the Capital Corral and Glitter Gulch, Raleigh's new gay bar down by the railroad tracks, and brought him back to my childhood home. It was a risky act, but a thrilling one, and Mimi's room had its own outside entrance through which my hot-blooded country boy could vamoose before sunup. It felt good to bring something of my new life into my old home.

"You have to promise me you won't sell it if money gets tight."

This was troubling to hear, but not out of the realm of possibility. She knew me too well. "I promise. Okay?"

When the shipment arrived in San Francisco it had to be unloaded on Montgomery Street at the top of Telegraph Hill and hauled down several wooden flights of the Filbert Steps. The bed came in four pieces, including the head and foot portions of the "sleigh." Taped to the headboard was a collection of hand-hewn iron bolts and a dedicated instrument for tightening them. The unfinished planks that supported the mattress, which looked easily as old as the bed itself, had been freshly drilled with dime-sized holes so they could be wired together for shipment. I couldn't help but see that as a desecration of sorts. I knew Daddy had hauled out the drill in the name of practicality, and you could not see the holes once the bed was assembled, but it still bothered me. It felt like a document that had been angrily initialed at the last moment. I wondered if it indicated how Daddy felt about shipping an heirloom to California for occupancy by his eldest son and God-knows-who.

IN LATE NOVEMBER of that year, a few months after my novel was published, my mother called to say that she and Daddy wanted to come pay me a visit.

"Just for a few days," she said. "A long weekend. I can meet your friends."

She knew I had a group of guys I was hanging out with on Telegraph Hill. For a while she had tried to convince herself I was "dating" Nancy Bleiweiss, my friend who was playing Glinda the Good Witch in *Beach Blanket Babylon*, but she seemed to have finally abandoned that notion and decided to see for herself what my life was all about while she could. "I would love that," I told her. "I'll make it special for you."

I'd always enjoyed showing San Francisco to my parents. Over the course of the five years I had lived there, they had been treated to sev-

eral versions of my Grand Tour: Muir Woods, the Cliff House, China-
town, the postcard version of things. That would not be possible this
time, given my mother's fragility, but I could plan a little gathering of
friends and show off Grandpa Branch's bed in its new setting. Even
the Edenic landscape in which my new apartment was nestled was
an attraction in its own right. It had once been an enormous garbage
dump that straggled down the hill past a rock quarry before a woman
named Grace Marchant moved onto Telegraph Hill in 1949 and began
a garden that would grow so lush and beautiful that it would officially
bear her name after her death.

Grace had been a Mack Sennett bathing beauty during silent film
days. Now she was a sassy, white-haired old lady who lived two doors
down. She didn't approve when, a year or so later, in need of a bigger
apartment, I moved farther up the Filbert Steps to what she called
"the wrong side of Montgomery Street." Grace cherished her bohemian
enclave on the lower steps with its dozing cats and plank sidewalks.
She maintained that the steps got snootier the closer you got to
Coit Tower. She teased me about one of my new neighbors, Whitney
Warren Jr., a fussy old socialite closet case who threw parties for the
likes of George Cukor and Princess Lee Radziwill and had opened
his home in the past for large USO events. ("Well," Grace said with a
wink, "at least you'll know when the fleet is in town.")

I introduced my folks to Grace on their final visit to the city. We
couldn't have missed her. She was there in the garden, that Seuss-
ian landscape of tree ferns and fried eggplants and electric-purple
princess trees, and she was yanking weeds with a vengeance in her
big straw gardening hat. My parents were impressed that I knew this
glorious creature. I pointed out Grace's wonky old shingled house,
which stood nearby, where the steps met Napier Lane. "It used to be a
saloon," I told them. "Back in the last century. They would drug men

at the bar and drop them through a hole in a floor. When they woke up, they would find themselves doing indentured service on a ship to Shanghai. That's where they got the term *shanghaied*."

Daddy loved that story and looked to Grace for verification. "Is that true?"

She shrugged. "More or less. Your son, as you know, can be vivid." She gave the old man a wink. "By the time I'm gone he can tell that story however he likes."

There's an obvious question here, and the answer is no. Grace Marchant was not my inspiration for Anna Madrigal. I had already created that character and her secret garden at 28 Barbary Lane several years before meeting the doyenne of the Filbert Steps. The truth is that back then there were many such homegrown eccentrics still tucked into the nooks and crannies of San Francisco. Hard to imagine, I know, in a time when quaintness is just another selling point on an Airbnb listing. I cringe when real estate agents today describe any property with wooden back stairs and a bit of shrubbery as "a real *Tales of the City* charmer." There is nothing charming about those prices. And the people who might have lived in such a place once upon a time, myself included, could not even contemplate living there today.

While we were still down there in the garden, I led my parents down Napier Lane to a narrow path winding across the hill to the Greenwich Steps and another enchanted garden, this one tended by Grace's daughter. In one way it was even more enchanted, because there was someone who lived there in a hidden lean-to just above the old seawall. I had stumbled across him one day by accident, and he invited me in for coffee. His name was Olin L. Cobb. He was a former merchant seaman, maybe in his late forties, roughly dressed and missing a few teeth. The term *homeless* wasn't used much in those days, but Olin would have balked at it. This *was* his home; he had built it out of black plastic sheeting and packing crates. He had a cot and a few charming knickknacks. He used it to do "earthquake research," recording in a log the behavior of small animals who came to visit. It was the lair of Bilbo Baggins. You would never have seen it if you weren't looking for it.

When the *Chronicle* got word of Olin (not from me, by the way), they dubbed him "The Hermit of Telegraph Hill." That was way off. He was extremely sociable, not a recluse by anyone's definition. He proved it the day I took my dying mother to meet him. I had deliberately not told them where we were going, so my father muttered *What the hell* as I pushed away a curtain of shrubbery to reveal the lean-to. Olin had a fire going and looked up with a welcoming smile.

"This must be your folks," he said.

My parents, though completely blindsided, mustered their graciousness in a way that warmed my heart. Despite their private social judgments about people, they knew how to behave in a remarkable variety of situations. When I introduced them to Olin, my mother said, "Lovely to meet you, Olin. This place is so . . . cozy."

"Coffee?" asked Olin.

"Uh . . . no thank you. I'm afraid my tummy won't let me."

Olin brushed off the only chair so my mother could sit down. Then he turned to my father. "So, Mr. Maupin . . . how are the horses and the hounds?"

I've never forgotten the dumbfounded look on my father's face. He turned to me for an explanation. "Did you tell him that?"

"Hell no," I replied with a grin.

It was true. I hadn't.

Stirring sugar into his coffee mug, Olin took his time explaining things. "Well, you see . . . when Armistead told me you were coming,

I went to the library and looked you up in *Who's Who in America*. The fox hunting is right there under your name."

"Well, if that don't beat all," said my father.

Olin had been a hit with my folks. As I drove them back to their hotel, my father was still relishing the afternoon. "You know, I spent fifty dollars to be in that book, and that fella back there is the only goddamn person who's ever remarked on it."

Olin was eventually driven out of his garden hideaway by too much publicity and the developers of a new condo adjacent to the seawall who didn't want him to be part of their "million-dollar view." I preserved the notion of Olin's home in *Further Tales of the City*, though I moved it to Golden Gate Park and gave it a sinister inhabitant who was nothing like Olin. Steve Beery and I had scouted a perfect location: a gardener's shed on the edge of the Rhododendron Dell.

Several months after Olin vanished from Telegraph Hill, he sent me a postcard (from Portland, as I recall, but with no return address).

It said, "Hello from Olin L. Cobb."

I never heard from him again.

MY FRIEND DAVE KOPAY, who knew about my mother's failing health, offered to throw a brunch for my folks on their last day in town. Earlier that year, Dave and I had ridden on the back of a convertible in the San Francisco Gay Freedom Day Parade. We had waved to the crowd like athletes after a big game, which came naturally to Dave, a former running back in the National Football League and the first professional athlete to come out of the closet. We were an unlikely duo, to say the least, this sweet lunk of a jock and a storyteller who didn't give a good goddamn about sports, but our willingness to be open about our lives in the public eye had made us brothers. Dave had even roomed with me briefly—nonromantically—in another house on Telegraph Hill. There were a quarter million people cheering us on at that parade, the first one to be held after Anita Bryant launched her ugly campaign. It was good for everyone's soul, healing in fact, but I remember looking up at the people in the tall buildings along Market Street and thinking that any one of them would have a pretty good shot at us. The more the movement grew, the more we thought about such things.

The plan for my parents' last day was for six or eight of us to meet with them at Dave's house on Upper Market Street. I was proud of my friends and knew my mother would love them, and Dave would be the perfect poster child for selling homosexuality to my old man. For me (and for so many people across America) Dave was living proof that We Are Everywhere.

When he called me early that afternoon, he began by saying, "Oh, man."

I assumed he was having trouble with brunch preparations, since it was really hard to picture him toiling over a casserole.

"Is there anything I can help with? It doesn't have to be fancy, Dave."

"You haven't heard?"

"No . . . what?"

The terrible weight of this thing, whatever it was, hung in the silence between us.

"Harvey and George have been shot dead at City Hall. Dan White did it."

Dave and I had been at more than one gathering with our cool straight mayor and our new gay supervisor. We knew them well enough to call them by their first names. Harvey and I headlined benefits together all the time. I had once introduced George Moscone onstage at the Castro and surprised him with a kiss on the cheek. I had seen Harvey and Dan White in the same chamber at City Hall when the Board of Supervisors voted on our new Gay Rights Ordinance. White had been the only supervisor to vote against that antidiscrimination law, claiming his constituents wanted it that way. Supervisor Dianne Feinstein had also expressed concerns, wondering aloud if the ordinance would, say, allow male schoolteachers to show up at school wearing dresses. In the end, though, she voted for the ordinance; and in the very end, it was her voice, cracking with horror, that announced the gruesome murders to the world. It was the Wild West all over again, and my mother, on her very last visit, had landed in the middle of it.

"Should we cancel the brunch?" I asked Dave.

That immediately sounded so shallow and stupid and, well, gay. I wanted to rephrase the thought, but Dave's sensible nature prevailed.

"No," he said. "I wanna be with you guys."

I knew what he meant. I wanted to be with us, too.

I NEEDN'T HAVE worried about Dave making too big a fuss over brunch. In reliably jocklike fashion he had buckets of Kentucky Fried Chicken waiting for us on his dining table. My parents had watched the news at their hotel, so there was a brief, sober discussion about the murders after they arrived by cab and met my friends. Then, for a while, at least, we more or less pretended that it hadn't happened. No one there wanted my mother's last day in town to be about that. It was sweet to look across the room and see her in smiling conversation with Daniel Katz, a cherubic twenty-one-year-old New Yorker whom I had already come to think of as my little brother. Daniel himself would be gone in four years, one of the earliest victims of pneumocystis pneumonia, and the person whose death inspired the first AIDS fatality in fiction, Dr. Jon Fielding in my fourth "Tales" novel, *Babycakes*.

As expected, my father and Dave hit it off immediately. Dave moved into a sort of jovial man-to-man mode, a style that came naturally after years in locker rooms with the 49ers and the Redskins. At one point he took my father into his bedroom to show him a Polaroid of a naked woman, a shot he himself had taken during a three-way with a straight couple, one of his favorite activities back then.

By that time the old man had been exposed to all manner of gay ribaldry, but Dave's gallant effort at putting him at ease seemed to have quite the opposite effect. When Daddy emerged from the bedroom he pulled me aside with a frown. "What the hell's the matter with that boy? Doesn't he know he's queer?" (He got a laugh out of me, as he had fully intended to do.)

As the afternoon wore on we got word of a memorial service for Harvey and George to be held down at Castro and Market. I wanted very badly to go to it, as did everyone else at Dave's house. It was hard telling my mother, since we had planned on a quiet last evening together, and I think she had counted on it. She made a good show of saying that it was fine, that she was feeling tired anyway, that it had already been a wonderful day so I should join my friends and not think twice about it.

We all piled into Dave's little black Toyota pickup. My mother rode in front with Dave, since that was infinitely more comfortable than the back, where half a dozen homosexuals and my father were jammed in tight for the short ride into the Castro. I looked on in mild horror as someone lit a joint and passed it around. When it came near my father, he said, "Gimme that goddamn thing," then snatched it and took a puff.

"I'm surprised at you," I told him, grinning.

"Well, I gotta do something. Your mother's up front with that god-damn bisexual."

He got a huge laugh from all of us, owning the moment completely, showing my friends he wasn't nearly the stuffed shirt they'd imagined him to be.

I PARTED WITH my parents at the corner at Market and Van Ness, where they said they would catch a cab back to their hotel. They would be leaving for the airport early in the morning, but we pretended it wasn't the last time for anything. My mother looked so brave and small in a silk headscarf she had donned to ward off the November chill. She smiled at me wanly as if she were memorizing something, and then kissed me on the cheek, leaving a lipstick smudge that she wiped off with her thumb. My father, knowing how fraught the moment was, socked me on the arm. All his goodbyes were like that, but this time was different, and we knew it. I was aching with the weight of too much left unsaid. I hated myself for being so much like the old man in a moment that called for something big and true. I promised to call my mother as soon as they got back to Raleigh, then walked away with my friends.

The crowd that gathered at Castro and Market had grown too large for that space and began heading down Market Street, with hundreds of people joining it at every intersection. They were carrying candles in paper cups—a surging sea of candlelight, almost phosphorescent in its beauty, like plankton on a night tide. And I had never heard such silence. This was not a march or even a protest. It was a conscious act of love in response to a conscious act of barbarism. It was the very best of us made visible.

My friends and I merged with that tide and let it carry us into the

Civic Center, where City Hall, the scene of the crime just eight hours earlier, now became the temple of our grief. As the plaza began to fill with mourners the silence somehow remained intact until a slender, stately woman walked across a stage, stood at a microphone, and began to sing "Amazing Grace." She had not been announced, but the crowd recognized her voice with a single sigh. She had lulled me to sleep sometimes during that bittersweet summer before college when Clark and I were living at the beach, and he was extolling the virtues of pussy, and I had longed, all too fearfully, for a beautiful Navy diver in faded red shorts.

I once was lost, but now am found, was blind, but now I see . . .

When I began crying it was for everything at once: For Harvey and George. For my mother. For my father's inexpressible pain. For my own awkward journey of self-discovery. For the comfort of friends and lovers in the darkest of hours.

It was my youngest friend, Daniel, who spotted the miracle in our midst.

"Look over there," he said excitedly, tugging my arm.

What on earth was I supposed to look at? We were surrounded by thousands of people.

"Over there," he said. "Under that lamppost."

I looked again and saw my parents about forty feet away. They were holding on to each other in the midst of all that heartbroken humanity. They had not taken a cab to their hotel after all but followed the river of light to its destination.

And they had not seen us yet. I stood frozen in amazement.

"Go get them," said Daniel, giving me a gentle shove.

So that's what I did. I hurried up to them and took their arms and led them closer to the stage with my friends. They seemed every bit as surprised as I had been.

"Is this your doing?" I murmured to my mother when the old man was talking to Dave.

She didn't answer, just squeezed my arm and looked toward the stage.

"This woman's voice is lovely. Do you know her?"

"That's Joan Baez," I told her.

"Oh no," she said with a crooked little smile.

My father had hated Joan Baez ever since her days of antiwar activism.

"That's okay," I told my mother. "What he doesn't know won't hurt him."

SIXTEEN

IT'S TIME TO TELL YOU ABOUT the way my friend Steve Beery and I met.

In the last month of his life, Harvey Milk had been introduced to Steve at the Beaux Arts Ball in San Francisco. Steve was dressed as Robin from the *Batman* comics, so the supervisor had tossed out an effectively corny line—"Hop on my back, Boy Wonder, and I'll fly you to Gotham City." On their first date Harvey had asked Steve if he was happy being gay, because Harvey, always on the run, wondered how much on-the-job training would be required. Steve took this to mean that Harvey saw him as serious boyfriend material.

I can't tell you for sure how many times they got together—half a dozen at the most. On mornings when Harvey slept over, he would drive Steve to work at a credit union on Geary Boulevard and they would make out in Harvey's Volvo in full view of Steve's coworkers, much to Steve's delight. They had made plans to spend Thanksgiving together, but a last-minute crisis at City Hall—reports of the mass suicides in Jonestown—kept Harvey working late again. On another occasion Steve recalled Harvey shrugging off a grisly death threat that had arrived in the mail. "I can't take it seriously," he said. "It was written with a crayon."

Their last night together was the Friday before Harvey was murdered. Steve remembered a night of leisurely cuddling that turned into gentle lovemaking. On Monday morning, Steve got the news from a coworker who'd heard it on the radio. His boss took pity on him and drove him home, where Steve found a note from his roommate saying that Harvey had called that morning with plans for getting together that evening. Numb with disbelief, Steve had walked all the way across town to City Hall, where throngs of other people sobbing in the street finally made the tragedy real for him. He didn't try to push his way past the police barricades; he had come into Harvey's life too late to be a part of his official history. He had just been in love with the guy.

When Steve worked up the nerve to call Harvey's office, Harvey's aide, Anne Kronenberg, arranged for him to attend the memorial service. Arriving alone at the Opera House, he searched for a seat in the reserved section up front and finally found one next to me. Introducing himself as a friend of Harvey's, he asked if he could take the seat. He was crying, so for most of the service I held the hand of this stranger. His face was blurry with grief, but I could see what Harvey must have seen: a bright, inquisitive, tenderhearted young man.

We parted after the service. Two weeks later, only a block from Macondray Lane, I saw Steve walking down Union Street. We stopped and spoke for a while. He still seemed distraught, and not just because of the loss of a month-long romance with Harvey. His dreams of being a free gay man had been shattered by those bullets at City Hall. He admitted to feeling that suicide was the only way out.

What was the point of anything, he asked, if the world could be like this?

I asked him if he'd like to have dinner sometime.

Thus began a fifteen-year friendship that was every bit as epic as a great romance. Steve was the buddy I had sought since childhood, someone to roam the woods with in search of adventure. He had a childlike appreciation of life. His little studio at the top of Telegraph Hill felt almost monastic with his treasures of the moment laid out like icons—a rubber Mighty Mouse doll, a Nancy Mitford novel, a Batman poster signed by Bob Kane. He was so self-contained that he could snuggle in anywhere and make it home. I saw him do this in a cabin on a cruise ship and in a villa in Lesbos and a cottage in the Cotwolds. In the end, when he was too weak to live by himself, he adjusted to the inevitability of Maitri, the Zen hospice in the Castro.

"I looked around," he told me one morning, "and saw the garden out back, and all the nice people who bring food, and I realized I could live here."

SEVENTEEN

MUMMIE HAD THE TOY FOX IN bed with her at the hospital in Chapel Hill.

She was on morphine by then, pale as an ivory Quan Yin, and getting some things off her chest. She wanted me to know, for instance, that I had neglected to pay back the thousand dollars she had bailed me out with back in the day.

"That was my mad money," she reminded me.

I told her I was mortified to hear that. I had just been careless.

"I want credit for getting you on your feet."

I told her I would think of a way to do that.

"It isn't about the money."

"I know."

I had wondered all these years, so I asked, "Why was it 'mad money'?"

"Because it was mine."

"I mean, where did you get it?"

Daddy had a Japanese sword, she said, a souvenir from the war that had been packed in the attic for years. She read somewhere that a knife-and-sword vendor was passing through town, and she wanted to see how much she could get for it. Daddy gave her permission and said she could keep whatever she got. She went down to the auditorium and talked with the dealer, and made a good deal. She kept that thousand dollars for years.

"It was the only money I'd earned since the war, so it meant something to me."

I told her I was so sorry I hadn't paid her back.

"And I want you to write a sweet book one day, something like *The*

Snow Goose." She had always loved Paul Gallico's tale of a bitter hunch-backed artist who retreats to a lighthouse but is rescued by the love of a sweet young girl and a goose whose wing he mends before rowing troops to safety in the great evacuation at Dunkirk. I told her I would work on that. It stung a little to realize that she didn't think of my current book as sweet—the one about the pot-growing transgender landlady who offers one last chance of love to a dying businessman. I had certainly been going for sweet.

"Do you want to see a trick?" she asked.

"Sure."

She extended her leg from beneath the sheets and splayed out her toes in every direction, wiggling them. Each toe was its own little puppet show. It was mildly grotesque, not what I'd expected.

"I've always been able to do that," she said proudly. "I did it for the nurses at the hospital on the day you were born."

"Why? Because I was coming out backwards?"

"No! I wasn't in labor yet. They were very impressed."

She started wiggling her toes again, so I grabbed her foot and sub-dued it for a while. It was more intimate than anything I could possibly have imagined.

"It's a very nice trick," I said, still holding on.

It was devastating to think that she saved something from the very beginning to share with me at the very end.

"Go on, Teddy. Go home. Get some rest."

I let her foot slip out of my hands.

"And come back early in the morning. I've got an orderly I want you to meet."

EIGHTEEN

I NEVER KNEW MY GRANDFATHERS. Both were dead before I was born. My maternal grandfather had been a bona fide Victorian—born in England in 1865—almost thirty years before my grandmother. He gave her six children to raise while scattering seed elsewhere with great abandon. My other grandfather had been a quieter sort, that Raleigh businessman who had been home with his wife and kids, as usual, the night he killed himself with a shotgun.

Both men were phantoms to me, rough sketches at best of what a living grandfather might have been. I cannot claim to have felt the absence of a male elder in my youth. My grandmothers had been enough for me—*a gracious plenty*, as my Southern grandmother used to say—a talcum-scented tag team of Old England and Old South. For years, nice old ladies were all I needed. It wasn't until I left my twenties and finally claimed my manhood in all its clumsy, unregrettable glory that I realized that a gay grandfather figure might come in handy, someone to tell me how things used to be, and how they might be in the years to come, for men like me.

I met Christopher Isherwood at an Oscars Night party thrown by one of the producers of *Saturday Night Fever*. That should nail the era for you. John Travolta was up for Best Actor, but there was a whiff of disgruntlement in the room, since the Academy had already declared the Bee Gees ineligible for a Best Song nomination. "Stayin' Alive" and those other monster hits in *Saturday Night Fever* had not been written specifically for the movie. The party was lively, if not exactly star-studded. (We were in West Hollywood, after all; the studs outnumbered the stars.) For me, the main attraction was the bantam rooster standing at the edge of the room with a drink in his hand. His eyes were the tip-off: piercing blue and all but parenthesized by tumbling eyebrows. I recognized that gaze from a television interview in which he had spoken with breezy candor about being "hommo-sexual."

Isherwood had already been my hero for most of the seventies, having written *The Berlin Stories*, the source material for *Cabaret*, a film that had not only set the tone for my life in San Francisco but had also offered a template for my fictional newspaper serial. (It was no accident that "Tales of the City" took place in a shabby apartment house with an all-seeing landlady and carnally adventurous tenants.) My love for Sally Bowles (and, okay, I'll just say it, Liza Minnelli) had been my gateway drug to the literary addictions of *Down There on a Visit* and *A Single Man* and *Christopher and His Kind*. Isherwood struck me as the obvious tribal elder for our new breed of open queers. He *called* himself queer, in fact, way back then, believing that the blithe use of the word was the way to embarrass our enemies. He never dodged his sexuality with coy semantics, the way Gore Vidal did, or equated it with decadence like Truman Capote and way too many others. He was sassy in his public presentation, but never bitchy. Kindness, in fact, seemed important to him.

I wriggled through the Oscar revelers to get to him. He was there with his sweetheart, the artist Don Bachardy, a beach-bred stunner in his early forties whose glossy gray mane suggested some higher breed of blond. Both men were drunk and jolly. I remember telling them about my serial in the San Francisco paper, and how convincingly Isherwood had mumbled, "Oh, that marvelous funny thing," as if he had actually heard of it. I offered to send him the book when it was published in the fall. He graciously acquiesced, so I confirmed my shamelessness by asking him if he could maybe, possibly, if he liked it, review the book for the *Los Angeles Times*. He countered shrewdly with the offer of a blurb, and told me, as he often did with hyperventilating pups like me, that he was listed in the Santa Monica phonebook.

That's just my version of things, of course, a memory I cherished for years like a smooth stone found on a beach. Thirty-four years later, when the final volume of Isherwood's diaries was published, I found that he had recorded nothing about that night at the party. He was feeling especially slothful that week, he said, so he was using a tablet called Dexamyl to kick-start writing. Both his left eye and "Old Mr. Right Knee" were giving him trouble, but he was proud of the fact that he could still make it down to the beach and back up the steep stairs to his house. His sleeping hours, tucked into bed next to Don, were the only ones that never felt squandered.

He told his diary that he was seventy-three and a half years old, adding the fraction the way a child would do, only more in urgency than eagerness. He said he did find "a curious strength in the terminal condition of being old [since] it cuts out such a lot of shit." Still, he was ashamed of what he called "senile resentments" when asked to autograph books for strangers. "It's very seldom that I really enjoy being a celebrity, though I guess I would miss it if I weren't one. The young need so much support and one should give more and more. That's the only creative way of keeping one's mind off oneself and one's ailments."

I have taken comfort in Chris's diaries, since there are parallels in my own life now that I am seventy-two and a half years old. I am slower now, lazy more often than not, and have diabetic neuropathy in Mr. Right Foot. Like Chris, I try to curb my grumpiness, though I sometimes surrender to it in private. My writing doesn't come as easily as it once did, so, when I need inspiration, I vaporize a strain of cannabis called "Girl Scout Cookies." Like Chris, I've finally found lasting love with a younger man (named Chris, as fate would have it), a photographer whose career dovetails with my own, since words and pictures naturally complement each other. Chris and Don distinguished fidelity from monogamy, preferring, as my Chris and I do, the durability of the former to the folly of making sex the deal-breaker in a union between men. When jealousy arose, as it inevitably did upon occasion, Isherwood took it as proof he wasn't indifferent. "It's so *French*," he once told me not long before he died, "that thing of not being jealous."

Isherwood and Bachardy slept intertwined with each other; so do Chris and I. Chris the elder believed he and Don could communicate with each other in the midst of sleep. We believe that, too. Isherwood once remarked to me that "life gets so much simpler once you've narrowed it to one other person." Now I know what he meant.

As Chris grew older he cared less and less for air travel, especially if it took him away from Don. When it came to cars, he was a reluctant driver and a jittery passenger, so he made a practice of lying down flat in the backseat when Don was behind the wheel. (He explained it to me this way: "I believe I'm the only person who's fit to be on the road at all, therefore I prefer to just miss it when other people drive.") I can relate to that. I'm grateful that my husband does the driving these days, but I can't keep my mouth shut when he looks down to his cell phone for traffic conditions or Shazams a song that catches his fancy on a freeway full of tractor trailers. True, my backseat driving is still happening in the front seat, but Chris assures me—*my* Chris, that is—that banishment always remains a possibility.

In one way or another, it's hard not to think of Chris Isherwood every day.

THE BOOK I mailed him—that first edition of *Tales of the City*—was an oversized trade paperback, a broad, floppy thing with the cartoon map on the cover that made it look less than literary. I was anxious for weeks until I received a letter—written by hand, if you can remember that quaint custom—telling me he couldn't put my book down and that he loved it for the same reasons he loved the novels of Dickens.

He even apologized for the delay in sending the blurb, saying that he found them to be as difficult to write as sonnets, since there was the same necessity to be brief.

Not long afterward I was invited down to Santa Monica to sit for a portrait by Don at their house on Adelaide Drive. This would be the first of many sittings for Don. The portrait that remains most memorable for me is the one that opens this chapter, drawn less than a month after my mother's death. For some reason I had yet to cry over that loss, but thanks to Don's gift for psychological insight, the pain of it is clearly visible in my eyes.

The place struck me as grand and rambling at the time. It's not— just a few smallish rooms and a studio tucked into the hillside, with only their tile rooftops visible below the street above. You can't see the house from anywhere nearby, so it has to be experienced from the inside out, where the glint of the sea through the tall, blue-shuttered windows wildly inflates the imagination.

And Chris and Don had a similar effect on me. These fabled lovers had met on the beach below the house when Chris was forty-eight and Don was eighteen. They had lived here since the fifties, playing host to movie stars and writers while scandalizing a tight-assed company town with the very fact of their love. I had entered their aerie through a carport containing an old beige VW bug and a set of barbells, but I felt as if I were arriving at Noël Coward's Goldenhurst or Somerset Maugham's Villa Mauresque. I was already in awe when I descended to the garden.

And what had Isherwood expected of his visitor that afternoon?

Thirty-four years later, his diary provided the answer: "Armistead Maupin was unexpectedly attractive and youthful. Not all that much so, but I realize I was expecting something terribly closet-elegant."

Not all that much so? Okay, fair enough. But *closet-elegant?* I was a fledgling writer, a lowly newspaper serialist whose only substantive achievement was being out of the closest. I can't help wondering if Isherwood had found something in my work that suggested age and pissiness, the same arch quality, perhaps, that had prompted him to remark that his friend Wystan (Auden) would have loved *Tales of the City*? Or had he simply reacted to my behemoth of a name, a name like Addison DeWitt or Sheridan Morley that immediately suggests some grand old windbag? I had endured this impression since childhood. At summer camp in North Carolina, a counselor had decided that Armistead was too much of a handle for an eight-year-old and announced to the cabin that he would call me Butch for the next two weeks. You can make your own joke here: I'm pretty sure that counselor had.

After that first day on Adelaide Drive, Isherwood wrote in his diary that he and I might become friends, but he was still waiting to see. Who could blame him? When you're seventy-something and a half years old, young writers who come on strong about your brilliance are not to be trusted. Only middle-aged artists believe in their own genius: the old know better. Listen to how Isherwood described a gay rights benefit he addressed in San Francisco in 1981: "Armistead Maupin introduced me, going much heavy on the praise, exalting me, in fact, to the position of America's Old Mr. Queer. But he is basically a friend, I feel—not one of those flattering foes." Knowing this would have disturbed me at the time, but now it makes perfect sense. We old-timers tend to squirm at eulogies delivered before our funerals.

As it happened, Chris had only four years left. If I had been his kind of diarist, or any kind of diarist at all, I could offer a richer array of my limited time with him. What's left now, I'm afraid, are a few over-honed anecdotes and the sweet afterglow of laughter and fellowship in that house on Adelaide Drive. Whenever I was in Los Angeles, Chris and Don generously folded me into their circle of friends, a variable feast that could mean anyone from David Hockney to roving poets and porn actors. I remember chicken dinners dished out by a poker-faced Romanian housekeeper named Natalie while the men at the table gabbed about movies or gave literal blow-by-blows of a sex club on Fairfax called Basic Plumbing. Natalie must have had an earful in her time. I wasn't there myself the night John Travolta gave an impromptu performance of a scene from *Cruising*, but I can't help wondering if Natalie was. According to Chris, Travolta knew the scene by heart and shoved his jeans below his Jockey shorts for Pacino's campy, climactic "Hips or lips?" line. If there are better ways to thank your hosts for a nice evening, they don't immediately come to mind.

Then there was a chilly night when the dinner guests were gathered with drinks around the living room fire. Chris looked almost preppy in jeans and a tweed jacket with elbow patches, bouncing on the heels of his loafers as if to syncopate the conversation. When talk turned to Eddie Murphy, Chris recognized the name and declared: "Oh, yes, Eddie Murphy! Marvelous, funny man!" One of the guests, the actress Rae Dawn Chong, said what some of us were already thinking: "But, Chris, he's terribly homophobic." To which Isherwood replied without a moment's hesitation: "Well, *fuck* him, then! Just *fuck* him!"

There was always an imp at play behind Chris's eyes. More than once I was prompted to offer him a toke off a joint, but he invariably declined, explaining that he and Don had once had nightmarish reactions to a bowl of kif Paul Bowles had given them in Morocco. Then, thoughtfully, he would add: "I don't mind if *you* do, though. I love the smell of it around me." I'm sure there was plenty of it around him the night a group of us piled into a car to see a cabaret singer performing in the San Fernando Valley. Don was driving, so Chris was stretched out across the three men in the backseat. The singer was a female friend of a friend, an unknown commodity, so there was speculation in the car as to whether or not the cabaret would be gay. Chris offered clues along the way by gleefully reading aloud the signs that passed his limited field of vision. "Midas Muffler!" he would crow. "That's very bad news indeed!" But, finally, as Don came to a stop in a decidedly lackluster mini-mall: "Pioneer Chicken! Thank God! It *is* a gay place!"

It was not a gay place—at least not until we arrived. The singer was touchingly earnest and untalented. Savoring the irony, I leaned over to Chris and murmured "Sally Bowles" in his ear. By then he'd had a drink or two, so he replied a little too loudly: "Sally was never this dreadful!" He was indulging me, of course. I remember looking around the table and realizing that six different decades of gay men were represented in our group. Isherwood had his arm around Steve Beery, the youngest one. Across the table sat Gavin Lambert, the almost-sixty-something novelist who had given me the endearing tomboy character Daisy Clover even before I met Sally Bowles.

I remember thinking at that moment: *This is how it should be.* This is how the camaraderie of queers can span generations, offering solace between young and old, bonding us through friendship and sex and art. And not just among the living. Chris was part of a lineage that reached back through Forster and Maugham to Wilde and Whitman and Carpenter and every unknown soldier and working-class rough-neck who had ever rolled in the hay with them. I found this genealogy far more appealing than the one I had been taught to revere in North Carolina, that bone-dry roster of long-gone planters and generals with their broodmare wives standing invisibly in the background. Here, at last, was ancestor worship with hot blood in its veins.

QUEERS WHO EMBOLDEN one another to be honest about themselves can feel real exhilaration in that moment, and it can last them a lifetime. Your tribe, as Isherwood called it, becomes a source of great sustenance. A terrible weight that you have borne for years becomes apparent by its sudden absence.

Ian McKellen and I had met in the early eighties through a mutual friend in San Francisco. Ian had just finished playing D. H. Lawrence in the film *Priest of Love* in New Mexico. I drove him and his then-partner Sean Mathias around town, giving them my usual rap for visitors. "This is where Kim Novak jumped into the bay in *Vertigo*. That's the house where Bacall hid out Bogart in *Dark Passage*. That's where Dirty Harry had the big showdown with the serial killer." And so on and so forth until he could finally take no more. When I showed him a pretty view from Russian Hill without elaboration, he gave me a devilish side-eye and said: "What's the matter? Wasn't anything filmed here?"

I had hit a nerve, I realized. Ian's film career had yet to catch fire (he was still many years away from having his Wizardly visage immortalized on a New Zealand postage stamp), and I had managed to remind him of that at, literally, every turn. I knew, of course, that Ian was a titan of the British stage, but I was wary of talking Shakespeare with him. I wanted for us to be friends, and thought that my shaky grasp of the classics might disqualify me.

It didn't. He didn't care about that. We bonded through laughter and queer cheekiness, launching a friendship that has prospered for forty years, though we have rarely been in the same city for long. Ian sometimes tells the press he decided to come out after a night of pot-fueled conversation with me and Steve Beery and my partner at the time, Terry Anderson. It began, quite simply, with Ian asking, "Do you think I should come out?" The three of us gave him an earful. Our friends were dying, and we had lost patience with people whose silence perpetuated the notion that there was shame in being queer.

Steve and Terry had both recently tested positive when the four of us drove up the coast together on a road trip. Back then a positive diagnosis was an almost certain death sentence. I remember how Ian kept our hearts light under the weight of that knowledge. He had signed the register at our inn as Tom Courtenay (an actor for whom he was often mistaken), then called the front desk shortly thereafter to inquire graciously about the pubic hair he had found on his pillow. In the sauna, he mooned us when the other patrons weren't looking. We giggled in the face of the Reaper when Ian was around.

When a fiftieth-anniversary stroll on the Golden Gate Bridge devolved into human gridlock (a quarter of a million San Franciscans had the bridge sagging visibly on that May day in 1987), Ian pressed on, though our merry band had just reached the first stanchion, and the crowd was quite obviously at a standstill. "C'mon, lads," he called, "We can do it. There's a big open patch up ahead where there are jolly picnickers and mothers pushing prams." He was joking, but he meant it, too, in his own way. Ian had survived the Blitz as a child. He remembered sleeping under a steel plate until he was five years old. His mother had died when he was twelve, his father when he was twenty-two; he was more than experienced in the art of pressing on. He was just what we needed, just when we needed it.

There was, in fact, an open patch up ahead—the AIDS drug cocktail that would begin to save lives in the nineties, or at least prolong them dramatically. Steve, as I've told you, wouldn't get to the cocktail in time. Terry would. And the prospect of a future made him realize that he didn't want to spend it with me. One morning in our tenth year together he climbed onto a new motorcycle and drove away. I had braced myself for his death, but not for this. "Cocktail divorce" was what they called it back then. There were more of them than you'd think.

WHEN I INTERVIEWED Christopher Isherwood and Don Bachardy for the *Village Voice* in 1985, I didn't know Chris was already enduring the pain of prostate cancer. I certainly didn't know it would be his last interview. Looking back now, I realize that he had already pushed off from the solid shores of his diaries and was drifting at sea on a raft with Don. The interview was about the two of them (I had already titled it "The First Couple"). Chris seemed foggy at times, so Don would answer for them both, or gently nudge Chris toward the answers they both knew to be true. When I asked them about the early days of their romance, Don directed his gaze toward Chris. "I'd never met anyone like him. He was so easy to be with. I was delighted. In fact, wasn't it I who proposed to you?" Chris blinked at him as if this were some sort of trick question and replied: "That's not the kind of thing you ask a gentleman. You *remember*."

The interview went well, but what stays with me now is the humiliating way it began. I had arrived from San Francisco with the only tool of my trade, a fancy Sony microcassette recorder about the size of a Tarot card. I had already used it on jobs for Andy Warhol's *Interview* magazine for taped encounters with Bette Midler, Dyan Cannon, Joan Rivers, and others, but eventually, even tiny technology overwhelms me. (I had once left the little microbastard behind at Shirley Temple's house, so she was forced to run down her circular drive, waving it over her head as I drove away. The interview, what's more, had not gone well. When Shirley reminisced about the "sweet little geckos" she had encountered when she was ambassador to Ghana, I told her I had similar memories of geckos in Vietnam. Since she was chain-smoking by then and we seemed to have bonded through laughter, I figured it was safe to bring up my other favorite lizard. "We had fuck-you lizards, too. Did you have those in Ghana?" Seeing the murderous gleam in her eye, I hastened to explain the lizard's cry, mimicking it for her. Her eyes shot to the tape recorder, then back at me. "You know," she said quietly, "when I was a little girl and there was profanity on the set, they would close down the set and there would be no more filming that day." Ambassador Black was lobbying her former costar Ronald Reagan to "give her another country," and she was not about to fuck it up on account of a profane lizard.)

That tape recorder set off another kind of consternation the day I interviewed Chris Isherwood on Adelaide Drive. I had forgotten to replace its batteries before leaving for L.A., so it whirred to a stop less than three minutes into the conversation. My mortification was so apparent that Chris made it his job to console me. "Think nothing of it," he said. "I once had the same thing happen to me." *Sure you did*, I thought, *you kind old sweetie pie.*

Chris assured me we still had plenty of time, so I should take his VW into Santa Monica to look for batteries. I was forty years old that spring, but I felt an almost boyish exhilaration as I drove past the tall, rattling palms of the palisades on my way to a Radio Shack. How could I not be a little giddy in that moment? There was warm ocean air on my face and the scent of some flower we didn't have up north, and my own best version of a grandfather, Old Mr. Queer himself, had just entrusted me with the keys to his car. As far as I was concerned, all was right with the world.

IT WAS DON, naturally, who saw Chris off. He sat with him every day of the last month of his life, drawing the man he had loved for the past thirty-three years. Chris was a willing participant in this effort, naked and often in pain, yet free of all vanity, giving himself to his Darling in the ultimate act of intimacy, the only one still available to him. And Don kept on drawing for several hours after Chris had died, recording the flight of spirit from his face, the inescapable absence of him, so that Don and the rest of us who loved him could actually believe that he was gone.

It's still hard to believe even after thirty years, thanks to the time-released revelations of the Isherwood diaries. There are always new angles on that life, ones that are utterly human and flawed and always irresistible. At times, to me, Chris seems to be in the very air of Santa Monica. In that lovingly haunted house on Adelaide Drive, in the portraits of Chris that still vibrate from the walls of Don's studio, in the tanned, glistening young men who still jog along the median strip of San Vicente where once they had earned the appreciation of a great man of letters.

And there is Don himself, of course, who is not only the keeper of Chris's flame but the keeper of his voice. The eerie similarity in their diction, which Don has always attributed to his unconscious mimicry, was vexing to me in my youth when I called their house and could not for the life of me tell whether it was Don or Old Mr. Queer who had answered the phone. Now I find great comfort in that quirk, because it offers a precious link to the past, a sort of two-in-one deal.

NOT LONG AGO I arranged for my friend Laura Linney to meet Don at the house on Adelaide Drive. Laura and I have known each other for almost twenty-five years, ever since she created the role of Mary Ann Singleton in the 1993 miniseries of *Tales of the City*. It has been one of those relationships where you don't just finish each other's sentences, you finish each other's thoughts. A crooked smile shared across a room is pretty much all it takes. I poured a lot of myself into Mary Ann's outwardly pleasant but guarded personality, and Laura seemed to relate to that as she inhabited the character. Put simply, we understood each other. Our genteel Southern parents had taught us all too well how to look like good children.

When we were both single, Laura had asked me to escort her to the Academy Awards when she was nominated for Best Actress for *You Can*

Count on Me. In her suite at the Four Seasons I helped her pick out a red Valentino gown only to step on its train repeatedly as we made our way down the red carpet, since the train was exactly the color of the carpet. "It'll be calmer inside," Laura reassured me. "It's like a bunch of well-behaved kids at a prom." We sat in the front row between Julie Walters and Ben Stiller while John Leguizamo, seated behind us with his gay brother, riffed on the hokey props for the *Crouching Dragon* number and whispered, "Look, it's Salvador Dalí!" when Bob Dylan's pencil-thin mustache appeared on a huge screen above us.

I couldn't imagine any experience more wonderful than that night until Laura and her husband, Marc Schauer, called me from a hospital room, giddy with joy, to tell me that they had named their newborn son Bennett Armistead Schauer. Marc and Laura had met only a month after Chris Turner and I had. Laura and I had read the same love poem at each other's weddings. It's been like this for a dozen years. We have mirrored each other's bliss, a bliss that, believe me, had been a long time coming.

And now here's little Bennett Armistead, already walking and just released by his mother onto the floor of Isherwood's office. This is the room where Chris did his writing and where his books still live and where Don now sleeps on a daybed to be closer to his spirit. There is a framed poster leaning against the wall on the other side of the room, the cover of *Liberation*, the last volume of Isherwood's diaries. The child, seeing Isherwood's kindly lined features, makes a beeline for the poster, pressing his hand against the old man's cheek, then turning to laugh with delight.

Such moments are all the god I'll ever need.

NINETEEN

MY MOTHER HAD BEEN DEAD FOR five months when I saw my English grandmother for the last time. The Madwoman was living in a red-brick high-rise in Alexandria, Virginia, one of those genteel "assisted-living facilities," where residents are assisted ever closer to heaven on the elevator. Grannie had yet to reach the top floor, the floor reserved for the dying. "But I should warn you, Teddy," my aunt had told me downstairs, "she's not like she used to be. She's a lot . . . um . . . smaller, and her hair has gone quite white." I had taken that in with a mute nod. *Okay. I can deal.*

"And she may not recognize you at all."

That was unimaginable, but I let it go. My aunt let me into the apartment, a dim, Yardley-scented glade where Grannie's old furniture—a damask chair, a Wedgwood lamp, an heirloom chest—seemed as awkwardly placed as strangers at a wake, already incompatible with the gleam of the invading chrome. I found her sitting upright in a chair, her back to the door, her small frame supported by a cane, her handbag in her lap. (She kept her chocolates there, among other closely guarded secrets.) She looked like someone waiting, very patiently, for a bus.

That, in effect, was what she was doing. From all reports, she was done with what she called "this bally body" and was ready to inhabit the next one.

She was ninety-five.

GRANNIE HAD GROWN up in Derby, in the East Midlands, a town that boasts about being the birthplace of the Industrial Revolution. Her fey watercolorist mother had been a follower of Madame

Blavatsky, the Russian occultist who founded Theosophy, so Grannie had been awash in those early tides of the New Age: séances, numerology, fairies, reincarnation, and, intermittently, before her Englishness prevailed, vegetarianism. In her teens she had studied piano at the Royal Conservatory of Music in London, the youngest girl to graduate at the time. She remained single throughout her twenties and recommended that course of action to everyone. "Just wait, Teddy," she had told me many times. "You don't know who you are until you're thirty. You're in no position to judge anything."

Grannie had kept busy in her twenties with magazine writing and dramatic recitals and a passionate new political life as a suffragist. ("A suffra*gist*, not a suffra*gette*," she had insisted. "I didn't pour acid in postboxes or chain myself to the prime minister's carriage.") Marguerite Norma-Smith made speeches all over England—rousing, charming, often very funny speeches—on the subject of "Why Women Want Votes." She was said to be one of the three women in England whom men would pay to hear speak. Once, when the issue came before Parliament, she made six speeches in a single day in London. She reveled in telling me about the time she had spoken on a village green in direct competition with a scheduled event. She ended up hijacking the audience of a livestock auctioneer, whose effort at selling rams proved no match for her elocution. Or so said the local newspaper. "I projected from the diaphragm," she told me more than once, pressing her fingers to her tummy. "And that's what you must do, Teddy." Then her fingers would trail up her torso to her mouth. "Stand up straight and project from the diaphragm."

When the Great War came, Grannie took a crash course in nursing and volunteered to care for critically wounded soldiers returning from the front. It traumatized her to witness so much mangled youth— "All those beautiful young men, some of them my own friends"—and

for years I (and many others in the family) took that as the reason
that she and my grandfather emigrated to America for the solace of
the Blue Ridge Mountains. According to lore, she had met Albert Edward Barton at one of her lectures, and he had been instantly taken
with her charm. Which lecture could that possibly have been? "The
Poets"? "Eastern Philosophies"? "Physical Culture for Women"? Certainly not a suffragist meeting, considering what I eventually learned
about my grandfather. He was over twenty years Grannie's senior, a
Victorian man in every sense of the word, but he was charismatic and
craggily handsome and had built a successful career in the steel industry. He had also suffered a wartime trauma of his own: his beloved
airman son, Robin, offspring of a previous marriage, had been shot
down in a dogfight over France. It wasn't hard to imagine how Grannie and this heartsick titan might have found comfort in each other,
might have wanted to leave everything behind and build a whole new
life somewhere else.

Their original plan had been to settle in Miami, but their motor trip from New York ended in Asheville, where the beauty of the
mountains stopped them in their tracks. After my mother was born,
they built a grand mountaintop house that my grandfather named
Birkland Brae in a proud nod to his Scottish ancestry. (Claiming kin-
ship to Bonnie Prince Charlie, he wore a kilt when he strode about
his property with his Great Danes.) Despite his insistence that "children should be seen and not heard," that ideal must have been hard
to enforce since Grannie bore five more children over the course of
a decade. When, at seventy-one, he died of a cerebral hemorrhage,
Grannie bore the burden of supporting that brood in the midst of the
Depression.

For a while she tried running a roadside sandwich stand she had
named The Scarecrow after the whimsical straw man that an archi-

tect friend had crafted for the roof. Business was brisk in the beginning, if not especially profitable. Grannie's sons habitually raided the Pepsi-Colas, and Grannie herself was too softhearted to charge penniless drifters for her lavish turkey-and-chutney sandwiches. It became clear that something more was required, so Grannie summoned her lady steel and moved her six children to Alexandria, Virginia, where they could be closer to colleges and she could be paid for teaching speech to Episcopal seminarians. She left her husband behind in Asheville, buried on a knoll not far from their second home, which they'd named Pine Burr Lodge to render it more ancestral, though it was a much humbler place than Birkland Brae.

When I first saw Pine Burr, forty years ago, its cinderblock walls and adjacent tourist cottages did not jibe with the childhood idyll of the 1920s that my mother recalled with such fondness. There was now a flaking sign that said "Sanders Court and Cafe," because Harland Sanders—yes, *that* Harland Sanders—had opened a business there at some point after Grannie had left for Virginia. That was almost too farcical to process immediately: the family seat of my immigrant British grandparents had become the second restaurant in the world (after the one in Corbin, Kentucky) to serve the colonel's secret recipe for fried chicken. Sanders had fared better in Asheville than Grannie had done with her sandwiches, but even his enterprise failed after a few years, when a new highway redirected tourist traffic.

When I was young, it didn't occur to me to wonder why the widow of a successful British steel magnate would have to sell sandwiches by the roadside. I would not know until the late eighties that my grandparents had never been married. They had left England under delicate circumstances. The "previous marriage" that had produced the airman son who had died in the war was still very much intact when they boarded a steamship bound for America. There was still a wife and three daughters, who, in the absence of a divorce, would naturally receive any inheritance after my grandfather died. My grandmother had been left high and dry.

I can't begin to speculate about anyone's morals or motives a century after the fact. What I feel mostly is even greater admiration for my grandmother, who raised a large and interesting family under great hardship and somehow kept her dignity intact. That can't have been easy, since my grandfather's philandering continued even after he and Grannie arrived in the States. In Asheville, when a ballerina touring with the Bolshoi Ballet was injured in a car wreck, my grandfather invited her to recuperate at Birkland Brae. There, under the same roof as Grannie and her children, he sired yet another child, a son who would be born elsewhere but eventually take his last name. I tracked down Martin Barton last year at his home in Plano, Texas. We talked for over an hour on the phone. He was ninety-three years old, and I was touched by his desire to meet his never-before-seen half siblings. I might very well have tried to help with that introduction had he not told me in a moment of sharing that he thought Pat Robertson, the Christian media mogul who attributes catastrophic weather to the "gay agenda," was the greatest political thinker of our era. After that, I lost interest in helping.

We've already had enough men like that in the family.

I KNEW NONE of these things during my last audience with my grandmother—not her inescapably unmarried state, not the Colonel Sanders connection, not the injured ballerina or the son she raised. My memories of her were of that sharp-edged aluminum suitcase and hot Virginia nights and periodic palmistry. As I stood there in her room, preparing to say goodbye for the last time, I dwelt on something my aunt had just told me: my grandmother had not been informed of my mother's death—that is to say, her eldest daughter's death. The general consensus was that Grannie was too far gone for the knowledge, so I was not to mention it to her, please. It would only upset her fragile equilibrium.

Once my aunt was gone I took a seat across from Grannie. The politeness she had already marshaled in her watery blue eyes told me not to hug her right away.

"It's Teddy, Grannie."

"How do you do," she said.

Her white hair was just as unsettling as advertised. It seemed to me that Grannie's hair had always been beige—"champagne beige," according to my sister, Jane, who had actually seen the dye box. Grannie had been very big on beige. Her suits, her gloves, her floppy feathered picture hats. She was not in the least vain, but she must have known how well that color complemented her eyes.

I leaned forward slightly, trying to come into focus. "Wren told you I was coming, didn't she?" I was hoping the mention of my aunt might jar something.

"Oh, yes?" It was clearly more of a question than an affirmation.

"You look very elegant."

"Thank you, kind sir."

I was too rattled to reaffirm my identity, so I just continued with a recital of the facts:

"I have a new apartment in San Francisco. On Telegraph Hill."

"Ahh."

"There are wild parrots outside my window. I can hear them flying over in the morning."

"In Asheville? Imagine that!"

"No, Grannie. San Francisco."

"I beg your pardon?"

"The parrots are in San Francisco. Where I live. I've never lived in Asheville." She was obviously back on her beloved mountainside with her husband and her six children and her thundering herd of Great Danes.

"That's a pity," she said. "Asheville is lovely."

I soldiered on. "I had a novel published last fall."

No response.

"It got a good review in the *Washington Star*."

This was pretty much the *only* review the book had received, but I was desperate for Grannie to know what I'd accomplished in my thirty-five years. I wondered if anyone in the family had sent her a copy of the book or if they had deemed it unfit for elderly eyes. My father's response, scribbled on yellow legal paper, had camouflaged his displeasure with ornery wit. "Your mother and I read Tales of the City today. Moving to Zanzibar tomorrow. Love, Daddy."

Grannie blinked at me graciously. "Well . . . good for you."

She might as well have been talking to some boastful stranger.

"Grannie . . . it's Teddy."

Her eyes registered nothing, though they were the same eyes that had gazed at me across a Ouija board when I was a boy. I could remember them dancing with glee as the planchette scooted beneath our fingertips past curlicue numbers and letters, predicting the future in gibberish. Even then I suspected that a piece of heart-shaped plywood from Parker Brothers was unlikely to be magical, and I'm pretty sure Grannie did, too, but there was something beyond that to keep me intrigued. *Is she steering this thing or am I? Are we doing this together?* It was a delicate dance of sorts, a gavotte between generations, and it was all about the eyes.

No more. The eyes were blinking at me but not in recognition.

Tell her, dammit. Fuck these fucking family secrets. Tell her you're Diana's eldest son. Tell her we have both lost the best person we have ever known.

But I couldn't. There had been a continent between Grannie and me for almost four years, so I had more or less forfeited the right to be remembered. I had been consumed with my new life in San Francisco, tethered to the golden shore by carnal self-discovery and a never-ending story in the newspaper that demanded my attention on a daily basis. Or so I had always assured myself.

"How lovely to meet you," she said at last, looking lost and mortified.

I felt the same way. I knew I had already tumbled from Grannie's mental family tree and was heartsick about it. She had been the first member of my logical family, the first person who had taken me as is. Why had I not visited more often? The easy excuse was my mother's recent decline and death, but not even that had brought me back to the South as often as it should have. I was done with the place for good. I had found a home out West that would love me for myself.

I was making a gloomy retreat from Grannie's apartment when I had an idea. Returning to her chair, I thrust out my hand with the palm turned upward for her perusal. She seized it immediately and began reading the lines in rapt silence, like a book she'd laid down the night before and couldn't wait to return to.

Then, without even looking up, she said, very softly, "Teddy."

"Yes!" I said, laughing. "Yes!"

"You're in your thirties now."

"I am indeed."

When her eyes finally moved up to my own, they were as open and lively as the sea. "And you've written a novel, you say?"

"Yes. And you're in it."

"Oh, dear."

I laughed again. "Not literally, but your spirit is there. Your loving, accepting spirit. She's a landlady in San Francisco, and she's a little . . . spooky about things."

Grannie took that in for a while. "I'll be coming back to visit you, you know."

Shortly before I moved to San Francisco, I had taken Grannie to see *On a Clear Day You Can See Forever,* knowing she would appreciate its reincarnation theme. We had both been charmed by the moment at the end when Barbra Streisand says, "See you later," to Yves Montand just before the elevator door closes, indicating she will join him in the next life. "See you later" had been our private joke for days.

Now, it seemed, Grannie was actually saying it.

"How will I know you?" I asked.

"You'll feel a little breeze in the room," she said.

The Madwoman's eyes were dancing as she built the drama.

"And when you turn around . . . there will be no one there."

TWENTY

MY FATHER'S ARCH-CONSERVATISM DEEPENED AS THE years wore on, even after his party climbed into bed with the fundamentalist "Holy Rollers" he had once openly disparaged. The platforms of the candidates he supported—including, of course, Jesse Helms— were growing more virulently antigay. He claimed—as my brother, Tony, would later claim—that his political beliefs were independent of his love for me. To me that meant that his love for me simply wasn't important enough to make him challenge the relentless fag-bashing of his party. I should be grateful for his tolerance, he seemed to be saying, since I was the one who wasn't playing by the rules. So I withdrew.

My brother, Tony, had begun to march in lockstep with my father's politics when he reached middle age, much as I had done in my youth. It must have been a bonding experience for them—and a relief for the old man to have a son on his side again. According to Tony's Facebook page, he embraced the Tea Party after Pap died, and once drove out to Oakwood Cemetery, where he listened to Rush Limbaugh with the car door open, so the old man could enjoy the broadcast from his grave.

In 2008, when Chris and I were married, Tony and his wife, Jean, flew to San Francisco for the wedding, where my little brother treated the other guests to the sort of almost-charming blunt talk for which the old man had been known. ("Y'all are mighty pretty for lesbians.") But any hope that Tony had finally understood that love was love went south when he voted for Amendment 1, the measure that would alter the North Carolina constitution to ensure that marriage in that state would always be between one man and one woman. "It's a matter of states' rights," he told me on the phone, using the argument my father had used to oppose integration. "What's right for California might not be right for North Carolina."

In 2014, when the University of North Carolina awarded me an honorary doctor of letters degree, I invited Tony to attend the hooding ceremony at the football stadium in Chapel Hill. He's a big fan of Carolina sports, and I thought he might enjoy seeing me honored in such a setting, but he declined with a painfully inept excuse about a Mother's Day luncheon. When, a year later, I finally confronted him about his absence, he apologized in an email: "I should have listened to my heart and not my head." His head, I suppose, had told him it wouldn't do to be seen celebrating the work of a liberal gay activist from California.

As of this writing, Tony is celebrating the ascendancy of Donald Trump and what I regard as a new fascist regime in Washington that has left our country more divided than at any time since the Civil War.

Brother against brother, then and now.

IN 2001, I published a novel called *The Night Listener*, which revolves around a San Francisco writer who drifts away from his aging conservative father because too much has been left unspoken over the years: a family suicide, the son's resentment of the old man's homophobia, et cetera. Four years later the book was made into a film starring Robin Williams and Toni Collette. We shot on location in New York City. It was there, as my snake-eating-its-tail life would have it, that I got word that my father was close to death. My sister was urging me to come home. Chris, my husband-to-be, thought we should go.

"What would be the point in that?" I asked him.

"He's your father," he said.

Great, I thought. *The love of my life sounds just like my mother.*

I nurtured no hopes of a deathbed epiphany with the old man. To me this was just one last chance to be hurt, probably with Fox News droning in the background. And my stepmother, who was roughly my age, always avoided intimacy with empty chatter about shopping and cocktails. For a while that had made her perfect for Pap. They didn't have to talk about anything real.

We went to Raleigh, of course, in the end. Robin Williams, who was playing "me" in the film (and whose beard I was mimicking to make him *look* like he was playing me) approached us as we were leaving the set for the airport. "Give my love to Pap," he said, looking directly into my eyes. As fellow San Franciscans, Robin and I had known each other for almost thirty years. He called me Armo sometimes, and had a habit of breaking into Tennessee Williams when he saw me. But he had never met my father beyond reading the novel and the screenplay. He had his own version of Pap, however, another gruff patriarch who was petrified of being close to his sensitive son, so I think he knew what I was about to face.

Chris, in fact, had never met my father either, since we'd only been together for a few years. When I consider that he might never have done so, I'm even more grateful that he had insisted on this last chapter.

In Raleigh, in that green-shuttered ranch house with the Howard Johnson's cupola and the muddy creek still trickling down below, I introduced my husband-to-be to my father. When we moved about the house, Pap was wobbly on his feet, so we ended up settling in the Chimney Room, where, beneath his Confederate flag, he told tales of our selectively abridged family history. His illness had made him more docile than I had ever known him to be. He seemed swallowed up by his chair. There were ugly bruises on his arms from various falls. Skin cancer surgery, a legacy of his South Pacific days, had left a shiny pink patchwork on his nose. He looked small and frightened, not like himself at all. I hated this meek version of him. I wanted him to rise up and bark like an old elephant seal. Just once. So Chris could see it.

"Robin Williams said to give you his love," I told my father.

He smiled. "How's my favorite funnyman?"

That sounded wrong, so completely out of character. Pap had never used the word *funnyman* (who does, anyway, beyond the announcers on *Entertainment Tonight*?), and the old man, as I remembered, had been furious when Robin came out publicly against the war in Iraq.

He's trying to be sweet, I realized. *He's scared and he needs company.*

I could see why. There was an air of grim submission in the house, a mute anticipation of the end. When Chris suggested we go for a ride in the rental car, everyone liked the idea, including my stepmother, who told us, right there in front of Pap, that she'd be glad to have him out of the house for a while. She must have had her reasons—I'm sure she did—but I was suddenly so grateful that I had found someone like Chris, someone kind and self-aware who wouldn't disconnect with me before the end has come. Someone who wouldn't talk about me as if I were no longer in the room.

Chris drove. Pap was up front, riding shotgun, giving directions.

I loved sitting in the back, listening to their back-and-forth. It felt miraculous.

"Take a left up here, then swing around the bend and follow her straight up to Canterbury."

"This neighborhood is nice," said Chris. "So leafy."

"Yes it is. You're a damn good driver."

"Thanks."

"Much rather have you drive than that fella in the back."

Chris chuckled.

"You know what I mean, doncha?"

"Oh yeah."

"I can hear you two back here," I said.

"Take a left on Canterbury," said the old man.

We drove downtown, connecting the dots of my childhood, of Pap's childhood, a jagged constellation of memories. We passed the historical marker honoring Grandpa Branch, who had died defending slavery and whose bed had been shipped to me in San Francisco as a gesture of my mother's acceptance. (The general's house was no longer there, even as a funeral home, having long since been replaced by a plain red-brick office building.) We rounded Capitol Square, past the Confederate monument and the steps where I'd spoken against Jesse Helms at Raleigh's first Gay Pride March. On the other side of the square I pointed out Christ Church, with the incongruous rooster on its steeple, the inspiration for Dansapp's "collection of cocks."

Then we moved on to Oakwood Cemetery, where my mother had been buried for over a quarter of a century. I showed Chris her tombstone and its inscription—"All Things Bright and Beautiful"—chosen by my father because of Mummie's favorite hymn, the one about "all creatures great and small."

Then, still following my father's directions, Chris drove us out to the far end of Clark Avenue, to the big old house where my father had grown up and my grandfather had killed himself. We didn't talk about that; we didn't need to. Under the comfortable cloak of fiction I had written of my grandfather's suicide in *The Night Listener*, and Pap had loved the book, though he made a point of saying that "that business" hadn't affected him as much as I'd imagined. When he had come to my appearance at a Raleigh bookstore he even became part of the show. During the Q & A portion, the inevitable question arose about where I get the inspiration to write, so I did what I always do and pantomimed a long, hard toke on a joint. It got the usual laugh, but Pap stole it from me by barking, "Shut the hell up!" from the audience. Suddenly we were a comedy act. "Ladies and gentlemen," I said. "Have you met my father?"

After our tour, back at the house, when conversation began to flag, Pap said, "I reckon you've got a plane to catch." It had been a perfect afternoon, a perfect summing-up in the presence of a sympathetic witness, and neither one of us wanted to screw it up. I hugged the old man goodbye—or as much of a hug as he would ever allow—and headed for the door. I thought that was the end of it until Pap pulled Chris aside and said something he thought I couldn't hear:

"You take care of that boy, you hear?"

It was just an instruction, delivered almost brusquely, but in that moment of our last goodbye, it felt like a benediction.

EPILOGUE: LETTER TO MAMA (1977)

Dear Mama,

I'm sorry it's taken me so long to write. Every time I try to write to you and Papa I realize I'm not saying the things that are in my heart. That would be OK, if I loved you any less than I do, but you are still my parents and I am still your child.

I have friends who think I'm foolish to write this letter. I hope they're wrong. I hope their doubts are based on parents who loved and trusted them less than mine do. I hope especially that you'll see this as an act of love on my part, a sign of my continuing need to share my life with you.

I wouldn't have written, I guess, if you hadn't told me about your involvement in the Save Our Children campaign. That, more than anything, made it clear that my responsibility was to tell you the truth, that your own child is homosexual, and that I never needed saving from anything except the cruel and ignorant piety of people like Anita Bryant.

I'm sorry, Mama. Not for what I am, but for how you must feel at this moment. I know what that feeling is, for I felt it for most of my life. Revulsion, shame, disbelief—rejection through fear of something I knew, even as a child, was as basic to my nature as the color of my eyes.

No, Mama, I wasn't "recruited." No seasoned homosexual ever served as my mentor. But you know what? I wish someone had. I wish someone older than me and wiser than the people in Orlando had taken me aside and said, "You're all right, kid. You can grow up to be a doctor or a teacher just like anyone else. You're not crazy or sick or evil. You can succeed and be happy and find peace with friends—all kinds of friends—who don't give a damn *who* you go to bed with. Most of all, though, you can love and be loved without hating yourself for it."

But no one ever said that to me, Mama. I had to find it out on my own, with the help of the city that has become my home. I know this may be hard for you to believe, but San Francisco is full of men and women, both straight and gay, who don't consider sexuality in measuring the worth of another human being.

These aren't radicals or weirdos, Mama. They are shopclerks and bankers and little old ladies and people who nod and smile to you when you meet them on the bus. Their attitude is neither patronizing nor pitying. And their message is so simple: Yes, you are a person. Yes, I like you. Yes, it's all right for you to like me, too.

I know what you must be thinking now. You're asking yourself: What did we do wrong? How did we let this happen? Which one of us made him that way?

I can't answer that, Mama. In the long run, I guess I really don't care. All I know is this: If you and Papa are responsible for the way I am, then I thank you with all my heart, for it's the light and the joy of my life.

I know I can't tell you what it is to be gay. But I can tell you what it's not.

It's not hiding behind words, Mama. Like *family* and *decency* and *Christianity*. It's not fearing your body, or the pleasures that God made for it. It's not judging your neighbor, except when he's crass or unkind.

Being gay has taught me tolerance, compassion, and humility. It has shown me the limitless possibilities of living. It has given me people whose passion and kindness and sensitivity have provided a constant source of strength.

It has brought me into the family of man, Mama, and I like it here. I *like* it.

There's not much else I can say, except that I'm the same Michael you've always known. You just know me better now. I have never consciously done anything to hurt you. I never will.

Please don't feel you have to answer this right away. It's enough for me to know that I no longer have to lie to the people who taught me to value the truth.

Mary Ann sends her love.

Everything is fine at 28 Barbary Lane.

Your loving son,
Michael

ACKNOWLEDGMENTS

In the making of this book I am deeply grateful to the following people:

My longtime literary agent, Binky Urban, for telling me that she knew the perfect editor for a memoirist.

Jennifer Barth, for turning out to be exactly that, an editor of great tact and taste who saw what I was trying to do and saw to it that I did it.

Steven Barclay, Sara Bixler, and Emily Hartman of the Barclay Agency, for helping me tell my stories onstage before I pinned them to the page.

Jane Maupin Yates, Louise Vance, Darryl Vance, Kathy Barton, and

James Lecesne, for reading early drafts of this text and offering invaluable suggestions and corrections.

Kirk Dalrymple, for holding down the family store and for being Philo's loving uncle.

Edward Ball, for his enthralling book *Peninsula of Lies*, which helped me fill in the blanks about Dawn Langley Simmons.

Patrick Gale, my dear old friend, for coaxing some of these memories from me for his 1999 biography, *Armistead Maupin*.

My husband, Chris, for loving and indulging me through the usual tremors of writing and for insisting that a term I coined a decade ago would be just the right title for this book.

PHOTOGRAPHIC SOURCES

All images courtesy of the author with the exception of the following:

Chapter 10: Photograph by Kim Komenich/The LIFE Images Collection/Getty Images.

Chapter 11: Courtesy of the Crawford Barton Collection, the Gay, Lesbian, Bisexual, Transgender Historical Society.

Chapter 18: Courtesy of Don Bachardy.

Acknowledgments: Photograph courtesy of Fred R. McMullen.

ABOUT THE AUTHOR

ARMISTEAD MAUPIN is the author of the nine-volume Tales of the City series, which includes *Tales of the City, More Tales of the City, Further Tales of the City, Babycakes, Significant Others, Sure of You, Michael Tolliver Lives, Mary Ann in Autumn*, and *The Days of Anna Madrigal*. His other novels include *Maybe the Moon* and *The Night Listener*. Maupin was the 2012 recipient of the Lambda Literary Foundation's Pioneer Award. In 2014 he was awarded an honorary doctor of letters degree by the University of North Carolina–Chapel Hill. He lives in San Francisco with his husband, the photographer Christopher Turner.

About the author

About the book

Read on

Insights,
Interviews
& More...

Meet Armistead Maupin

The *Tales of the City* author on his past as a closeted young conservative and his fears over America's 'fascist regime'

by Paul Laity

ARMISTEAD MAUPIN IS DIVORCING HIS FAMILY—that's how he puts it. The particular problem is his brother, Tony, a Donald Trump supporter with a fondness for the Confederate flag. "That's what Facebook has done," Maupin tells me: you see a family member's page "and you want no part of it anymore. Life is too short to pretend the poison isn't there. Their religion and their politics automatically make me, as a gay man, a second-class citizen. So fuck it."

Maupin (pronounced "Mawpin"), whose much-loved Tales of the City novels are soon to have an updated treatment on Netflix, has long made a distinction between his problematic biological family and his "logical family"—close friends and soulmates. The idea was expressed in fiction by Anna Madrigal, the transgender matriarch of the Tales, who gathers around her a familial group of misfit tenants at 28 Barbary Lane, San Francisco. Now the author has chosen *Logical Family* as the title for his long-awaited memoir.

There have been two Maupins: the young, virginal, archconservative Vietnam volunteer who shook Nixon's hand and kept his sexuality a secret, desperate to impress his white supremacist, homophobic father. And, from his late twenties, the openhearted ambassador of homosexuality, a writer who, in his own words, revealed "the gay experience" to a readership of millions (and the even bigger audience of the 1990s *Tales* TV miniseries).

He wanted to write a memoir, he says, "to show that I had made a journey ▶

from a position of darkness and narrow thinking to quite the opposite. I wanted credit for overcoming the influences of my childhood." He also wrote it, he has said, to "get over the fact that I was cross with myself for waiting so long to come out." Given that he's an author who has "looted his own life for his fiction," an autobiography of some kind was all but inevitable: "I've been anecdotalising my life since I was a child," he chuckles. As Maupin's stand-in character Gabriel puts it in the *roman à clef The Night Listener*: "I'm like a magpie, I save the shiny stuff and discard the rest."

This shiny stuff is also on display in a new biographical documentary, *The Untold Tales of Armistead Maupin*, directed by Jennifer M Kroot. In the film, Maupin's friend Neil Gaiman recalls how *Tales of the City* began in 1976 as a daily serial in the *San Francisco Chronicle*, and was "almost a Trojan horse." It "smuggled in all sorts of themes"—hook-up culture, everyday drug use, gay bathhouse sex, transgender identity—while remaining a frothy, funny narrative with characters for whom readers felt a deep affection. "The idea that he was doing this in a family newspaper—that is not just groundbreaking," Gaiman reflects. "That takes chutzpah, it takes testicles the size of asteroids."

Gaiman comments too on Maupin's current life with his husband, Christopher Turner, thirty years his junior, whose picture he admired on the website Daddyhunt.com ("porn and personals") before bumping into him on the street. They are "a strange storybook couple; each is the other one's ideal. . . . It's like Armistead was being written by a beneficent creator with a plan," who said: "OK, you are going to be this repressed, right-wing kid from North Carolina, but just stick with the story and in the end you will get your happily ever after."

My conversation in Maupin's ground-floor apartment in the Castro district of San Francisco ranges from his friendships with Robin Williams and Ian McKellen to David Hockney's early ▶

5

passion for Cliff Richard. At its centre,
however, remains the family he was
born into: he is still "ashamed of the
degree to which I did not rebel when I
was a young man."

Maupin's father, a lawyer with grand
ancestors, painted "The South Will Rise
Again" above the porch of his children's
playhouse. He walked his family out of
church when black worshippers were to
be given communion, and ridiculed
anyone with a hint of gayness as a "fairy
nice fellow." "The arrogance runs so
deep among upper-class southerners
that it won't go away anytime soon,"
Maupin says now. "It's tied to their
whole identity: all that *Gone with the
Wind* shit." Knowing he was gay from
an early age, he remembers feeling
"there was every indication that I
shouldn't be this thing: it was a sin, a
crime and a mental illness." He wanted
electroshock therapy but it was never
the right time to ask.

Maupin wasn't just a run-of-the-mill
young conservative but a highly
successful young one (having embraced

his father's politics "because I was terrified of who I was"). He was given his first writing job by the notorious racist, homophobe and future senator Jesse Helms and set out for Vietnam to prove he was a man: "My mother said I had a Lawrence of Arabia complex, which was a lot closer than she knew." He even got involved in a propaganda exercise to show how young Americans supported their country's involvement in Southeast Asia, dreamed up by the infamous "dirty tricks department" later behind Watergate. This was how he met Nixon: "My father was over the moon. I was doing everything I needed to make him happy."

The edifice had already begun to crack before Maupin moved to San Francisco: he recalls losing his virginity after a twilight tryst in a park in Charleston, when he was still in the navy. The sex wasn't great, but he "can still feel to this day" the following morning's "exhilaration . . . riding to the ship in my Sunbeam Alpine, listening to 'Good Morning Girl' on the radio." ▶

After leaving the navy he became a reporter, but it was his move to the West Coast, and in particular the San Francisco bathhouse scene, that finally shattered his identity. He writes in *Logical Family* that "if anything delivered me from the privileged white elitism of my youth it was the red-lit cubicles and darkened hallways and even darker mazes of Dave's Baths."

"Once you see how you've been oppressed," he says, "you understand different types of oppression."

"You can tell the difference between a bastard and a nice guy in the dark," Maupin remembers. "Where everything is a silent and tactile experience, gentleness is a very potent language. And the racial divides are largely gone. It wasn't so much the fact that I was having sex as the fact that I was lying naked in someone else's arms, feeling tenderness. And that's why I went back night after night"—with amyl nitrite in a container "like a silver lipstick" around his neck. Maupin had lots of anonymous sex with men and "close friendships with women;

it took me a while to learn to be friends with gay men." For a "romantic with a slut side," it was an "amazing" time to be cruising the streets of the Castro.

Then the serial that became *Tales of the City* was commissioned, and he "danced down Polk Street, because I knew I had something, a subject that wasn't being covered." The soap-operatic stories offered the opposite of the standard account of a ghettoised gay experience, and Maupin cringes when the *Tales* are described in narrow terms as a "portrait of gay life in San Francisco. The triumph was that I got everyone in … the whole point is that we're all in it together." They were also a valentine to his new West Coast home: Quentin Crisp once introduced Maupin as the man who had "invented San Francisco."

The writing of 800 words a day, five days a week, for the first two years of *Tales* was "agonising but exhilarating." Maupin notes the influence of *Cabaret*, based on Christopher Isherwood's *The Berlin Stories*. He met Isherwood "at an Oscar party thrown by one of the ▶

producers of *Saturday Night Fever*. That should nail the era for you." It was Isherwood, soon a friend, who first remarked that *Tales of the City* has a Dickensian flavour, blending comedy with social comment. Maupin notes that the serial, each episode with its own cliffhanger ending, "revived something that hadn't been done in a hundred years."

He looked around him for inspiration, folding current events and new lifestyles into the narrative. Maupin depicted "lesbian mothers before that was anywhere in the culture" and "invented Anna Madrigal the same year Bruce Jenner won male athlete of the year." He has "always been a political creature": from day one, "I was gleeful that I was getting some radical concept out there in a way that was palatable, affecting and amusing."

Maupin chose to come out to his parents in 1977—via *Tales* character Michael Tolliver's celebrated "Letter to Mama" (itself prompted by a right-wing antigay "Save Our Children" crusade):

"… you are still my parents and I am still your child." After a long wait, the author finally received a curt reply from his father: "Dear Teddy, As you know your mother is very ill, so any additional stress can only exacerbate the situation." In other words, as Maupin summarises it: "Shut up before you kill her."

But as San Francisco's newest celebrity, he "was having so much fun. The personal and the political had merged for the first time in my life … When I auctioned off jockstraps in a rabbit suit at a Folsom Street bar, I was doing it to benefit lawyers who were fighting for our rights." He slept with Rock Hudson (after a first encounter when, intimidated by the star, he failed to perform), had a Palm Springs drugs epiphany and was a frequent guest at Isherwood's house in Santa Monica: "When I visit now, I shiver with the memories of how it felt to sit there and listen to people tell the truth about their lives."

He published the Tales novels throughout the 1980s; they were among the first fictional accounts of the AIDS ▶

epidemic. "Everyone around me started to die. We thought we were all going to die," Maupin has said. When he killed off his character Jon Fielding, who had the disease, a proportion of readers, gay and straight, accused the author of "ruining our morning's entertainment with your political agenda." But he "had to put it in," because AIDS was "happening all around me"—not least to Hudson, whom Maupin controversially outed before he died. Both Terry Anderson, the author's boyfriend of a dozen years up to 1996, and Turner were HIV-positive when the relationships began. How has Maupin escaped becoming infected? "By being boring in bed."

A reminder of the extent to which conservatives still considered the Tales outrageous came when the TV miniseries starring Laura Linney as Mary Ann Singleton was aired in the US in 1994 (having been broadcast in the UK the year before). A heated controversy developed over the show's depiction of LGBT relationships, nudity and drug use: this was still a time, the show's producer

Alan Poul recalls in *The Untold Tales*, when "man-on-man kissing was a big taboo" on TV. While the right accused the series of being incendiary and salacious, Poul thought it was simply about "everybody's right to search for love." It was a big ratings success, and still enjoys a high reputation.

Linney, a good friend, and Olympia Dukakis, who played Anna Madrigal, are destined to reprise their roles in the forthcoming Netflix series (which draws on the final three Tales novels published between 2007 and 2014). According to Maupin, it's to be set in the present day, and begins with Madrigal's ninetieth birthday party featuring "a whole new and diverse set of people living at 28 Barbary Lane. Mary Ann has a dark secret she's bringing with her, and it unfolds from there." As executive producer, Maupin is overseeing the writing team—Michael Cunningham, author of *The Hours*, has reportedly written the first script.

The money from Netflix will come in useful: times are relatively hard, and ▶

with highly-paid techies invading the Castro, Maupin could no longer afford to buy a house there. "My books have sold over forty years, but the bulk was at the beginning," he explains. Yet he still finds the city "enchanting," and has said he feels "lucky to be alive. . . . There are friends who aren't with me who don't have the luxury of griping about the Google bus."

Maupin still has many pleasures—walking his labradoodle to the dog park, vaping a cannabis strain called "Girl Scout Cookies" (a diabetic, he no longer drinks alcohol) and spending time with Turner, "the love of my life." He enjoys his continued renown, especially in this—very busy—year, and has no time for the "snobby literary crowd" who look down on his work as "popular entertainment."

But his despair at last year's election result is unabating: *Logical Family* refers to "a new fascist regime in Washington." "I wrote that six months ago," he tells me, "and I thought: you'll be sorry you used that term. But I'm not at all. I think we're closer than ever." And it means that after decades of struggling with his "mean, tight, selfish" father (who, having mellowed a little, died in 2005), Maupin is finally calling time on his biological family. Trump has, he writes, "left our country more divided than at any time since the civil war. Brother against brother, then and now." ॰॰

The Making of
Logical Family

by Paul Constant

This article originally appeared in the Seattle Review of Books *in October 2017. Reproduced with permission from the* Seattle Review of Books.

THE ONE THING about hosting author interviews in public spaces is that you've got to "yes, and . . ." the hell out of them. No matter what the author throws at you, you have to make it an additive experience. If they tell an anecdote about fox hunting, you've got to find the connective tissue to tie that anecdote to the next question somehow, even if the next question is related to the stock market. Dead air in an onstage interview is . . . well, death.

I bring this up because onstage recently in Seattle, Armistead Maupin knocked me on my butt at least three times. I mean, he literally left me speechless. Maupin is a sweet and generous public speaker. He's kind in his recollections, he's full of explosive anecdotes and hilarious observations. And every few minutes, he'll say something so fantastically filthy that it'll make you laugh until the wind's knocked out of you.

Maupin fired off quips about sign language interpreters miming acts of masturbation, about oral sex, about orgies. A few times, those jokes were so quick and so funny that I had nothing to say in response. Maupin seemed to relish catching me flat-footed. The last time it happened, he said, "I saw the color was coming back into your face, so I decided to do something about that."

Of course, it wasn't all dirty jokes. We talked about why he decided to write his memoir, *Logical Family*, now ("I'm seventy-three," he noted wryly, asking when else he was supposed to publish his memoirs.) We discussed how he feels about his legacy (he seems rightfully proud of what he did to represent gay and trans populations in mass media.) He shared whether he's comfortable with his role in the outing of actor Rock Hudson (yes, although Maupin admitted that he does have dreams where Hudson, a ▶

former flame, appears to him and says he's happy with how things worked out.) He talked at length about Barry Manilow and what it means to be a closeted artist.

Maupin also revealed that he's working with Netflix to create a television series based on his popular Tales of the City books. The series, he says, will be set in the present day and will track the lives of his most popular characters more than four decades after the first publication of the first "Tales of the City" in the *San Francisco Chronicle*.

If you've read all of the series, you'll likely want to read *Logical Family*. If you've never read a single word of *Tales of the City*, you'll find *Logical Family* to be a concise and fascinating introduction to Maupin's world. It's such a personal and specific book that it has universal appeal. I wouldn't be surprised to see it become one of his very best-loved titles.

The book tracks his early career as a writer—from the first thing he wrote as a toddler to his time as a writer of serial fiction in newspapers to his long path to bestselling novelist. And it also follows his transformation as a human, from his youthful conservatism to his stint in the navy during the Vietnam War to his rebirth as a gay celebrity at a time when San Francisco was the most exciting city in the world.

Maupin writes freely about the drugs he took, the orgies he attended, the enemies he made. It's the kind of book that only a man satisfied with the course of his life could write. He knows who his friends are, and he knows his enemies, and he knows what his accomplishments are, and he's at peace with that. And if he can drop a few jaw-dropping sex jokes along the way? Well, that's just a bonus. ∾

Have You Read?
The Tales of the City Series

❝ These novels are as difficult to put down as a dish of pistachios. ❞

—Charles Solomon,
Los Angeles Times Book Review

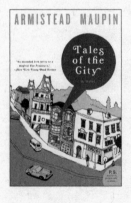

TALES OF THE CITY

For almost four decades, Armistead Maupin's *Tales of the City* has blazed its own trail through popular culture—from a groundbreaking newspaper serial to a classic novel, to a television event that entranced millions around the world. The first of nine novels about the denizens of the mythic apartment house at 28 Barbary Lane, *Tales* is both a sparkling comedy of manners and an indelible portrait of an era that forever changed the way we live.

MORE TALES OF THE CITY

The tenants of 28 Barbary Lane have fled their cozy nest for adventures far afield. Mary Ann Singleton finds love at sea with a forgetful stranger. Mona Ramsey discovers her doppelgänger in a desert whorehouse, and Michael Tolliver bumps into a certain gynecologist in a seedy Mexican bar. Meanwhile, their venerable landlady takes the biggest journey of all—without ever leaving home.

FURTHER TALES OF THE CITY

The calamity-prone residents of 28 Barbary Lane are at it again in this deliciously dark novel of romance and betrayal. While Anna Madrigal imprisons an anchorwoman in her basement, Michael Tolliver looks for love at the National Gay Rodeo, DeDe Halcyon Day and Mary Ann Singleton track a charismatic psychopath across Alaska, and society columnist Prue Giroux loses her heart to a derelict living in a San Francisco park. ▶

BABYCAKES

When an ordinary househusband and his ambitious wife decide to start a family, they discover there's more to making a baby than meets the eye. Help arrives in the form of a grieving gay neighbor, a visiting monarch, and a dashing young lieutenant who defects from her yacht. Bittersweet and profoundly affecting, *Babycakes* was the first work of fiction to acknowledge the arrival of AIDS.

SIGNIFICANT OTHERS

Tranquility reigns in the ancient redwood forest until a women-only music festival sets up camp downriver from an all-male retreat for the ruling class. Among those entangled in the ensuing mayhem are a lovesick nurseryman, a panic-stricken philanderer, and the world's most beautiful fat woman. *Significant Others* is Armistead Maupin's cunningly observed meditation on marriage, friendship, and sexual nostalgia.

SURE OF YOU

A fiercely ambitious TV talk-show host finds that she must choose between national stardom in New York and a husband and child in San Francisco. Caught in the middle is their longtime friend, a gay man whose own future is even more uncertain. Wistful and compassionate yet subversively funny, *Sure of You* could only come from Armistead Maupin.

MICHAEL TOLLIVER LIVES

After a hiatus of nearly two decades, Armistead Maupin resumes his classic Tales of the City saga with this tender portrait of his all-too-human hero, Michael Tolliver, now a fifty-five-year-old gardener who has survived the plague that took so many of his friends. When a family crisis arises in Michael's boyhood home in Florida, he journeys there with his brand-new, much-younger husband, and finds his loyalties tested as never before. ▶

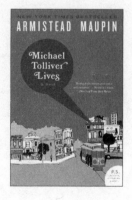

MARY ANN IN AUTUMN

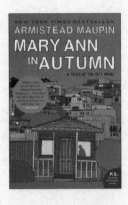

Tales of the City heroine Mary Ann Singleton, having abandoned San Francisco twenty years earlier for a career in New York, returns to the city of her youth in flight from a pair of unforeseen calamities. When she seeks a fresh start with her oldest friend, Michael "Mouse" Tolliver (now living in domestic bliss with his husband), she discovers that her speckled past has crept up on her in a most unexpected way.

THE DAYS OF ANNA MADRIGAL

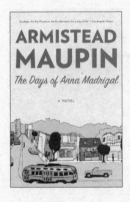

The ninth and probably final novel in Armistead Maupin's bestselling Tales of the City series, following Anna Madrigal's family road trip to Burning Man and told through the interweaving tales of several familiar characters. With the aid of Brian and his beat-up RV, Anna journeys east from San Francisco into the dusty troubled heart of her Depression childhood, facing some unfinished business she has so far avoided.

Also from Armistead Maupin

MAYBE THE MOON

"Though Cadence Roth, the heroine of Maupin's captivating novel, is only thirty-one inches tall, her impact on the reader's emotions is enormous. . . . A suspenseful story whose subtly foreshadowed ending delivers a dramatic clout."
—*Publishers Weekly*

THE NIGHT LISTENER

"With rare authority, humor, and stunning grace, Maupin explores the risks and consolations of intimacy while illuminating the mysteries of the storytelling impulse."
—*Chicago Tribune*

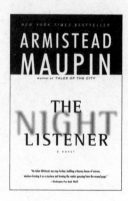

Discover great authors, exclusive offers, and more at hc.com.